Communicating Differences

Communicating Differences

Culture, Media, Peace and Conflict Negotiation

Edited by

Sudeshna Roy
Stephen F. Austin State University, USA

and

Ibrahim Seaga Shaw
Northumbria University, UK

First published 2016 by
PALGRAVE MACMILLAN

Palgrave Macmillan in the UK is an imprint of Macmillan Publishers Limited,
registered in England, company number 785998, of Houndmills, Basingstoke,
Hampshire RG21 6XS.

Palgrave Macmillan in the US is a division of St Martin's Press LLC,
175 Fifth Avenue, New York, NY 10010.

Palgrave Macmillan is the global academic imprint of the above companies
and has companies and representatives throughout the world.

Palgrave® and Macmillan® are registered trademarks in the United States,
the United Kingdom, Europe and other countries.

ISBN 978-1-137-49925-7

This book is printed on paper suitable for recycling and made from fully
managed and sustained forest sources. Logging, pulping and manufacturing
processes are expected to conform to the environmental regulations of the
country of origin.

A catalogue record for this book is available from the British Library.

A catalog record for this book is available from the Library of Congress.

Typeset by MPS Limited, Chennai, India.

This book is dedicated to my mother, Kalyani Chowdhury,
whose love and dedication reminds me to be the best
I can be, every day.

– Sudeshna Roy

This book is dedicated to my mother Haja Hassiatu Shaw of
blessed memory, who passed away in October 2011.

– Ibrahim Seaga Shaw

Contents

List of Figures and Tables

Figures

Tables

Foreword

In a world scarred by conflict and confrontation, intercultural under-standing and accommodation is becoming increasingly important both as a policy imperative and in the everyday reality of life. Society is undergoing rapid changes due to forces of globalization, mobility and migration, technological evolution, and the media's presence in all fac-ets of life. As a result, the essence of how we communicate in relation-ships, between and across cultures, in organizations, through education and in moments of conflict and crisis, is undergoing an unprecedented transformation.

This collection of readings deploys multi-disciplinary perspectives to highlight the growing importance of intercultural communication in a wide range of contexts, from conflict mediation and negotiation, to war and peace journalism, human rights and peace education. The contribu-tions examine these issues in a holistic fashion, promoting intra-field dialogue and a more rounded approach towards peace-building, social justice and change. The essays in this volume provide an extremely useful compendium for scholars and students of communication and media studies and highlight the many connections between and among these distinctive areas of the discipline.

The increasing diversity of human societies, due to global forces of mobility and migration, brings people closer geographically and virtu-ally, and requires new discourses and approaches to concepts of differ-ence and multiculturalism, inclusion, and intercultural awareness. Such debates in the arenas of public policy and education can be fruitfully informed by the contributions of communications scholars and practi-tioners. The chapters, specially commissioned for this volume, deploy diverse theoretical and methodological approaches and include exam-ples from different parts of the globe, demonstrating the variety and vitality of intercultural interactions.

What makes this particularly interesting and useful for students and scholars, as well as policy-makers, is its capacity to strike a balance between engaging with theoretical debates about cultural dimensions of communication and rich empirical research, based on various case studies. These span the globe: from peace initiatives in Kenya to an educational program for US students in Northern Ireland, to Canadian efforts to promote indigenous–non-indigenous reconciliation; from

Pakistan's Right to Free and Compulsory Education Act, to a Jewish-Muslim dialogue program among women undergraduates in the midst of the Israeli-Palestinian conflict, and the role that faith-based organizations can play in peace-building.

Other themes included in the book are the representations of minorities and 'Islamic' terrorism in the mainstream media and popular cinema, and how Afghan songs were promoting peace during the years of conflict. The terrain thus covered is diverse, fascinating, and full of extremely interesting and innovative descriptions and analyses of the importance of cultural communication that enriches our understanding of how it could be used for conflict resolution and reconciliation. The other major strength of the volume is its successful combination of the work of established and emerging scholars in this field – such academic conversation is extremely valuable.

The book is neatly divided into four parts. Essays in the first part address the need for and effectiveness of intercultural communication at the macro as well as micro levels. Part II of the book focuses on issues surrounding identities in conflict areas, and examines how cultural constructions of ethnicity and identity affect conflicts. Education about culture, peace, and conflict is discussed in essays in Part III of this volume, while the final part explores alternative theories and approaches to communicating culture, peace, and conflict.

There are implications for race, gender, ethnicity, ideology, and institutional power in these essays and together they pave the path for alternative approaches to teaching, talking, and educating about culture, peace, and conflict. The peace-building measures discussed in the book would be useful for academics, policy-makers, and non-governmental organizations dealing with conflicts and their aftermath. The editors, Sudeshna Roy and Ibrahim Seaga Shaw, deserve commendation for putting together an extremely useful and timely read.

Daya Kishan Thussu
Professor of International Communication
University of Westminster, London

Acknowledgements

We are indebted to Palgrave's anonymous reviewers whose comments and suggestions sharpened and enhanced the focus of the volume immensely. We acknowledge with thanks the permission granted by Dr Elizabeth Bloodgood and Dr Shelley Dean to cite their article titled 'Where Have All the Protest Songs Gone? Social Movement's Message and Their Voice in Politics'. We also acknowledge with gratitude the support, patience, and guidance provided by Palgrave senior acquisitions editor for Film, Culture, and Media Studies, Ms Felicity Plester. Many thanks also go to Ms Sneha Kamat Bhavnani, Palgrave editorial assistant for Film, Culture, and Media Studies. She was always understanding, patient, and ready to help in any way she could. Last, but not the least, my heartfelt love and thanks to Sudeshna Roy's sweet daughter, Trishala, for spending hours of her time in helping me standardize the references and in-text citations for half the chapters in this volume.

Notes on Contributors

Garry Bailey is an associate professor at the Duncum Center for Conflict Resolution at Abilene Christian University teaching conflict resolution courses in the areas of Conflict and Communication Theory, Ethics, and Culture. His background is in intercultural and organizational communication, and his research interests are in seeking peace in the contexts of gender roles, race conflict, and restorative justice practices.

Patrick Belanger is Assistant Professor of Humanities & Communication at California State University, Monterey Bay. Drawn to the challenge of bridging diverse publics, he researches communication-based approaches to peacebuilding. He holds a BA and MA from Simon Fraser University and a PhD (Communication) from the University of Southern California.

Mariam Betlemidze is a doctoral candidate in the Department of Communication, University of Utah. Her current research focuses on multimedia activism at its intersection with affect, sexuality, and social change. Through the French poststructuralist lens, she studies how human and non-human actors create networks and assemblages that traverse spatial and temporal barriers. Prior to her graduate career in the United States, she worked as a journalist and a communication officer for media, humanitarian, and non-governmental organizations covering the conflict zones of the South Caucasus.

John S. Caputo is a professor and Walter Ong, S. J. Distinguished Scholar of Communication and Leadership Studies at Gonzaga University. He holds a PhD from the Claremont Graduate School. His areas of expertise include intercultural communication, media and social values, and communication theory. He is the author of five books, and more than 35 articles and chapters. His guest editorials have appeared in newspapers, he has been a guest on radio and television programs, speaks internationally about media and social values, and has been honoured as a Visiting Scholar-In-Residence at the University of Kent at Canterbury, England. He has received numerous teaching awards and directs the Gonzaga-in-Derry and Gonzaga-in-Cagli, Italy Projects.

Jinbong Choi is an associate professor in the Department of Media & Communication at the Sungkonghoe University and the author of seven books. His research papers appear in several academic journals including

Public Relations Review, Journal of Business & Technical Communication, TEXT & TALK, Global Media Journal, Journal of Media and Communication Studies, and so on. He holds a PhD from the Department of Communication Studies at the University of Minnesota, Twin Cities. He has taught at the Texas State University-San Marcos, Minnesota State University-Mankato, and the Bemidji State University.

Mary Jane Collier is Professor of Communication at the University of New Mexico. She has published *Community Engagement and Intercultural Praxis: Dancing with Difference in Diverse Contexts* (2014) and various journal articles on peacebuilding and conflict. She has been awarded the National Communication Association International and Intercultural Communication Division Distinguished Scholarship Award.

Sachi Edwards is an adjunct faculty member in the Higher Education, Student Affairs, and International Education program at the University of Maryland, College Park. Her research and scholarship focus on pedagogical pathways to peace and social justice, indigenous, and spiritual approaches to learning, and the impact of religious identity on sociocultural power dynamics.

Claudia L. Hale is Professor Emerita of Communication Studies at Ohio University. Her research interests include interpersonal and organizational communication, conflict management, and peacebuilding. She holds a PhD from the University of Illinois.

Sahar Khamis is an associate professor in the Department of Communication at the University of Maryland. She is an expert in Arab and Muslim media and former Head of the Mass Communication Department in Qatar University. She is former Mellon Islamic Studies visiting professor at the University of Chicago. She holds a PhD in Mass Media and Cultural Studies from the University of Manchester.

Julia Khrebtan-Hörhager is Assistant Professor of Communication at the Colorado State University, Fort Collins, a leader of education abroad programs, and recipient of a 2012 International Communication Association Top Paper Award for her work on German–Italian intercultural relations. Her research and teaching interests include intercultural/international communication, European studies, conflict, international cinematography, and critical media studies.

MiSun Lee is an ABD doctoral candidate at the School of Communication & Arts, Yonsei University, Seoul, South Korea. She completed her BA and MA at the School of Journalism and Mass Communications, University of Minnesota, Twin Cities, US. She has presented at many national and international conferences.

Yanqin Liu is a doctoral student in the Hugh Downs School of Human Communication at Arizona State University. She focuses primarily on social influence and health communication as well as interpersonal communication in intercultural contexts. Prior to starting her doctoral work, she studied intercultural conflicts at the University of Utah.

Jing Lin is Professor of International Education Policy at the University of Maryland. She has published extensively on Chinese education, culture, and society, and East–West dialogues. Other important strands of her research are peace education and environmental education, and spirituality, religion, and education.

Rebecca Merkin is Associate Professor at Baruch College – City University of New York in New York. Merkin completed her PhD at Kent State University and her Graduate studies at Boston University. Her research interests lie in the area of intercultural communication, focusing on cultural differences in order to communicate beyond those differences.

Roshan Noorzai is a native of Afghanistan. His research interests include peace and conflict studies, political communication, and ICTs for development.

Sudeshna Roy is Associate Professor of Communication Studies at Stephen F. Austin State University, USA. She has co-edited the book *Transatlantic Relations and Modern Diplomacy* (2014) and is writing her first solo-authored book on media representation in the BRICS countries. Her articles have appeared in peer-reviewed journals such as *International Communication Gazette, China Media Research and Media, War and Conflict.* She is the chair of Diaspora and Media Division of International Association for Media and Communication Research (IAMCR) and has chaired the Peace and Conflict Communication Division of the National Communication Association (NCA).

Elesha L. Ruminski is Associate Professor of Communication Studies at Frostburg State University (FSU) in Western Maryland. She holds a PhD in Rhetoric from Duquesne University in Pittsburgh. She has coordinated and facilitated community dialogues supported by the Maryland Judiciary's Mediation and Conflict Resolution Office, Mountainside Community Mediation Center, and the Maryland Commission on Civil

Rights. Also the coordinator of Leadership Studies at FSU, she co-edited the scholarly collection *Women's Communicative Leadership Development: From Ceilings of Glass to Labyrinth Paths* (2012).

Max Saito is Associate Professor of Communication at Westfield State University in Westfield, Massachusetts. He teaches communication courses focused on addressing the intersection of race, gender, sexuality, class, nationality, and consumption.

Ibrahim Seaga Shaw is Senior Lecturer in Media and Politics at Northumbria University in Newcastle-upon-Tyne. He is the author of two books, *Human Rights Journalism* (2012) and co-editor of *Expanding Peace Journalism* (2012). He is also author of *Business Journalism: A Critical Political Economy Approach* (2015). Shaw holds a PhD from the Sorbonne, and has a background in journalism spanning 20 years having worked in Sierra Leone, France, and Britain. Shaw is also Secretary General of the International Peace Research Association (IPRA).

Daya Kishan Thussu is Professor of International Communication at the University of Westminster. Author or editor of 17 books, among his key publications are: *Mapping BRICS Media* (2015); *Communicating India's Soft Power: Buddha to Bollywood* (2013); *Media and Terrorism: Global Perspectives* (2012); *Internationalizing Media Studies* (2009); *News as Entertainment: The Rise of Global Infotainment* (2007); *Media on the Move: Global Flow and Contra-Flow* (2007); *International Communication – Continuity and Change*, third edition (2016).

Nur Uysal is Assistant Professor of Strategic Communication in the Diederich College of Communication at Marquette University, Wisconsin. Uysal conducts research in intercultural communication, corporate social responsibility, and public diplomacy and holds a PhD from the University of Oklahoma. Uysal's research is published in top-tier strategic communication journals, including *International Journal of Strategic Communication, Public Relations Review,* and *Journal of Public Affairs*.

1
Introduction – Communicating Differences: Toward Breaking the Boundaries for Peace and Conflict Research in Communication

Sudeshna Roy and Ibrahim Seaga Shaw

Society is undergoing rapid changes due to forces of globalization, mobility of people, technological evolution, and the media's ubiquitous presence in all facets of life. As a result, the essence of how we communicate in relationships, between and across cultures, in organizations, through education, and in moments of conflict and crisis, is undergoing multi-faceted transformation. This volume brings together an eclectic and significant collection of essays representing influential theories, ideas, methods, and case studies in culture, media, conflict, and peace communication from diverse scholars who provide a thorough understanding of what entails processes of communicating differences in a conflict-torn world.

The problems of communicating about culture, conflict, and peace resonate with what founder of conflict and peace research Johann Galtung (2004) called cultural violence, and which he categorized as Attitude in his ABC *(Attitude, Behavior, and Contradictions)* Conflict Triangle. Most of the violence and conflict/crisis we experience in the world today can be traced back to the idea of *Attitude* (cultural violence) represented in, for example, hate speech, persecution complex, myths, and legends of war heroes, religious justification for war, discrimination on the basis of skin color, gender, religion, sex, etc., 'choseness'/being the chosen people', civilizational arrogance, and more (Galtung, 2004; Lynch and McGoldrick, 2005, p. 38; Shaw, 2012, p. 12).

This notion of cultural violence as an invisible indirect form of violence, which Chow-White and McMahon (2012) call 'cold conflict', suggests a clear overlap between the theories of communication, human rights, social justice, and peacebuilding. When one takes part in a communication exercise, one is essentially contributing to the creation of peace, which can also be central to the promotion and protection of human rights and bring about social justice in many instances. Yet, as we continue to witness acts of extremism and terrorism in this world, it is important to understand that it is not just the lack of the human right to communicate that can lead to indirect forms of cultural or structural violence, or direct forms of physical violence, but also the failure to strike the right balance between this right and the right of others to enjoy their religious freedom without being subjected to hate attacks.

What is more, the problem of communicating differences can lead to direct political violence as well as the clash of cultures involving Islamophobia on one hand and extremism and terrorism on the other. Moreover, there are other challenging issues of patriarchy and gender discrimination that fall well within the purview of cultural conflict, as well as other forms of discrimination. Take for example the shooting incident in 1989 in Montreal by a young man which left 14 young women dead. The burning issue of discrimination against women appeared to be the root cause. Marc Raboy described the emotional event in the following way:

> On 6 December 1989, late in the afternoon, a young man armed with a semi-automatic rifle burst into a classroom at the Ecole Polytechnic de Montreal (the engineering faculty of the University of Montreal). He separated the people present into two groups, men and women. Then, according to witnesses, he cried: 'You're all a bunch of femi- nists. I hate feminists', and opened fire. In a rampage through the building lasting barely 15 minutes, he murdered 14 women. Then, he killed himself.
>
> (Raboy, 1992, p. 133)

This might have largely sounded, at the time, like an act of a lunacy per- petrated by a single member of society. However, the underlying cause of this act is not exposed in such an explanation. Such an act comes from the influences of the ideological, invisible crises of everyday life associated with the idea of the growing empowerment of women in a society that was, and perhaps still is, largely characterized by patriarchy and gender discrimination.

The question is obviously raised as to how this shooting to death of 14 young female students can be compared to present day politically and ideologically motivated conflict, and acts of terrorism motivated by religious extremism. They are similar mainly in the sense that they are all categorized as direct visible violence, which is the manifest *Behaviour* in Galtung's ABC Conflict Triangle (2004). They are also similar in that they all happened as a result of some form of cultural violence or failure of intercultural communication: Islamophobic discourses in the case of contemporary acts of terror, and anti-feminist discourses in the case of the Montreal shooting. Examples of such failures abound, and appear, in fact, to be on the increase.

Although communication processes have enormous potential to bring about conflict transformation and peacebuilding, scholars need to focus more on the 'what' and 'how' of constructive contributions, as well as the underlying conceptualization of peace and communication. It is clear that there are many 'fields' within the field of Communication that are feeding conflict and peace studies in largely insulated ways. There needs to be more cross-pollination within the field in order to enable a greater understanding of the field and thorough engagement with what is an important and increasingly vibrant area of activity. While there have been few isolated cases of research on issues of cultural identity, intercultural communication, and communication diversity, there is little evidence of a scholarly volume that looks at the idea of communicating differences using the lenses of culture, media, peace, and human rights. It is in the context of addressing this gap that the current volume has been conceived.

The present volume brings together essays from scholars and practitioners from the various fields within the discipline of Communication Studies whose work demonstrates the importance and viability of approaching issues of conflict from an intra-disciplinary perspective. The various fields within Communication Studies that are integrated in this volume are intercultural communication, media studies, rhetoric, peace journalism, human rights journalism, conflict management and mediation, peace education, and peacebuilding. The volume highlights the many connections between and among the distinctive areas of study in order to tease out the possibilities of promoting intra-field dialogue and a more holistic approach towards peacebuilding, social justice, and change.

Individuals and groups with diverse backgrounds, values, and beliefs, situated in a variety of cultural, political, economic, and institutional structures need to grapple with ideas of diversity, difference, and multiculturalism. The ways in which these fundamental issues are debated in today's society helps pave the path towards a more inclusive, culturally conscious world that allows for dialogue and debate with regard to public policy, educational reform, and sustainable peace. Communication scholars and practitioners have made rich contributions in advancing the causes of intercultural awareness and a more peaceful society for the past several decades. Many of them have made these contributions from different focus areas. Some examples of approaches with different foci are: peacebuilding from an intercultural perspective; conflict resolution at the workplace; interpersonal conflict mediation; critiques of conflict reportage in the media; and a multitude of other approaches. Their work has made an impact in a variety of social arenas including but not restricted to social justice, citizen participation, student education, information dissemination, global north-south dialogue, intercultural understanding, gender perspectives, and critiques of existing peacebuilding and conflict management practices and institutions. However, continuous social changes around us engender the inclusion of nuanced perspectives about peace and conflict management as well as insight into newer forms and forums of expression in communication. For example, research in new media provides fresh avenues of reaching peacebuilding objectives and goals, or approaches to conflict management from grassroots women workers and organizers.

There are several important contemporary factors that need to be considered as scholars and practitioners contend with the ideas of sustainable peacebuilding and greater understanding between people across the world. Some of these factors are simultaneously oppositional and complementary in nature, such as: forces of globalization and the historical specificity of the nature of conflict; cultural diversity and indigenous perspectives about peace and conflict; traditional representation of interests; and technologically evolving forms of the portrayal of involved constituents. It then becomes imperative that scholars and practitioners keep the channels of dialogue and mutual understanding of each others' works open in order to further contribute to bodies of work in this area. Longitudinal research as well as short-term case studies offer newer understanding of causes of conflict. Challenging existing frameworks and co-constructing more relevant approaches to conflict management and cultural dialogue provide all involved with tools that are crafted from contemporary social processes and offerings. Critiques of political, economic, cultural, and other macro-social issues igniting overt and covert forms of conflict become a necessary step towards the prevention of the same in the future. These undertakings and pursuits need to be thorough, consistent, and continuous through inevitable change. The nature of conflict is changing and so are cultures and peacebuilding endeavors.

This volume helps to build bridges across perspectives to provide for a larger array of solutions for sustainable peace and cultural understanding in intercultural and global contexts. The volume is a meeting ground of ideas and approaches in the form of essays that identify areas of convergence between the aforementioned disparate fields within Communication Studies. The essays embrace a variety of theoretical and methodological approaches including critical, interpretive, rhetorical, social scientific, and pragmatic.

What is conflict?

The very conceptualization of conflict encompasses the idea of intra-disciplinarity within it. An attempt to fix the meaning of conflict is futile since almost all the fields within Communication deal with some aspects of it. Just a cursory examination of the top professional Communication associations in the world, such as the International Communication Association, the National Communication Association based in the US, the International Association for Media and Communication Research, and the Association for Education in Journalism and Mass Communication, shows that the various divisions within the field are dealing with multitude of conflict issues. While different divisions facilitate communication scholars' congregation around clusters of similar ideas, and tease out theoretical and practical solutions to conflicts, the divisions also sometimes hinder scholars from seeing useful connections and creative approaches towards conflict negotiation and peacebuilding.

This volume lets the reader take a peek at a variety of conflicts spanning from interpersonal, intercultural and mediated to folk and peace studies, and a multitude of theoretical implications and innovative practical implementations of the theories. The scope of a reader is frequently witnessed in learning about various theories and case studies within a particular area of communication. This volume is able to go a step beyond and demonstrate the integration of theory and its application not only within such areas, but also amongst them.

Organization and overview of the book: main themes and objectives

We have organized *Communicating Differences* into four main parts, each covering a complex set of related ideas that reflect the changing nature of culture, conflict, and peace in a mediated world.

The volume begins with Part I, From Macro to Micro – Intercultural Communication at the Heart of Conflict Negotiation, consisting of four chapters that address the need and effectiveness of intercultural communication at the macro as well as micro level, theoretically and empirically. This part identifies for the reader the variety of ways in which cultural settings influence the way conflicts are managed, negotiated, and interpreted. A theoretical framework for the necessity of intercultural communication in processing issues of conflict is also discussed. In Chapter 2, Mary Jane Collier extends the framework for intercultural communication and peacebuilding co-developed with Benjamin Broome, by featuring the benefits of orienting to connections and intersections of elements and processes. This approach is applied to a case study of the work of International Peace Initiatives (IPI) in Kenya. The value of incorporating this framework is illustrated by attending to context as overlapping macro, meso, and micro level frames; recognizing the interrelated personal, relational, and structural dimensions of peacebuilding; demonstrating how these dimensions are intersecting, contextually contingent, and communicatively constructed as well as produced; and showing how the framework can accommodate integrated theoretical perspectives. In Chapter 3, Ibrahim Seaga Shaw draws on cultural studies, critical theory, and Galtung's idea of indirect cultural violence to provide an analysis of how micro conflict events are portrayed through the discourses of macro events to represent UK Muslims in a largely negative light based on systemic and deliberate patterns of stereotyping. The micro event he analyses is the framing of the isolated incident of the murder of British soldier Lee Rigby in Woolwich in May 2013 by two Muslims. The macro discourse he refers to is the general framing of Muslims who support right-wing extremist groups in the UK. The conflation of the micro and the macro happens in the media representation of these events and alleged Islamic extremist phenomena in the UK. In Chapter 4, John S. Caputo interweaves theory and practice, intercultural and international communication, and micro and macro, with the help of dialogic theory. In order to understand the role of intercultural communication in peacemaking, Caputo describes a project that brought US students to Northern Ireland to work collaboratively with a grassroots organization named *The Junction: Community Relations and Peacebuilding in Derry*, who have used the process of dialogue, ethical remembering, and healing to facilitate working with former combatants to build a lasting peace. This chapter is a wonderful example of theory in action, where intercultural communication adds a measurable understanding of causes and history of a conflict leading to the development of a shared community through storytelling. In Chapter 5, Mariam Betlemidze brings to light factors of intercultural, interethnic, and international cooperation that are hidden under transcendent strategies of the conflicting stakeholders of the

South Caucasian conflicts. This chapter offers Deleuzo-Guattarian and Badiouian ideas to challenge existing perspectives on South Caucasian conflicts that reveal multiple images of dynamism, desired productions, and states of endless becomings. The multiplicity of understanding of the conflict is at once beneficial and problematic in nature. However, the author demonstrates how affirmative philosophy is a useful tool for unlocking the potentials of these multiplicities in a way that helps stakeholders move from confusion to clarity.

The second part of the volume, From Local to Global: Mediated Identities in Conflicted Cultures, moves on to issues of identities in areas that are experiencing conflict in the world. In this part, the reader begins to understand the complexities brought about by cultural conflicts that heavily influence the construction of identities of stakeholders with local as well as global impacts. The identity construction process is further complicated by the pervasive presence of media, at a pace that has never before been experienced. The part contains four chapters that focus on case studies from particular areas of the world as well as theoretical understandings of ideological underpinnings and processes of ethnic conflicts. In Chapter 6, Sudeshna Roy strives to deconstruct the politics of representation of the many Indian ethnicities represented in Bollywood movies in the new millennium. The author conducts a critical discourse analysis of the ten highest grossing Bollywood Hindi movies of the current century to unearth discourses of marginalization, extreme stereotypes, and disenfranchisement embedded in the ideological 'othering' of minorities in these movies. The case studies highlight how the global econo-political scenario has a local influence through the extension and cementing of popular stereotypes of Indian ethnicities that may or may not parallel social and political conditions in the country's complex class, ethnic, racial, and religious hierarchies. In Chapter 7, Julia Khrebtan-Hörhager demonstrates how intercultural cinematography brings the local and the specific to the levels of the global and the universal. Cinema assumes a pedagogical role in the lives of audiences, and serves as a means of teaching culture and conflict. Using intercultural cinematography as a peacebuilding methodology and epistemology, the author focuses on the dynamics between the 'self' and the 'other' as represented in the Italian film *Quando sei nato non puoi più nasconderti*. The film addresses particularities and possibilities of communication dynamics between the local population in Italy and the incoming immigrant population, a subject increasingly relevant and currently being debated in the contemporary context of the European Union response to the immigration crisis brought on by the Syrian civil war. The author provides concrete examples of the *reel to real* inclusive strategies of de-escalating the complex relationships between the European 'self' and the immigrant 'other'; and examines its impact on the multicultural dynamics in the European Union. In Chapter 8, MiSun Lee and Jinbong Choi conduct longitudinal analysis of news media coverage of South Korean immigrant community. The South Korean government has promoted immigration within the last decade. As a result the foreign population (mostly from South Asia) has soared in the country. The authors highlight how Korea is in a transitional period. They adapt from Western experiences of immigration, acknowledging the importance of journalists' role in social change and apply those learnings to the news media experience in South Korea, providing a local application of global theories of news media with regard to immigration. They explore four Korean national newspapers in 2005 and 2011 to examine how newspapers represent immigrants and whether the attitude of news coverage has changed over the time that the government has concentrated its efforts on inviting more immigrants to the country. Rounding up this part, in Chapter 9, Yanqin Liu applies a comparative approach to examining the construction of human rights in China and the US. Human rights are a controversial topic in most countries and especially between the US and Chinese cultures. Although both cultures emphasize the importance of human rights, the US and China have different understandings of what constitutes human rights. These differences derive from a variety of factors, including historical, cultural, and philosophical contexts. By using qualitative discourse analysis, this chapter focuses on the origins of human rights in the US and China, as well as the differences and similarities of human rights construction, in order to explore the possibility of sharing common philosophical foundations for human rights dialogue between the US and China.

The third part, From Deconstruction to Reconstruction: Rebooting Frameworks of Education on Culture, Conflict, and Peace, focuses on how peace and conflict is constructed, deconstructed, co-constructed within frameworks of educational institutions and what changes they are undergoing in the various case studies identified in the essays. There are implications for race, gender, ethnicity, ideology, and institutional power in these essays, and together they pave the way for alternative approaches to teaching, talking, and educating about culture, peace, and conflict. In Chapter 10, Patrick Belanger addresses the Truth and Reconciliation Commission of Canada's work to promote Indigenous–non-Indigenous reconciliation through public narrative. Since truth and reconciliation are not concomitant, the author is reluctant to assume that merely accurate knowledge of the historical events of racism will catalyze a realignment of socio-political relations. He therefore examines a communicative model for motivating both conceptual *and* material evolutions: the theory of interest-convergence. The author demonstrates how crucial it is to challenge racism in school curricula as well as in broader media discourses, and the usefulness of a rigorous communication strategy that covers multiple bases rather than relying on sanguine assessments of audience motivations. In Chapter 11, Rebecca Merkin describes the different forces attempting to improve education for women in Pakistan, including the famous case of Malala Yousafzai. She then deconstructs the text of the Pakistani government's newly enacted constitutional amendment, known as the Right to Free and Compulsory Education Act, in order to elucidate how this text is inadequate to effect improved education for women in Pakistan. In addition, its cultural dimensions are analysed and updated using data collected on the basis of Hofstede's (1994) Value Survey Module. The results of the updated cultural characteristics from the Pakistani data are applied to the current situation of women's education in Pakistan. Finally, given Pakistan's cultural characteristics, this chapter concludes with ideas for possible peacebuilding efforts to improve women's education in Pakistan. In Chapter 12, Elesha L. Ruminski examines how a community slogan has prompted dialogue about a particular college town's identity while supporting a broader initiative of promoting alternative dispute resolution supported by the Maryland Judiciary's Mediation and Conflict Resolution Office (MACRO). The slogan, formed through a MACRO-sponsored community dialogue series, inspires a dialogic process that calls for Frostburg community members to ask themselves – and each other – who they are and what is unique and important to them and their community, providing an opportunity to examine dialogic outcomes rhetorically and to understand opportunities for dialogic peace education. The chapter provides reflections on the considerations and implications of the dialogue process for peacebuilding and peace education. In Chapter 13, Jing Lin, Sachi Edwards, and Sahar Khamis present a case study of a Jewish-Muslim dialogue program called the Women's Leadership Initiative (WLI). The program brought together Jewish and Muslim undergraduate women to explore the possibility for peace in the midst of the ongoing Israeli-Palestinian conflict. This chapter describes the processes, challenges, and outcomes of the WLI, and shares insights for future intergroup dialogue facilitators, practitioners, and participants. Specifically, the chapter discusses the difficulty and importance of learning about, and accepting, multiple perspectives; the participants' desire to focus on religious beliefs as a unifying factor, and the implications of doing so; and the participant-led initiatives that resulted from the semester-long program.

The final part of the volume, From Singular/Static to Multiple/ Dynamic: Creative and Alternative Approaches to Cultural Communication, Peacebuilding, and Social Change, includes essays that have a variety of alternative theories and approaches to commu-nicating culture, peace and conflict phenomenon. In Chapter 14, Garry Bailey looks at gender roles in relationships with a particular interest in processes of peacemaking. Gender roles are shown to range from patri-archal and hierarchical complementarian to egalitarian and radical feminist. Because gender roles differ and are often the focus of conflict for people, there are differing and disparaging arguments about these roles. Gender peacemaking is suggested as a response to gender threats using dialectical peace processes. In Chapter 15, Makato Saito explores how ordinary grocery shopping can contribute to the promotion of peace and justice both nationally and globally, while strengthening local food and economic systems. In the chapter, the author compares and contrasts shopping practices in conventional stores and food co-ops highlighting how the same communicative practices of grocery shopping may manifest themselves in the light of food and economic systems, public health and environmental stewardship, and reducing fossil fuel consumption. Using the Cultural Discourse Analysis theory, Saito demonstrates how being a conscientious shopper at a food co-op can outsmart being a smart shopper at a conventional supermarket that constitutes patriotic communicative practices as civic engagement. In Chapter 16, Roshan Noorzai and Claudia L. Hale explore the effective-ness of Afghan songs promoting peace during years of conflict. For this study, the authors analysed songs and interviewed a number of singers. The authors conclude that songs were used as an alternative channel of communication not only to express opposition to war but also to inform and educate masses and warring parties about peace and co-existence. In fact, protest songs became a major cultural capital for peace activism in post-Taliban Afghanistan. Finally, in Chapter 17, Nur Uysal builds on Abu-Nimer's (2001, 2002, 2003) work on religion as a source of peace to explore some of the ways in which faith-based organizations can play a key role in contributing to peacebuilding. Through qualitative field research, this chapter aims to explore the value of interfaith dialogue. A case study on a faith-based organiza-tion inspired by a transnational movement originated in Turkey was conducted. The findings from the case study revealed that interfaith dialogue plays a multifaceted role in the peacebuilding process. The study suggests that faith-based NGOs could be a viable opportunity for future peacebuilding processes and that a cultural communication perspective to interfaith dialogue could further increase the role of faith-based NGOs in peacebuilding processes across the world.

All the essays together argue that if social justice, social change, and peace are to be accomplished at various degrees of incremental success, then readers need to widen their horizons, and become creative in the ways in which they approach cultural conflicts or sustainable peace-building ventures. The essays point to learnings from the mistakes and successes of the past by deconstructing the underlying structural causes of political, economic, and cultural similarities and differences, recon-ceptualizing the taken-for-granted and identifying unconventional, cross-disciplinary methods to educate and inform ourselves in order to take action in matters of culture, peace, and conflict.

References

P. Chow-White and R. McMohan (2012) 'Examining the "Dark Past" and "Hopeful Future" in Representations of Race and Canada's Truth and Reconciliation Commission', in I.S. Shaw, J. Lynch and R. Hackett (eds) *Expanding Peace Journalism: Comparative and Critical Approaches* (Sydney: Sydney University Press) pp. 345–373.

J. Galtung (2004) Violence, War, and their Impact: On Visible and Invisible Effects of Violence, them.polylog.org/5/fgj-en.htm, date accessed 27 May 2015.

J. Lynch and A. McGoldrick (2005) *Peace Journalism* (Stroud: Hawthorn Press).

M. Raboy (1992) 'Media and the Invisible Crisis of Everyday Life', in M. Raboy and B. Dagenais (eds) *Media, Crisis and Democracy: Mass Communication and the Disruption of Social Order* (London: Sage) pp. 133–143.

I.S. Shaw (2012) 'Stereotypical Representations of Muslims and Islam fol-lowing the 7/7 Terrorist Attacks in London: Implications for Intercultural Communication and Terrorism Prevention', *International Communication Gazette*, 74, 509–524.

Part I
From Macro to Micro – Intercultural Communication at the Heart of Conflict Negotiation

This part is dedicated to providing a jumpstart to conceptualizing the variety of cultural contexts within which conflict can raise its head. Conflict could be part of a macro-culture, crossing local boundaries to encompass issues that transcend regions and may exist among groups internationally, or may even be found within a dominant group in a culture. Collier's Chapter 2 takes the reader through an intercultural communication-based peacebuilding framework to her work with the International Peace Initiative in Kenya. Shaw, in Chapter 3, highlights how macro-cultural conflicts such as Islamophobia spread across countries and cultures and how media depict such conflicts. Conflict could also be localized amongst a group of people who share patterns of learned and shared behaviors and ideas in localized regions, among particular groups, such as ethnic groups, racial groups, genders, and age categories. Readers will be able to discern such a conflict in Caputo's Chapter 4 on the dialogic approach to cultural conflict negotiation in a small town in Northern Ireland. Another glimpse of a micro-cultural conflict can be found in Chapter 5, where Betlemidze highlights how a theoretical approach could clarify understanding of conflict in the Caucasus.

2
An Intercultural Peacebuilding Framework: Extending the Conversation through a Focus on Connections

Mary Jane Collier

I am grateful to Sudeshna Roy for the opportunity to expand an earlier conversation about intercultural communication and peacebuilding that Benjamin Broome and I began some years ago. We offered our first articulation of a framework for intercultural peacebuilding in Broome and Collier (2012). We continue to believe there is great potential for scholars interested in culture and communication to contribute to peacebuilding scholarship and practice. In this chapter, with Ben's encouragement and support, I build on that conversation. Below, I first conceptualize intercultural communication and describe its centrality in peacebuilding. Next, I introduce a case study and situated examples of my work with an international nongovernmental organization, International Peace Initiatives (IPI). I concentrate on several IPI projects with which I have been involved over the years in order to better illustrate the value of incorporating a framework with multiple dimensions, different contextual frames, and diverse perspectives on culture and communication into peacebuilding work.

Next, using that case study, I detail the importance of attending to context as macro, meso and micro level frames for peacebuilding. Fourth, I explain the value of recognizing the interrelated personal, relational, and structural dimensions of peacebuilding, as well as offer selected examples of how these dimensions are intersecting, contextually contingent, and communicatively constructed/produced. Fifth, I show how the peacebuilding framework accommodates multiple theoretical perspectives, goals, and diverse methods. Sixth, I argue that reflexivity and reflective practice are essential to address cultural difference, interculturality, and intersectionality; and to recognize levels of privilege, status positioning, equity, inclusion, and justice. I point out how these are essential to the orientation and framework of peacebuilding that Ben and I proposed (Broome and Collier, 2012), as well as to the work of IPI. Finally, I apply several strategies that we articulated previously to the peacebuilding work of IPI to illustrate how to keep the intersections front and center.

I have found that approaching the varied connections and intersections of peacebuilding research and practice as 'dances with difference' is very useful. I have applied this metaphor to discussing various case studies of international, national, and local community engagement as well as the conflict and peacebuilding that is often required in that work (Collier, 2014). Focusing on intercultural communication, on levels of context, and on structural, relational, and personal dimensions of peacebuilding, as 'dances with difference' captures the sense of dialectic tension and back and forth movement that Ben and I envisioned as central to our framework. In sum, my goals in this chapter are to spark interest in these 'dances with difference' and encourage conversation, dialogue, and debate, contribute to work inspired by this book, and to stimulate efforts to expand, revise, and refine our peacebuilding framework.

Overview/review of framework

Below, I review conceptualizations of key terms and concepts to provide readers with necessary foundations of the framework Ben and I co-created. I cite several sections from Broome and Collier (2012). First, we approached *peacebuilding* as working to reduce violence (Bertram, 1995; Hatay, 2005) and promote contextual and cultural transformation (Fisher, 1993). We argued that peacebuilding includes short and long-term, continuously evolving and developing relationships, institutions, and societies (Lederach, 2003).

Three key concepts/processes in our peacebuilding framework are: communication, culture, and context (Broome and Collier, 2012). We defined *communication* as '... the means through which cultures, as well as contexts, are structurally produced and socially constructed' (p. 252). We defined *intercultural communication* as:

> the set of processes through which cultural systems emerge and are contested, reinforced and modified, as well as the processes through which personal views, group identifications, inter-group relationships, group representations, relationships within and across groups, institutional policies, public and organizational discourses, social practices and norms are formed. (p. 253)

We defined *cultures* as:

> ... multi-level, dynamic and often contested communication structures and processes that evidence subject positions and past, present and future itineraries. Any encounter, site or period of time involves multiple cultural identifications, representations, structures and contextual factors. Cultures emerge as personal accounts and narratives, social interaction patterns that produce relationships between groups, institutional discourses, organizational policies and practices, and media discourses that circulate and form a momentary context. (p. 253)

Finally, we defined *context* as:

> ... material and environmental conditions which drive, and can be changed by, peacebuilding. Context includes such factors as histories and collective memory, climate and ecological conditions, food, housing, transportation, war/violence/safety conditions, organizations and services related to governmental, legal, and educational institutions, technologies in use, and resources. The context is more than the 'scene' of peacebuilding; it is a constitutive force and set of dynamic and material conditions. Contexts are both temporal and spatial, incorporating past, present and future. (p. 253)

Intercultural communication therefore is the process through which the three dimensions of peacebuilding: personal, relational, and structural, are constructed and produced. The peacebuilding processes and outcomes occur within dynamic, multileveled contexts. We outlined the dimensions in the following ways (Broome and Collier, 2012):

> The *personal dimension* includes the cognitive, emotional, perceptual, and spiritual aspects of individuals' orientations in conflict situations. Scholar/practitioners of culture and communication working at this level examine individuals' preferences and self-descriptions of social-psychological dimensions and orientations to conflict and peacebuilding. The focus is on maximizing potential for individual changes in self-perceptions, narratives, and perceptions of the other, reducing enemy images while increasing open-mindedness and willingness to engage with the other through dialogue and other forms of constructive conflict transformation.
>
> The *relational dimension* includes the communicative and interactive aspects of conflict. Scholar/practitioners of culture and

communication working at this level examine social relationships, inter-group relationships, the nature of hierarchies and status positioning of group members. The focus is on promoting *patterns* of communication and community engagement that contribute to conflict transformation, relationships that are equitable, inclusive, and enhance justice, and the work of intercultural alliances.

The *structural dimension* includes ways in which societal discourses, organizational policies, and institutional practices create and enable differential access to resources and status, levels of individual agency and equity, levels of inclusion and decision making, and societal norms. Scholar/practitioners working at this level examine how structures such as policies, laws, public and media texts and discourses, both enable and constrain individuals and groups. The focus is on what needs to be changed in institutional policies and practices, creating the means to enable broader inclusion of diverse voices, and creating conditions and relations that contribute to social justice and peace. Contextual factors and conditions (such as economic conditions, food and supplies, and travel restrictions) become structures when they exert constraining and/or enabling force on group members. (pp. 251–252)

A final essential component of our framework is reflexivity. We defined *reflexivity* as reflecting both individually and dialogically with each other and with those with whom we work about our various cultural identifications, locations of advantage and disadvantage, ideologies that we privilege, and approaches and assumptions we bring to peacebuilding. We argued that reflexivity is essential to confront the challenges of peacebuilding, collaboratively design relevant and sustainable interventions, and identify when it is time to step back or step out for good.

International Peace Initiatives (IPI)

I have been working with IPI since 1999, since its inception as the visionary idea of a doctoral student, and now colleague and dear friend, Dr. Karambu Ringera. As of 2013, IPI has sent over 1,000 children to school, impacted more than 2,500 families, and touched the lives of countless others in Kenya, Africa, India, the US, the UK, Austria, and Australia. IPI has numerous programs: the Institute of Nonviolence and Peace, the Orphans and Vulnerable Children's Education Fund, Community Support Initiatives, Amani Children's Homes, and the IPI College Scholar's Program. All these programs support primarily women and children to overcome vulnerabilities brought about by poverty, disease, and violence.

In Meru, Kenya, there is an environmentally friendly home for vulnerable children (Kithoka Amani Community Children's Home, or KACH) that includes a dining hall used for community meetings. There is an organic farm with an irrigation system. An eco-lodge for visitors has now been completed and is being expanded into a peace village. There is a vibrant workshop for enterprises such as weaving, making jewelry, detergent, and other products. There is a council/prayer building as well as a house nearby which is the IPI office. IPI is not only an international organization, but also a consortium of many different collaborators and funders; a place where community members and volunteers live and work; a set of structures for conflict transformation, problem-solving, and advocacy; and a set of spaces in which intercultural communication and inter-community peacebuilding deliberations thrive.

I am a founding US IPI Board member, (there is also a Kenyan IPI Board), and I have served as an evaluator, financial supporter, trainer, observer, and ally to the extensive community engagement and peacebuilding work. Dr. Karambu (as she prefers to be called) and I approach our relationship as a particular type of 'allyhood' (Collier and Ringera, 2015). We have also written about our collaboration as a series of 'intercultural dances with difference' (Ringera and Collier, 2014). I expand the conversation about the peacebuilding framework below by using IPI's important peacebuilding projects and work with various communities to demonstrate the value of a focus on *connections and intersections between* peacebuilding dimensions.

Working with the intersections: intercultural, contextualized dimensions of peacebuilding

Key concepts

Cultures, interculturalities, and dances with difference

My IPI collaborators and I approach culture and intercultural communication in IPI's peacebuilding work from decidedly critical as well as interpretive perspectives. Cultures are approached as itineraries to point to movement (Collier et al., 2002) and to acknowledge that contextually contingent interculturalities are being formed through communication. For example, Dr. Karambu's and my peacebuilding itineraries include both critical evaluation of some international development and calls for community based action planning. However, we bring different national, racial, ethnic, and class positioned identifications and goals into our itineraries. These itineraries and interculturalities as dynamic locations evidence the unfolding dances with difference (Collier, 2014) that are evident in peacebuilding and intercultural relationships.

Cultures are communicative systems associated with groups, organizations, and places/spaces; cultures emerge through structures that are institutional, such as government, churches, and legal and educational systems. Christianity is a strong institution in Kenya, for instance. Cultures are also evident in communicative texts and discourses in relationships between group members and in personal sets of values, representations of other groups, and so on. This approach to cultures as plural, dynamic, and multi-dimensional means that cultures pertain to socially constructed orientations as well as institutionally/organizationally produced ideologies, policies, and practices. Cultures and interculturalities need to be viewed through all the contextualized dimensions outlined below in order to ensure that views are contextually relevant, resonate to some degree with community members, and are useful in contributing to peacebuilding work that is just, equitable, and inclusive.

Contextual frames

When examining intractable conflict, community engagement and peacebuilding, scholars benefit from examining macro, meso, and micro contextual frames (Sorrells, 2012). To begin with a macro frame for contextual factors, in Kenya, national culture includes a government system of a political democracy, a history of colonial influences, a strong educational system, and a high rate of poverty due to a struggling economy and long-term drought. Male dominance is reflected in the low number of female members of Parliament and large business owners, and the high rate of abuse of women. While Christianity is strongly represented, Muslim groups and mosques are also growing in numbers. There are numerous international 'aid' agencies which are also positioned as oppressive by some and welcome by others.

At the meso contextual frame, ethnic cultural conflict erupted in violence in the national election prior to the last, and increasing numbers of refugees are changing the cultural composition of Nairobi, Mombasa, and other cities. Women have historically assumed, and are also in the present assuming leadership roles in community organizations. For instance, Dr. Karambu regularly initiates partnerships of IPI with numerous local and national Kenyan women's organizations, women's youth organizations, and women leaders. This is an important move in the broader context of longstanding patriarchy and male dominance, and an important move in pre-empting the need for international organizations to impose their views and offer resources to local communities.

> The idea that 'help' will come from the outside is challenged when people recognize that within us and our communities, we have adequate resources to bring about change. When people recognize that institutions and systems that are not working in our society must be changed from within, not from outside, then people start to be engaged citizens, looking for solutions and leading in this transformation themselves.
>
> (Interviewee quoted in Ringera and Collier, 2014, p. 114)

Micro-level contextual factors are also an important lens through which to understand intercultural peacebuilding praxis. Micro-level interactions and discourses in which I participated and observed do more than reveal individual views and experiences. They also evoke representations of groups and institutions such as the US government. In my work with IPI in Kenya, I experienced conversations in which a female chief described the needs of her struggling communities due to histories of colonial dependence and declining aid, as well as experiences with corrupt political candidates buying votes and not following through on promises to local groups. I conversed with a representative of the US State Department who offered overgeneralized and negative representations of Kenyans and their 'tendencies toward violence during elections' or the predictability of Kenyans in the US 'overstay[ing] their visas to remain in the US' At the same time, this official offered overgeneralized, one-sided, positive representations of US elections as 'unobstructed and fair' and US government programs in Kenya having a long history of providing 'essential resources and advice' that Kenyans 'couldn't do without'.

All three levels of context are important in intercultural communication (Sorrells, 2012) and keeping an eye on the intersections of these levels is essential in designing, implementing, and evaluating IPI's peacebuilding praxis. The examples above illustrate the overlapping and intersectional nature of micro, meso, and macro levels of context and communicative texts. Acknowledging the complicated context and recognizing the need to create independent, local processes of social change led IPI's founder Dr. Karambu to orient their work by emphasizing participant generated descriptions of needs and issues, and participant driven processes and practices. As Dr. Karambu describes, 'Through its various programs, IPI uses a holistic, participatory, empowerment and community-based approach to model how engaged communities transform disempowering circumstances into opportunities for self-reliance and sustainable peace and "development"' (Ringera and Collier, 2014, p. 113). This approach demonstrates the value of a commitment to community members driving discussions and actions related to the choice of issues that need to be addressed, outlining the nature of the problems, the resources needed and available, who is affected, contextual factors such as obstacles and resources available, development of action plans, and implementation of peacebuilding steps.

Connections between contextualized dimensions of peacebuilding

Intersecting structural and relational dimensions

IPI peacebuilding praxis emerges in the intersections of structural factors and forces, and relationships between and among groups. For my work with IPI my collaborators and I have found it important to not only analyse the range of extant and previous enabling and constraining structures that are relevant to each particular issue being addressed in a particular project, but also to talk about how to change or create new structures that will enable peacebuilding praxis. For example, Ringera (2014) argues that peacebuilding in Kenya is governed by histories of colonialism and a dominant ideology of war and peace founded in patriarchy, and models of conflict that are reactive (protectionist and exclusionist) rather than proactive (based on inclusion and equity). Ringera and Collier (2014) outline the impact of the United Nations Security Council Resolution 1325 in 2000, which positions women, and organizations and civil society organizations led by women, as taking center stage in ensuring the new constitution is enforced and peacebuilding occurs at the national and local level. These macro structures are of both the past and present scenes, and part and parcel of the local situated and material conditions impacting everyday relationships.

Thus, these structures are part of a range of relationships between and among groups and between and among leaders. It is valuable to assess not only what the extant relationships are but also which ones might become the most relevant relationships. What could be changed to enhance just, inclusive, and equitable peacebuilding? These assessment and design moves have a better chance of serving peacebuilding if they do not occur in isolation but are approached as intersecting forces and tensions between dimensions.

Historically, as well as currently, many international organizations and development organizations seem to overlook the role of women and their actions in organizing, protesting, and creating change at the local level. As Collier and Ringera (2014) describe, women note that many husbands and some male community leaders call for women to 'stay in the kitchen', while women have been organizing, innovating, and creating micro-enterprises to sustain their families, educate their children, and obtain antiretroviral medications to fight HIV/ AIDS for decades. Peacebuilding researchers and practitioners would be well served by examining relationships among and between groups as contextualized, and structured in part by globalization, global and national histories, various forms of patriarchy, as well as local norms, ideologies and 'traditional' practices around decision-making and problem-solving. As well, using the structural lens enables a clearer view of how feminist, inclusive, equitable relations are constructed among women leaders and among male and female feminists to take needed actions.

To increase the effectiveness of local relationships in a context of drought and economic challenge, IPI has created multiple Community Support Initiatives in networks with over 20 community-based groups to support women (as well as men) and youth in income-generating projects related to jewelry, bee-keeping, and detergent making. The women along with experienced community members, grow their own crops, and to expand permaculture, have built relationships and part-nered with local experts to build an organic farm and expand irrigation.

Intersecting structural and personal dimensions

The macro, meso, and micro contexts, and thus structural factors, are also part of the picture of the personal dimension of peacebuild-ing. I found that it was important to understand the strong role of Christianity and Christian churches in Kenya. For instance, in my trav-els and stays with families, as well as focus group interviews, I learned the importance for community members of beginning and closing sessions with Christian prayers. This move set a tone of reverence and respectful engagement, as well as reinforced some of the transcendent principles that motivated the groups. As another example, I heard many women, some quite ill with HIV/AIDS, describing their unwavering personal commitment to see their children educated. I also heard male community leaders and organizational staff describe their personal, moral call to overcome patriarchy, and prevent violence against women and children.

At a day long peace forum, I heard testimonials and narratives that resulted in an action plan for male elders to meet with their sons to hear their views and then problem-solve the extreme shortage of employment, poverty, and increasing frequencies of alcoholism and drug addiction that then resulted in increased violence. The value of family and community came through strongly as individuals contributed their views. However, understanding the constraints of the broader context in the form of economic conditions, social norms, and sometimes disappointing political leadership and funding, is essential to understanding the narratives I heard. These pointed to the limitations, as well as the opportunities for individuals to take action.

My personal orientation to my roles and relationships as an invited observer at the peace forum is another example of the value of attending to the intersections of structural and personal dimensions. Enabling and constraining structural factors included how histories, experience with international agencies, education, and treatment by government representatives from the US affected how my nationality, white race, and female body were positioned by diverse Kenyans and international visitors. My membership on the US IPI Board, my professor status, my having been Dr. Karambu's advisor, and my long-term relationship with Dr. Karambu, who was helping lead events such as the local peace forum in Meru, all worked in my favor. It was clear that I was invited as an observer, however, rather than any sort of a participant or trainer, which is consistent with the participant action approach and IPI values (Collier and Ringera, 2014). These examples show that peacebuilding researchers and practitioners are well served by keeping these contextually contingent intersections in view.

Intersecting relational and personal dimensions

Dr. Karambu and I have written elsewhere about our relationship as allies and our shared political itinerary as feminists (Collier and Ringera, 2015). It is important for peacebuilding researchers and practitioners to recognize that relationships take time to develop and individuals must commit to weathering conflict if the relationship is to be sustained. Because Dr. Karambu and I met when she was my doctoral student at the University of Denver over 15 years ago, our relationship has evolved and changed. We are now colleagues and Dr. Karambu is an internationally recognized activist, peacebuilder, local and national leader, and tireless advocate for IPI. When the US Board needed more insight about why funding planned for the expansion of the eco-lodge in Meru was diverted to pay for a security guard and building of a road, my relationship with Dr. Karambu meant that I could talk with her and get her point of view, knowing that it might be hard to hear that her decisions were been questioned by the US Board. Also, I could provide more context about 'on-the-ground' conditions to the US Board. During the period of time when there weren't regular visits by US Board members to Kenya (which are now occurring), my experience in Kenya also meant that I had the positioning that enabled me sometimes to call out US Board members and volunteers whose national, class-based, and racialized privilege and presumptions relating to 'how things ought to be done in Kenya' frequently colored their actions.

Additionally, my relationship and shared political itinerary enabled Dr. Karambu and I to talk about power relations pretty openly. As the leader of an international non-governmental organization receiving funds from the US and several European donors, Dr. Karambu had been 'under surveillance' by organizations for many years, and also had widespread experience seeing and hearing how dependencies upon international agencies depleted the abilities of local communities to exert their own agency. When I had to 'wear my US IPI Board cap' as Dr. Karambu put it, and interrogate the IPI budget line by line, this was challenging. When US-donated goods got stuck in Nairobi due to bureaucratic policies that often resulted in international organizations paying bribes for the correct signature to emerge, it came down to trusting that Dr. Karambu was doing everything possible to sort out the situation. She said at one point, 'Either you trust me or you don't'.

Reflexivity as a foundational commitment in peacebuilding

One of the ways to account for the complexities of the context, culturally diverse identifications and representations, the range of communication discourses and forms of communication including mediated, digital, cell phone and face-to-face interaction, and intersecting dimensions of personal, relational, and structural factors, is the praxis of reflexivity. Benjamin Broome and I gave an overview of our positionalities that impact our researcher and practitioner orientations to peacebuilding (Broome and Collier, 2012). Dr. Karambu and I wrote a narrative (Collier and Ringera, 2015) that also reflexively described the challenges, joys, and lessons of sustaining an international ally relationship. I have learned countless insights from my conversations with Dr. Karambu, the IPI staff, and leaders and participants in community organizations.

As one example of a lesson I continue to learn, my privileged locations, critical research itinerary, and desire for individual recognition regularly pop up amidst those who 'get' my whiteness, national, race and class privilege, among other things. As Warren (2010), among others, points out, researchers, practitioners, and certainly peacebuilders, should not assume that once we have a glimmer of understanding our own privileges, such as whiteness, that this will last, or position ourselves as superior to others, who don't 'get it'. Such positionings misrepresent how momentary awareness cannot be equated to taking actions to achieve structural change, and may act to reproduce status hierarchies. I consider myself extremely lucky to have developed a relationship with several international collaborators that can help remind me that this work is not about the personal dimension exclusively, and not about 'me'; it is about keeping the focus on the contextually contingent connections between the structural, relational, and personal dimensions. Reflexivity is therefore central in that we all bring a range of identifications, representations, ideological biases, and social justice sensibilities into tension and conversation to increase the relevance and sustainability of peacebuilding.

Selected strategies and stances enhancing peacebuilding

Particular strategies found useful in the peacebuilding work described by Broome and Collier (2012) are also found in my work with IPI; these speak to intersections and the communicative spaces between dimensions, context, communication, and cultural difference. As described earlier, cultures are plural, cultural identifications are intersecting as well as contested, and there are many 'dances with difference'. Not all US, British, or representatives of international organizations enact colonizer identifications. Male and female, wealthy and impoverished, young and elderly Kenyan community members enact and help reproduce both patriarchy and feminist cultural systems. Thus, acknowledging multivocality as well as intersectionality is important if peacebuilding work is to be relevant.

Histories are also multiple and contested; where one community leader valorizes a long history of partnering with organizations in Europe, for instance, there will be another whose goal is to create a new history of independence from those partnerships. There are clashing and contradictory histories around political conflict in Kenya, as in most sites of intractable conflict. Peacebuilders benefit from recognizing competing ideologies as well as histories related to peace and conflict; these also drive and are driven by intercultural communication and contextual factors, and affect the relationships between dimensions of peacebuilding.

Power relations are both produced by structures and constructed by groups and individuals. Several community groups and intercommunity organizations, such as those located in Meru, have begun to meet regularly for peace forums and problem solving. During my last visit, a community member explained that they no longer had patience with politicians whose promised resources, such as a larger police force, never materialized. They had decided to form their own security group who community members could call on. One community worked with their female chief and local women's groups to close down an illegal liquor distributor, and at the same time committed to protecting the female chief from retaliation from any of the male chiefs or local security personnel. Thus, it is evident that agency emerges in the intersections of group members' abilities to act within contextual enabling and constraining forces. Peacebuilders who want to work with communities in order that community members can develop sustainable and relevant practices are making presumptions about and influencing opportunities for exertion of agency. As Dr. Karambu and I have experienced in our work with IPI, to increase levels of agency for community members means attending to intersecting dimensions of the structural, relational, and personal; and working with the 'between-ness' of 'our dances with difference' (Collier, 2014).

Finally, a long-term commitment to engagement is essential to peacebuilding projects. IPI is clearly Dr. Karambu's life work, and IPI has a network of expanding, and continuing relationships with various groups and organizations. As mentioned earlier, my long-term relationship with Dr. Karambu and several members of the IPI staff has provided space for us to work through conflict, discuss privilege and power, and refine as well as reinforce our itinerary of peacebuilding work.

Continuing the conversation

My goal for this chapter has been not only to spark dialogue and discussion about how the elements of the peacebuilding framework developed by Ben Broome and me in 2012 can be fruitfully applied, but also to focus on the intersections and connections among the elements that may produce more nuanced, complex, and inclusive intercultural peacebuilding. Intercultural communication scholars and practitioners have much to offer to such a global, national, and local, and disciplinary and interdisciplinary, arena of research and practice. Ben and I look forward to many more and wider conversations that will spark critique and change in the framework, as well as demonstrate the potential for increased inclusion, equity, and justice in the connections between cultures, communication, and peacebuilding.

References

E. Bertram (1995) 'Reinventing Governments: The Promise and Perils of United Nations Peace Building', *Journal of Conflict Resolution*, 39, 387–418.

B. J. Broome and M. J. Collier (2012) 'Culture, Communication, and Peacebuilding: A Reflexive Multi-Dimensional Contextual Framework', *Journal of International and Intercultural Communication*, 5, 243–269.

M. J. Collier (2014) *Community Engagement and Intercultural Praxis: Dancing with Difference in Diverse Contexts* (New York City, NY: Peter Lang).

M. J. Collier, R. Hegde, W. Lee, T. Nakayama, and G. Yep (2002) 'Dialogue on the Edges: Ferment in Communication and Culture' in M. J. Collier (ed.) *International and Intercultural Communication Annual: Transforming Communication about Culture* 24 Vol. 24 (Thousand Oaks, CA: SAGE Publishing, Inc) pp. 219–280.

M. J. Collier and K. Ringera (2015) 'Intercultural Allies Dancing with Difference: International Peace Initiatives, Kenya' in K. Sorrells and S. Sekimoto (eds) *Globalizing Intercultural Communication: A Reader* (Los Angeles, CA: SAGE Publications, Inc).

R. J. Fisher (1993) 'The Potential for Peacebuilding: Forging a Bridge From Peacekeeping to Peacemaking', *Peace & Change*, 18, 247–266.

A. J. Hatay (2005) 'Peacebuilding and Reconciliation in Bosnia and Herzegovina, Kosovo and Macedonia 1995–2004', Uppsala: Department of Peace and Conflict Research, Uppsala University.

J. P. Lederach (2003) *The Little Book of Conflict Transformation* (Intercourse, PA: Good Books).

K. Ringera (2014) 'The Role of Women in Grassroots Peacebuilding in Kenya', in S. B. Maphosa, L. DeLuca and A. Keasley (eds) *Building Peace from Within: An Examination of Community-Based Peacebuilding and Transitions in Africa* (Pretoria, South Africa: Africa Institute of South Africa) pp.172–198.

K. Ringera and M. J. Collier (2014) 'Beyond Development to Grassroots Dances: International Peace Initiatives in Kenya' in M. J. Collier *Community Engagement and Intercultural Praxis: Dancing with Difference in Diverse Contexts* (New York City, NY: Peter Lang) pp. 112–136.

K. Sorrells (2012) *Intercultural Communication: Globalization and Social Justice* (Thousand Oaks, CA: SAGE Publishing, Inc).

J. T. Warren (2010) 'It Really Isn't about You: Whiteness and the Dangers of Thinking You Got It' in T. K. Nakayama and R. T. Halualani (eds) *The Handbook of Critical Intercultural Communication* (Chichester, England: Wiley-Blackwell) pp. 446–460.

3
Reporting the Lee Rigby Murder and Anti-Muslim Hostilities in the UK in 2013: The Cultural Clash Communication and Human Wrongs Journalism Nexus

Ibrahim Seaga Shaw

The way different cultures are mediated in the mainstream press goes a long way in influencing how people are perceived across cultures. According to recent research (Khiabany and Williamson, 2012, Shaw, 2012a, and Ogan et al., 2014) the representation of Islam and Muslims in the mainstream press in the past two decades has largely been influenced by Samuel Huntington's prediction in his ground-breaking book in 1996 that the source of the great divisions and conflicts between peoples of global society will be cultural, and not necessarily ideological or economic, as in the last century. Yet, not many people took Huntington's prediction seriously until the 9/11 terrorist attacks that have been followed by many others from Madrid, London, Mumbai, Philippines, and most recently, to Sydney and Paris. In the post-Cold War era, 'the friendly/enemy country dichotomy is determined not necessarily by east/west/communist/capitalist ideologies but by who is on our side in this "war on terror"' (Shaw, 2012a, p. 4). Thus Muslims and the Islamic World, who are largely perceived in the West as targets, and not helpers in the 'war on terror', have since the end of the Cold War replaced the 'Soviet Union' as the new 'uncivilised' enemy of the 'civilised' Western world.

This chapter builds on work by Shaw (2012a), who argues that the news media's discursive stereotypes and clichés, portraying Muslims as 'inferior', 'uncivilised', 'violent', and 'destructive' constitute 'fighting' and 'hate' words of cultural miscommunication. Shaw (2012a) notes that these words have the potential to incite hostility towards all believers of Islam on the one hand, and provoke Islamic radicalism or extremism on the other. However, while that work focused on the problem of miscommunication in the reporting of the 7/7 London Terrorist bombings, this chapter mainly compares the framing of one act of extremism and terrorism carried out by two Muslims against a British soldier, and the framing of the counter extremism and terrorism against Muslims allegedly blamed on right-wing extremist groups. This chapter refers to both as acts of extremism and terrorism largely caused by intercultural miscommunication, or what I now call cultural clash communication, which constitutes what Galtung (2004) calls 'cultural violence'. The acts of extremism and terrorism carried out are manifestations of 'indirect' forms of violence such as the 'hate' stereotypical representation of the 'other'. In this chapter I draw on cultural studies and critical theory perspectives (Weerakkody, 2009) and Galtung's idea of indirect cultural violence as part of his ABC conflict triangle (Galtung, 2004) in content-analysing the largely negative representations of Muslims based on systemic and deliberate use of varying patterns of stereotyping—that is, using negative characteristics unique to one or two individuals based on their behaviour in a particular situation to describe the general characteristics of a specific group to which that individual or those individuals belong. The danger of negative group stereotyping is that the blame and potential backlash of one human wrong committed by one member of a religious or political community are shared by all members of that community. For instance, by virtue of their being Muslims, coupled with their chanting some verses from the Koran when carrying out the murder of Drummer Lee Rigby in Woolwich on Wednesday 22 May 2013, Michael Adepolajo and Michael Adobawale have not been alone on the receiving end of blame and reprisal for their acts of extremism and terrorism. A plethora of evidence provided by the Islamophobia monitoring watchdog Tell Mama, and reported in mainstream media shows that right-wing anti-Islamic discourses and hostilities have been rising sharply since the Lee Rigby murder. However, while the two involved in the Rigby murder, and all Muslims, became recipients of blame and hostility, this chapter argues that the situation was completely different in the case of acts of extremism and terrorism carried out in light of right-wing discourses, and forms of violence against all Muslims. Here, interventions from the police and political authorities to prevent, or react to, the increasing anti-Muslim hostilities were lacklustre to say the least, while media coverage was seriously limited to few articles, and with very little context.

This chapter takes the following structure: first, a brief look at the intercultural communication and human rights journalism/peace journalism nexus in the context of reporting extremism and terrorism; second, the research objective, questions, and methodology; third, the extent of coverage and the sourcing patterns of the Lee Rigby murder and anti-Muslim hostilities; fourth, Islamophobia or anti-right-wing discourses; and finally, diagnostic discourses of the Lee Rigby murder and anti-Muslim hostilities.

Extremism and terrorism: the intercultural communication–human rights journalism/peace journalism nexus

There is a plethora of research that suggests that anti-Muslim prejudices and hostilities have existed long before the 9/11 terrorist attacks in the US in 2001. The 1997 Runnymede Trust report on Islamophobia produced by the Commission for British Muslims and Islamophobia and authored by Chris Allen noted in its opening sections, 'Islamophobic discourse, sometimes blatant but frequently coded and subtle, is part of everyday life in modern Britain … in the last 20 years … the dislike [of Islam and Muslims] has become more explicit, more extreme and more dangerous' (Allen, 1997, p. 6). Edward Said put the blame on the media when he wrote, 'there has been an intense focus on Muslims and Islam in the American and Western media, most of it characterised by a more highly exaggerated stereotyping and belligerent hostility' (Said, 1997, p. 11). As Khiabany and Williamson (2012) observe, anti-Muslim racism predates immigration from Muslim majority countries to the UK or the 'war on terror'. The 'backward, atavistic, barbaric and fanatical' stereotypical representations of Arab-Muslim majority countries date back to several centuries ago, during the eras of western imperialism and colonialism of the Middle East and North Africa (Khiabany and Williamson, 2012, p. 138). Italian Premier Berlusconi said: 'We must be aware of the superiority of our civilisation, a system that has guaranteed well-being, respect for human rights—and in contrast with Islamic countries' (BBC News, 2001).

However, according to a report by Amnesty International (2012), the events of 9/11 and a series of other terrorist attacks in Madrid, London, Mumbai, the Philippines, and most recently in Sydney and Paris, have created a general climate for increasing anti-Muslim attitudes in many countries in the West. According to Ogan et al. (2014), two reasons have been given for these latest rounds of Islamophobia: first, the

US-led Western wars in Iraq and Afghanistan; second, the US media, and by extension the Western media, which tend to employ Samuel Huntington's Clash of Civilizations understanding of Islam when reporting stories about Muslims or their religion (Seib, 2004). 'Huntington's controversial view of post-cold war global conflict was that culture—largely based on religion, rather than ideology or geography—would be the cause' (Ogan et al., 2014, p. 29). Yet the suggestion by Ogan et al. (2014) that 'many attribute these latest rounds of Islamophobia 'to the wars in Afghanistan and Iraq' is problematic to say least, not least because it confuses the definition of Islamophobia to mean 'Islamic or Muslim extremism or terrorism, when in actual fact Islamophobia, according to the 1997 Rennymede Trust Report, is defined as anti-Islam or fear of Islam type of behaviour or attitude, but also because according to a maze of research (Khiabany and Williamson, 2012, Shaw, 2012a, Said, 1997), including that in this chapter, there is little evidence in the coverage of the mainstream media of extremism and terrorism allegedly carried out by Muslims to suggest that these acts of extremism and terrorism are attributed to Western wars carried out in Islamic countries such as Iraq and Afghanistan.

But it is not only the definition of Islamophobia that has attracted controversy in both academic and journalistic circles in recent times. The definitions of extremism and terrorism have also been controversial in the sense that the definitions of these two concepts vary according to which side of the divide you find yourself between the **us** (the Western culture) and the **them** (Islamic culture). The way we perceive acts of violence carried out by groups such as the Palestinians, the Kashmiris, the Tamil Tigers, and the Northern Irish Republicans can vary from person to person or from one place to another. This reinforces the cliché that 'one man's terrorist is another's freedom fighter' (McCoubrey, 1997, p. 258). For instance, Saddam Hussein, Osama Bin Laden, and the Taliban were all in the recent past described as terrorists, but they have all been at one stage hailed as friends of the West, and in fact regarded as freedom fighters and those fighting a just war (Thomas, 2002).

Thus the differences in the framing of extremism and terrorism in the mainstream media clearly reinforce the cultural clash communication. However, in the context of intercultural communication, all acts of extremism and terrorism, be it by Muslims or non-Muslims, must be presented and condemned as such, without any form of discrimination. It is the main aim of the research in this chapter to find out whether the mainstream media coverage of the Lee Rigby murder and the anti-Muslim protests and hostility fall-outs tended to result more from intercultural communication or cultural clash communication.

For the rest of this section I will look at intercultural communication as it relates to peace journalism and human rights journalism. First, what do we mean by intercultural communication. Klyukanov (2005) defines culture in terms of values and beliefs associated with groups based on gender, religion, nationality, ethnicity, or physical ability/disability. The term communication is defined as 'the practice of creating meanings or symbolic resources' (Klyukanov, 2005, p. 10). Based on this culture–communication nexus, Klyukanov (2005, p. 10) defines intercultural communication as a 'process of interaction between groups of people with different systems of symbolic resources'.

Intercultural communication based on constructive boundary lines that value and endorse individuals for what they are, and use supportive language when referring to them is largely similar to peace journalism, because the latter encourages a win-win approach to constructive dialogue with due respect given to the views and opinions of all parties in the conflict. Lynch and McGoldrick (2005, p. 5) define peace journalism as 'a set of tools, both conceptual and practical, intended to equip journalists to offer a better public service' and provide society at large with opportunities 'to consider and value nonviolent responses to conflict'. Both intercultural communication and peace journalism demonstrate empathy for cultures and peoples, and are orientated towards truth and solutions instead of propaganda (lies) and problems (conflict), respectively.

Intercultural communication based on constructive boundary lines that attach value and respect to the 'other' resonates with the idea of human rights journalism, which Shaw (2012b, p. 46) refers to as 'journalism without borders—a journalism based on human rights and global justice, a journalism that challenges political, economic, social and cultural imbalances of society at both local and global levels'. In fact human rights journalism (HRJ) goes one step further than peace journalism in resonating with intercultural communication in that it moves beyond the double win, that is win-win involving the cultural groups involved in the cultural exchange, to a triple win, that is a win-win involving not only the groups engaged in the cultural exchange but also third-party bystanders who are not directly involved. Moreover, HRJ goes further in resonating with intercultural communication in being more proactive in challenging indirect structural and cultural imbalances of society as cold conflicts, instead of waiting until they manifest as direct political violence, as hot conflicts. Chow-White and

McMahon (2012, p. 348) affirm that peace journalism research has largely focused on examples of 'hot conflict', such as media coverage of wars/conflicts.

Research objectives and questions

The objective of this chapter is three-fold. First, to use content analysis to compare the framing by six British national newspapers of the act of extremism and terrorism carried out in the murder of British soldier Lee Rigby and that of the acts of extremism and terrorism carried out in the attacks against Muslims and Islamic centres as fall-outs of the murder, to determine the extent and variation of intercultural miscommunication as a form of human wrongs journalism. Second, to use content and discourse analysis to investigate the extent to which Islamophobic or demonic stereotypical representations of Muslims in the first two-and-a-half weeks of coverage of the Rigby murder was far more than or less than the demonic representation of fascist and racist right-wing British activists who carried out the increasing anti-Muslim hostilities in the UK in the weeks that followed. Finally, to use content and discourse analysis to investigate the use of evocative descriptive distance frames or diagnostic critical empathy frames in the British press coverage of the Rigby murder and the anti-Muslim hostilities.

Based on the three main aims of the chapter outlined above, the following research questions will be explored:

1) What was the volume of coverage in the six British newspapers devoted to the Rigby murder and the anti-Muslim hostilities?
2) Which sources were most frequently cited in the coverage of the Rigby murder and the anti-Muslim hostilities?
3) What was the volume of Islamophobic frames compared to those condemning right-wing fascist attacks on Islam?
4) How did the six newspapers perform on the evocative-vs-diagnostic framing of the Lee Rigby murder and anti-Muslim hostilities?

Methodology

The methodology is inspired by a combination of thematic and textual analysis of the news coverage of the Lee Rigby murder in Woolwich and the following anti-Muslim hostilities, drawing on methods of content analysis, framing analysis, and critical discourse analysis (CDA). Manifest quantitative content and latent qualitative framing analyses will be employed to analyse news coverage to answer the first three research questions, while CDA will be used to analyse news coverage to answer research question four. A combination of quantitative and qualitative content analysis is undertaken to understand both the literal, denotative, and generally accepted meanings of textual messages on one hand and the hidden, implied, connotative meanings of textual messages (Weerakkody, 2009, p. 146) on the other.

I employ a frame analysis method to determine the extent of Islamophobic discourses (ID) in the British press reporting of the Lee Rigby murder and their demonisation of right-wing fascist discourses in the following anti-Muslim hostilities in answering research question three. Entman (1993, p. 51–53) defines news framing as the process in which we select 'some aspects of a perceived reality and make them more salient in a communicating text in such a way as to promote a particular problem definition, causal interpretation, moral evaluation, and/or treatment recommendation'. Media frames reflect broader cultural themes and discourses, providing audiences with ways to think about issues. They reflect how journalists emphasise or de-emphasise their expression of an issue. Framing news stories comprises persistent cognitive ways in which information is selected, excluded, emphasised, and organised into discourse (Chong and Druckman, 2007, p. 100). Van Ginneken (1998, p. 15–16) describes this as an arbitrary process of 'selective articulation' and argues that people's worldviews essentially influence how stories and issues are framed. Thus, in this study, the articles coded and analysed contain repetitive themes or stereotypical representations contributing to an essentialist negative portrayal of Islam and Muslims based on the extremist or terrorist behaviour of one or two Muslims, on one hand, and those contributing to an essentialist negative portrayal of British national identity based on the extremist or terrorist behaviour of one or two Britons, on the other.

CDA draws its strength from Gramsci's notion of hegemony as developed by a number of cultural studies theorists (Van Dijk, 1993, p. 251). It considers the ways in which social order and power relations are created and reproduced in discourse (Fairclough, 1995, p. 94, Van Dijk, 1993, p. 253). It is particularly concerned with the negative role of the media in creating and reinforcing inequality in social relations. The choice of CDA as one of the methodological approaches is informed by the fact that it strongly relies on linguistic categories such as modes or nuances of communication using idioms, clichés, vocabulary, metaphors etc. in contrast to other approaches to text and discourse analyses, such as content or conversation analysis (Titscher et al., 2000, Wodak and

Meyer, 2001). CDA is very helpful in determining the location and spread of hegemony in news media discourse. Stereotypical portrayals of particular social groups are firmly embedded in polarising discourses of extremism and terrorism. The chapter particularly draws on CDA's hermeneutic method of 'grasping and producing meaning relations' (Wodak and Meyer, 2001, p. 16) to determine the resonance between negative and destructive stereotypes, on one hand, and discourses of hate and hostilities, on the other, employed by the mainstream British press coverage of the 2013 Lee Rigby murder in Woolwich, especially in the West Midlands. The consequence of using the hermeneutic CDA procedure is that the line between data collection and analysis is blurred. The approach of this chapter in answering research question four is therefore similar to many CDA studies that 'deal with only small corpora which are usually regarded as being typical of certain discourses' (Wodak and Meyer, 2001, p. 25). The use of CDA as an additional methodological approach is considered necessary here to complement the content analysis and framing analysis which are in themselves considered to have their limitations.

The unit of analysis is corpora drawn from news coverage of the Lee Rigby murder and subsequent anti-Muslim hostilities by six British national newspapers (four broadsheets—the *Telegraph*, *Times*, *Guardian* and *Independent*, and two tabloids—the *Daily Mail* and *Daily Mirror*). The rationale for the choice of these six British national newspapers is informed by the fact that they are the most authoritative and widely read newspapers in Britain. They are newspapers of reference recognised nationally and internationally. They also represent a holistic ideological spectrum, with the *Daily Mail* and *Telegraph* leaning towards the political right, the *Times* centre-right, the *Guardian* and *Daily Mirror* centre-left, and the *Independent* left. The choice of such a diverse ideological spectrum of newspapers allows us to observe the extent to which ideology influenced the framing of Islamophobic and demonic right-wing discourses of the Lee Rigby murder and anti-Muslim hostilities. The press has been selected for this research because newspapers continue to play an important role in setting the news agenda for politically and ideologically charged issues of the day. Only articles collated from the Lexis-Nexis database of the six British newspapers in the study using the search words 'Woolwich murder' between 23 May (the day after the drummer Lee Rigby's murder in Woolwich on 22 May 2013) and 31 July 2013 were coded for analysis in this chapter. Analysis of research questions one and three will focus on news articles obtained between 23 May and 30 May and between 31 May and

10 June 2013, while analysis of research question four will be carried out on randomly selected articles obtained from between 23 May and 31 July 2013.

The Lee Rigby murder and the anti-Muslim hostilities: volume of coverage and sourcing patterns

In all 119 articles, which included news reports, features, opinion-editorials, and letters, were collapsed and coded from the Lexis-Nexis database of the coverage of the Woolwich murder of British soldier Lee Rigby and the successive right-wing anti-Muslim protests and hostilities, by the six selected British newspapers between the first two and half weeks following the murder on 22 May 2013. Duplicate articles and timeline briefs were not included in among the articles coded for analysis. In order to understand the variation in the volume of coverage, as well as in sourcing and framing patterns across the six British newspapers, I divided the two-and-a-half week period into two periods: the first spanning 23 May—that is, the day after the Rigby murder—to 30 May, marking one week, and the second spanning 31 May to 10 June, marking one-and-a-half weeks.

Drawing on De Bonville's (2000) model of quantitative content analysis, all 119 articles of the six British newspapers were content analysed to determine the volume of coverage in answer to research question one (RQ1), and the use of official state sources vs non-official civil society sources in the framing of the Rigby murder and the anti-Muslim/anti-right-wing protests and hostilities that followed in answer to RQ2. I will use statistical tables and figures to support the analysis in this section.

I will start by using Tables 3.1 and 3.2 and Figures 3.1 and 3.2 to answer RQ1 (volume) and RQ2 (sourcing pattern), to be followed by discussions. Table 3.1 and Figure 3.1 will represent the volume of coverage and sourcing pattern data in the coverage between 23 and 30 May 2013, that is the first week following the Rigby murder, while Table 3.2 and Figure 3.2 will represent the volume of coverage and sourcing pattern data in the coverage between 31 May and 10 June 2013, that is the second week-and-a-half following the Rigby murder. Two main sourcing patterns were coded: official state sources (OSS) and non-official civil society sources (NCSS). The OSS included dominant elite sources such as the police, prison, fire officers, politicians, and politicians' spokespeople, while the NCSS included less dominant sources representing civil society individuals and organisations, some of which comprised Muslims or right-wing activists or their sympathisers.

Table 3.1 Official state sources' (OSS's) and non-official civil-society sources' (NCSS's) coverage of Rigby murder and anti-Muslim hostilities (23 May–30 May 2013)

Newspaper	No. of articles	No. of OSS	No. of NCSS
Daily Mail	18	56	34
Mirror	2	3	4
Guardian	13	25	11
Independent	26	27	34
Telegraph	21	34	25
Times	7	21	18

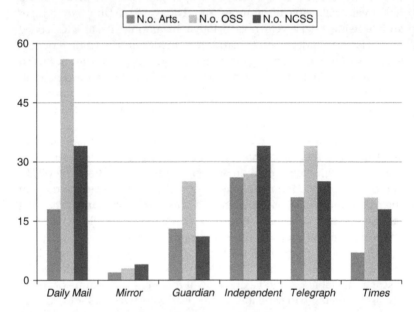

Figure 3.1 Representing data in Table 3.1: coverage of Rigby murder and anti-Muslim hostilities (23 May–30 May 2013)

Discussion: differences in volume of coverage and sourcing patterns (23 May–30 May 2013)

As we can see in Table 3.1 and Figure 3.1, by way of answering RQ1, there is a vast difference between the volume of coverage of both the Lee Rigby murder and the anti-Muslim protests and hostilities in the *Daily Mail* (18) and the *Mirror* (2), which shows that in terms of the two tabloid newspapers, the *Daily Mail*, which ideologically leans toward right-wing conservatism has more interest in issues of Islamophobia and right-wing extremism than the ideologically more centre-left, liberal-leaning *Daily Mirror*. We can also see that the *Mirror* performed relatively very poorly in volume of coverage compared to the centre-left and left-leaning quality newspapers of the *Guardian* (13) and *Independent* (26), respectively. Moreover, it was the left-leaning, liberal *Independent* newspaper that emerged as the paper with the largest volume of coverage, which shows that it has more interest in issues of Islamophobia and right-wing extremism than all five of the other newspapers in the study. The right-wing, conservative *Telegraph* emerged with the second largest volume of coverage (21) scoring far better than even the centre-right conservative newspaper, *The Times* (7) and better than the right-wing, conservative tabloid, *The Daily Mail*. The fact that two ideologically-polarised, quality newspapers (the *Independent* and *Telegraph*) did far better than the other two, the *Guardian* and *Times*, which are centre-left and -right, respectively, shows the importance of ideology in influencing coverage of issues of Islamophobia and right-wing extremism and terrorism. However, the fact that the left-leaning liberal newspaper had more coverage than the right-leaning conservative newspaper shows that left-wing politicians of the Labour and Liberal party and their supporters made the most political capital out of the Lee Rigby murder and anti-Muslim hostilities.

In order to determine whether the top-down approach to sourcing routine (Curran, 2011) exists (answer to RQ2) and to observe the extent to which the British political class or civil society set the news agenda in the framing of extremism and terrorism issues, I measured the number of times official state sources (OSS) and non-official, civil-society sources (NCSS) were used in the production of the articles coded and analysed in the coverage by the six selected British newspapers. I was also interested to see how these sourcing patterns differed across the six newspapers, and the role of ideology in this.

As we can see in the statistics in Table 3.1 and Figure 3.1, the *Daily Mail* employed the largest number of sources of all five newspapers, despite having far less coverage than some of them, for example the *Independent*, *Telegraph* and *Guardian*. However, it had more OSS (56) than NCSS (34), which meant that, for the *Daily Mail*, political and state elites played a far more dominant role in setting the news agenda than the rest of civil society. What is more, the *Daily Mail* used far more OSS than all the other newspapers, which shows that its construction of the reality of the Lee Rigby murder and its fall-outs was far more influenced by elite political power relations than all the other papers. The *Telegraph* was the only paper that came close to the *Daily Mail* in this respect, having employed 34 OSS, compared to 25 NCSS, showing that here, too, the elite political powers had more influence in setting the news agenda covering the Rigby murder and its aftermaths than in the remaining four papers. Since these two are pro-conservative, establishment newspapers, it is perhaps not surprising that they employed the most OSS over NCSS compared with the other four newspapers. One very interesting finding relates to *The Times*, the centre-right leaning conservative paper, which, despite its very limited volume of coverage, employed a very large number of sources and had little difference between the number of OSS (21) and NCSS (18). This meant that for *The Times*, the construction of the reality of the Lee Rigby murder was influenced by the political establishment in a very limited way compared to the *Daily Mail* and *Telegraph*. This, in a way, confirms the centre-right ideological positioning of *The Times*, as well as its professional neutrality or objective type of journalism when it comes to politically-sensitive issues of extremism and terrorism.

On the other hand, the left-leaning liberal newspaper, *The Independent*, employed more NCSS (34) compared to OSS (27), which meant this paper gave more voice to civil society organisations and individuals in setting the news agenda of the Rigby murder than any of the five other papers. The centre-left *Guardian*, for its part, employed far more OSS (25) than NCSS (11), which shows that, as far as the construction of reality relating to extremism and terrorism in the UK is concerned, this newspaper is fast drifting away from the concerns of the public to those of the conservative establishment. Even the *Times* referred to more civil society sources (18) than the *Guardian*.

Table 3.2 Official state sources' (OSS's) and non-official civil society sources' (NCSS's) coverage of Rigby murder and anti-Muslim hostilities (31 May–10 June 2013)

Newspaper	No. of articles	No. of OSS	No. of NCSS
Daily Mail	11	15	19
Mirror	3	3	2
Guardian	6	12	8
Independent	4	5	15
Telegraph	2	2	3
Times	5	5	2

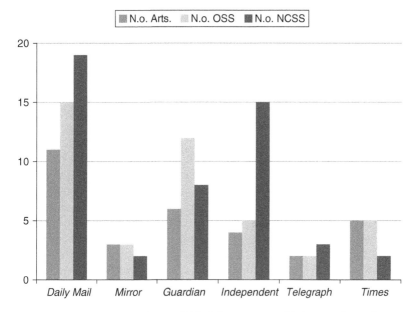

Figure 3.2   Representing data in Table 3.2: coverage of Rigby murder and anti-Muslim hostilities (31 May–10 June 2013)

Discussion: differences in volume of coverage and sourcing patterns (31 May–10 June 2013)

We can see from Table 3.2 and Figure 3.2 that in answer to RQ2, the volume of coverage in the first week following the Rigby murder (23–30 May) was significantly more than that in the second week-and-a-half (31 May–10 June) in all the six newspapers studied. This vast difference seems to suggest that the Lee Rigby murder allegedly carried out by Islamic extremists received more media hype in Britain than the anti-Muslim protests and hostilities allegedly carried out by extreme right-wing conservative activists. Although this could be due to the dramatic and brutal way in which the Rigby murder was carried out, one would have expected a bit more coverage of the even more dramatic explosions at Mosques and other Islamic centres as part of the revenge attacks for the Rigby murder.

Another interesting revelation is that the right-wing, conservative-leaning *Daily Mail*, despite having very limited coverage of the fall-outs from the Rigby murder, during the second week-and-a-half-long period employed more NCSS (19) than OSS (15). This shows that there are times when right-wing conservative newspapers, especially tabloids, echo more civil society voices than those of the establishment. Yet the

Mirror, in addition to its very limited coverage, employed more OSS than NCSS; this shows that this time around ideology was not an important agenda-setting factor for tabloid newspapers in framing extremism and terrorism. Despite its very limited coverage during this period, the *Independent* was more consistent in still having far more NCSS (15) than OSS (5), which shows that its allegiance to grass roots civil society is unflinching. Despite its limited coverage, the *Guardian* was also consistent in having more OSS (12) than FCSS (8), although this time the margin between the two was not as wide as in its coverage of the first week. This shows the *Guardian* taking its more traditional centre-left positioning in its reporting during the two-and-a-half weeks after the Rigby murder, a time when the focus of the coverage was more on the anti-Muslim hostilities fall-outs compared to the first week. Despite its very limited coverage, the right-wing, conservative *Telegraph* used slightly more NCSS than OSS, contrasting sharply from its first week's coverage, while the centre-right *Times* used more of the latter, consistent with its first week's coverage. These differences in sourcing patterns across various stages of a developing extremism story show that, after all, the ideological positioning of some of the newspapers becomes less and less evident as the tempo of the drama of the Lee Rigby murder wanes.

The Lee Rigby murder and anti-Muslim hostilities: Islamophobia or anti-right wing discourses?

In this section, I will draw on Entman's model (1993) of frame analysis to compare the framing of the Islamophobic discourses and anti-right-wing, fascist discourses in the six British newspapers' coverage of the Rigby murder and the following anti-Muslim hostilities in answer to RQ1 and RQ3. The aim of this question is to determine which of the two discourses—Islamophobia or anti-far-right-wing fascist discourses—was more foregrounded in the reporting of the Lee Rigby murder and the following anti-Muslim hostilities in the six British newspapers during the two periods (23–30 May and 31 May–10 June 2013), and the implication of this difference for intercultural communication and human rights journalism in Britain. On one hand, Islamophobic or anti-Muslim/anti-Islamic discourses in the articles were identified by looking for stereotypes that negatively portrayed the Islamic religion or Muslims as extremists and terrorists based on the extremist or terrorist behaviour of one or two alleged extremist or terrorist Muslims. On the other hand, anti-right-wing discourses in the articles were identified by looking for stereotypes that negatively portrayed far-right conservative English people as extremists and terrorists based on the extremist or terrorist the behaviour of one or two alleged far right English extremist/s or terrorist/s. Here I will also use the following statistical tables and figures to support the framing analysis. Each of the coded articles is examined to see whether there is any negative portrayal of Islam or its followers as extremist or terrorist and/or of far right-wing conservative English as extremist or terrorist. Only one negative portrayal of either Islam or far right-wing conservative English, or both, is coded for each article, even if there are many references to this in that same article (Table 3.3 and Figure 3.3).

Table 3.3 Islamophobic discourse (ID) and anti-far-right conservative English discourse (AFRCED) of the Rigby murder and anti-Muslim hostilities in the six British newspapers (23 May–30 May 2013)

Newspaper	No. of articles	No. of ID	No. of AFRCED
Daily Mail	18	13	2
Mirror	2	2	0
Guardian	13	7	2
Independent	26	11	8
Telegraph	21	12	0
Times	7	5	0

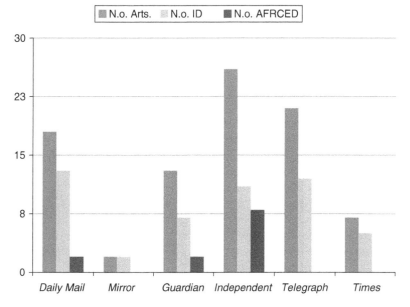

Figure 3.3 Representing data in Table 3.3: coverage of Rigby murder and anti-Muslim hostilities (23 May–30 May 2013)

Discussion: Islamophobia vs anti-right-wing fascist discourses (23 May–30 May 2013)

As we can see from Table 3.3 and Figure 3.3, Islamophobic discourses portraying Islam and Muslims generally in a negative light because of the extremism and terrorism carried out by the two killers of Lee Rigby claiming to be acting in the name of Islam were far more foregrounded in almost all the six British newspapers' coverage of the Lee Rigby murder and the anti-Muslim hostilities that followed than anti-fascist right-wing discourses against those accused of carrying out the anti-Muslim protests and hostilities, which included the burning and bombing of Mosques and Islamic cultural and educational centres. What this seems to suggest is that while the British mainstream press was very critical of the act of extremism and terrorism carried out by the two Muslim killers of Lee Rigby and their few sympathisers, such as Anjem Choudary, they were far less so of the act of extremism and terrorism carried out by the many far right-wing fascist activists against Muslims by way of revenge or reprisal attacks. The two right-wing conservative newspapers, *Daily Mail* (13 instances of ID and 2 instances of anti-far-right conservative English discourse or AFRCED) and *Telegraph* (12 ID and 0 AFRCED), took the lead in foregrounding Islamophobia by a very long margin compared to their framing of the anti-right-wing fascist discourses. What is even more glaring is the fact that neither the *Times*, *Telegraph*, nor *Mirror* carried any AFRCED which shows that for these three newspapers all that needed to be criticised were acts of extremism and terrorism carried out by Muslims, and not those against them carried out in the name of British far right-wing conservative politicians and activists.

It certainly does not help the cause of peaceful intercultural communication between Muslim minorities and non-Muslim majorities in the UK if only two out of 18 *Daily Mail* articles, for instance, published during the first week after the Rigby murder, turned out to be critical of far-right fascist, anti-Muslim hostilities, while as many as 13 articles carried Islamophobic discourses. Within the context of triple-win human rights journalism, journalists should help promote intercultural communication, instead of the zero-tolerance, winner-takes-all type of cultural clash communication that provokes violent extremism and terrorism. Unfortunately, however, as we have seen in the above framing analysis, the opposite was more evident in the coverage of the first week following the Rigby murder, not just in the *Daily Mail* but in all other British national newspapers in the study. Islamophobic stereotypes included all manner of pejorative and grossly offensive metaphors and messages depicting Islam and Muslims in a negative light, some of them even constituting 'fighting' words that were enough to mobilise far-right activists suspected to be from the English Defence League (EDL) to set fire to and trigger explosions in Islamic places of worship and education, especially in the West Midlands of England. However, among the six newspapers studied, the *Independent* did far better in foregrounding discourses that were critical of the far-right-wing fascist activists who had carried out the anti-Muslim protests and reprisal attacks on Muslim targets. Although it carried slightly more Islamophobic discourses (11) than anti-far right fascist discourses (eight), the disparity was at least very marginal compared to the other newspapers, especially the right-wing newspapers. *The Guardian* is the other newspaper that did not do too badly in this respect compared to the other four newspapers. This is perhaps not too surprising, given that, being centre-left and leftist newspapers, respectively, the *Guardian* and *Independent* are traditionally very critical of far-right political activism.

Discussion: Islamophobia vs anti-right-wing fascist discourses (31 May–10 June 2013)

As we can see from Table 3.4 and Figure 3.4, all the six British national newspapers generally carried more Islamophobic discourses depicting Islam and Muslims in a negative light compared to anti-fascist right-wing discourses depicting far right English politicians and activists in a negative light during the second week-and-a-half following the Rigby murder and the following anti-Muslim hostilities. However, during this period (31 May–10 June 2013), despite the very limited coverage compared to the first week following the Rigby murder, the difference between the foregrounding of Islamophobia and the anti-right-wing discourses was much smaller compared to that during the first week following the Rigby murder. Take for example the *Daily Mail*, where the difference was just limited to three, compared to the first week of coverage, where the difference was as wide as 11. This very marginal difference shows that, after all, the right-wing *Daily Mail*, which is traditionally known for its anti-Islamic and anti-immigration stance, is becoming increasingly critical of attacks of extremism and terrorism carried out by English far-right fascist activists. This demonstrates that when it comes to issues of Islam and immigration, the *Daily Mail* is gradually moving to a centre-right ideological positioning, compared to the *Telegraph*, which, as we saw in its coverage of both periods, failed to foreground any anti-right-wing fascist discourse and carried many

Table 3.4 Islamophobic discourse (ID) and anti-far-right conservative English discourse (AFRCED) of the Rigby murder and anti-Muslim hostilities in the six British newspapers (31 May–10 June 2013)

Newspaper	No. of articles	No. of ID	No. of AFRCED
Daily Mail	11	7	4
Mirror	3	3	0
Guardian	6	2	2
Independent	4	3	3
Telegraph	2	1	0
Times	5	4	1

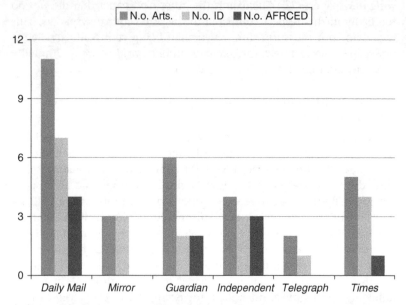

Figure 3.4 Representing data in Table 3.4: coverage of Rigby murder and anti-Muslim hostilities (31 May–10 June 2013)

more Islamophobic discourses in its coverage of the first week following the Rigby murder. The *Daily Mail* even did better than the centre-right *Times*, which managed to have one AFRCED compared to four ID. However, the *Times* did better this time, compared to its coverage of the first week where it had no AFRCED.

Moreover, during the second week-and-a-half period, there was no difference between the foregrounding of Islamophobic discourses and that of anti-right-wing discourses in the coverage of the *Guardian* and *Independent*, arguably making them far better in having a more balanced coverage of the ID and AFRCED, compared to the right-wing newspapers. The fact that these two left-wing newspapers demonstrated more objectivity in their framing of ID and AFRCED during the second week-and-a-half than the first week following the Rigby murder shows that as the tempo of the coverage of the Rigby murder began to wane, these two newspapers began to adopt a more professional than ideological stance. For the *Mirror*, in addition to very limited coverage, the no-AFRCED story was the same, and it even had three ID compared to the one it had had in its first week's coverage. It is difficult to draw a conclusion because of the very limited coverage but the *Mirror*'s statistics show that in terms of issues of Islamophobia and anti-right-wing discourses, it is fast moving from a left to right ideological positioning in the British press.

Despite the efforts of the left-wing papers, the *Independent* and *Guardian,* to foreground at least some anti-fascist discourses, the fact that they and the other four British newspapers foregrounded more Islamophobic discourses than anti-right-wing fascist discourses in their coverage of both the first week and second week-and-a-half periods following the Lee Rigby murder shows just how the British press helped to support the masking of the human wrongs (extremism and terrorism) of the people (the far-right English activists and politicians) who are like them (Us), at least in sharing the same Western Christian values, and focused more on exposing the human wrongs (extremism and terrorism) of the Muslim extremists, who are the Other. It is simply a question of out of sight, out of mind. As I argued earlier in this chapter, this type of representational imbalance in the British press has the potential to create a British society that is polarised along religious and ethnic lines and therefore more prone to producing future home-grown extremism and terrorism from both sides of the divide—extremist Muslims vs extremist far-right-wing activists.

Evocative vs diagnostic discourses of the Lee Rigby murder and anti-Muslim hostilities

The aim of this final section is to answer RQ4 on how the six British newspapers performed on the evocative vs diagnostic discourses of the Lee Rigby murder and anti-Muslim attacks that followed. The raison d'être of this question is to explore whether the British press, represented by the six newspapers in this study, provided context or diagnosis to explain the extremism and terrorism associated with the Lee Rigby murder and the anti-Muslim attacks, or whether they just focused on the simple evocative narratives of some crazy Islamists chasing and killing a British soldier on the street in London. I make the argument that an emphasis on diagnostic discourses of the Lee Rigby murder and the consequent anti-Muslim attacks was necessary to understand the big picture of the real root causes of the extremism and terrorism associated with the two connected events, to help readers make informed judgements about reducing the risks of further escalation of, or preventing future hatreds and hostilities. Because of the limited scope and space of this chapter I will use the hermeneutic model of Critical Discourse Analysis, instead of the quantitative and qualitative content analyses used in the last two sections, which allows me to randomly choose and critically analyse articles published in the six British newspapers between 23 May, that is the day after the Rigby murder, and the end of July 2013, studied here as examples that provided evocative or diagnostic discourses of the Lee Rigby murder and the consequent anti-Muslim attacks. This section will proceed to first look at evocative discourses which more or less dominated the framing of the Rigby murder and the anti-Muslim reprisals and then look at the relatively very few examples of diagnostic discourses.

Evocative discourses

Evocative discourses that ranged from shocking and dramatic messages evoking concern and human interest in the murdered victim Lee Rigby, and to a much lesser extent in the victims of the anti-Muslim attack, to a very large extent punctuated the coverage of the six British newspapers. I only have space and scope to refer to a few examples here. One such article is a news report in the *Daily Mail*, entitled: 'Every faith, every generation joined in the mourning' (28 May 2013), by Ian Drury. The article emotionally narrated how British soldier Lee Rigby 'had survived Taliban bombs and bullets during a gruelling tour of duty of Afghanistan' only to be tragically 'run over and hacked to death by Al Qaeda-inspired extremists near his military base', in the relative safety of his homeland. One of the well-wishers who came to leave flowers for the murdered soldier expressed how she felt sickened by what had happened, while another said 'it is really moving to see all these other people who wanted to pay their respects'. The *Daily Mail* had also earlier carried a story about the consequent anti-Muslim hostilities with the title 'Eleven people across UK arrested for making "racist or anti-religious" comments on Facebook and Twitter about British soldier's death' (25 May 2013). The opening sentence of the article has all the hallmarks of evocative reporting, which demonstrates human interest in the victims and outrage against the perpetrators:

> The murder of soldier Lee Rigby has provoked a backlash of anger across the UK, including the attacking of mosques, racial abuse and comments made on social media.
> (Daily Mail Opening sentence, 25 May 2013)

An even more evocative discourse appeared in a news report by Ben Farmer (2013) in the *Daily Telegraph*, the day following the Rigby murder, entitled 'Angry mob descends on Woolwich after EDL coaxing; RETALIATION' (23 May 2013). Both this title and the opening sentence of the article have all the trappings of an extremely charged evocative appeal:

> RETALIATIONS followed the Woolwich murder last night as hundreds of English Defence League demonstrators gathered in Woolwich and two people were arrested for separate attacks on mosques elsewhere.

The news report added that about 200 protesters had assembled at the main square near Woolwich train station, 'many wearing black balaclavas emblazoned with the EDL logo', throwing bottles at police and unequivocally chanting EDL and anti-Muslim chants. The protesters were apparently responding to a 'feet on the street' twitter call by EDL leader Tommy Robinson, according to the report.

Although the right-wing newspapers carried the lion's share of evocative discourses, the left-wing papers also had plenty of them in their coverage. An article in the *Guardian* by Simon Jenkins, one of Britain's most prolific and controversial commentators, dated 24 May 2013, provided a very evocative and dramatic discourse, presenting the Woolwich killers as commanders of the news agenda, having enjoyed the 'oxygen of publicity' from their act of terror. Jenkins's article adds: 'Front pages became their platform, authenticating their manifesto. The prime minister obediently raced home from important business in Paris. He slavishly "cleared his diary", plunged into his favourite Cobra bunker and summoned the mightiest in the land to co-ordinate a response'. Jenkins jokingly wonders whether Cameron would have reacted so dramatically if the British soldier had merely been shot by youths in the streets. However, Jenkins warned that 'it was medieval crudity of the weaponry, the brazen hacking and stabbing and blood splashed over the internet that had every politician homing in on Cobra, press officers in tow. Tabloid terror invited tabloid government'. He went on to add an even more loaded string of evocative words: 'The adjective mountain grows ever higher, depraved, sickening, horrific, barbaric, (and) unspeakable'.

Diagnostic discourses

While evocative discourses on the Rigby murder and the subsequent anti-Muslim attacks, which were for the most part dramatic, emotional, and sometimes entertaining, were abundantly evident in the coverage of the six British newspapers, especially the right-wing ones, diagnostic discourses that were really supposed to educate readers about why in fact monsters such as the killers of Lee Rigby, hate preachers of Islam, and the perpetrators of the anti-Muslim attacks had been created in the first place were very limited. I will refer to and analyse a couple of the very few diagnostic discourses here. By far the most telling diagnostic discourse that properly provides the big picture of why the Woolwich broad-daylight murder really took place is the link between it and the many wars, especially the drone wars, that Western nations, especially the US and Britain, are waging in the Gulf, Middle East, Africa, and Asia. One glaring example was the opinion article in the *Daily Mail* entitled 'Foreign Wars and A Chilling Legacy of Hate' (29 May 2013) by Andrew Alexander, who began by outlining two ways to respond to the Woolwich murder: One is pure anger and frustration plus a demand for tougher government control, and the other 'is to use our brains and our imagination to understand why young Muslims can be easily radicalised, i.e. turned into murderers'. Alexander's article explained how the illegal wars of the West in Iraq and Afghanistan, which have claimed hundreds of thousands of lives and created millions of refugees, have hardened and radicalised young Muslims to seek revenge. He compares the terrorism associated with the Woolwich murder to the killing of innocent civilians in Afghanistan:

> The spectacle at Woolwich may have been utterly disgusting. But was it any more appalling, Islamists can ask, than the spectacle of an Afghan child with its limbs blown off and all because a CIA agent in Virginia had hit the Go' button for his drone to fire without being 100 per cent certain that the targeted gathering was a Taliban gang not a wedding party.

Simon Jenkins's opinion article in the *Guardian* (24 May 2013) cited earlier in this section somehow reinforces Alexander's point: Jenkins notes that the British and Americans indeed use drones to 'kill Muslim soldiers and inevitably civilians' in Afghanistan, Pakistan, and Yemen.

'Retaliation for these killings may not be "justified" in our terms. But jihadists have no access to drones and must rely on car bombs, nail bombs, machetes and cleavers'. Diagnostic discourses like these two, albeit very limited indeed in the articles of the newspapers studied, have the potential to provide a better understanding and hence better judgement on the part of the public and policy-makers in making informed decisions to prevent future incidents of extremism and terrorism in Britain and global society at large. Moreover, the fact that we have some very good examples of diagnostic discourses means that the ideas or models of intercultural communication and human rights journalism are indeed possible and not just utopian ideals.

Conclusion

To summarise this chapter, the findings of the quantitative content analysis and the qualitative frame analysis show that the six British newspapers studied here foregrounded the acts of extremism and terrorism carried out by Muslims in their coverage of the Lee Rigby murder and issues related to Muslim hate-preachers far beyond the acts of extremism and terrorism carried out by far-right-wing fascist activists against Muslims and Islamic centres. Moreover, the findings of the CDA show that the British press foregrounded evocative discourses over those of diagnostic, and in this way ignored the root causes of extremism and terrorism by Muslims and non-Muslims in Britain. This chapter argues that this unbalanced coverage, foregrounding Islamophobic discourses over anti-right-wing discourses, and foregrounding evocative discourses over diagnostic discourses, could have undermined intercultural communication and human rights journalism/peace journalism and obscured policy interventions to reduce tensions between Muslims and non-Muslims, and by extension future extremism and terrorism, such as those we saw in Sydney in December 2014, and Paris in January 2015.

References

C. Allen (1997) 'The "First" Decade of Islamophobia: 10 Years of the Runnymede Trust Report "Islamophobia: A Challenge for us All"', *The Islamic Council of Western Australia,* http://www.islamiccouncilwa.com.au/wp-content/uploads/2014/05/Decade_of_Islamophobia.pdf, date accessed 27 May 2015.
BBC News (2001) 'EU Deplores "Dangerous" Islam Jibes', 27 September 2001.
D. Chong and J. N. Druckman (2007) 'A Theory of Framing and Opinion Formation in Competitive Elite Environments', *Journal of Communication*, 57, 99–118.

P. A. Chow-White and R. McMahon (2012) 'Examining the "Dark Past" and "Hopeful Future" in Representations of Race and Canada's Truth and Reconciliation Commission' in I. S. Shaw, J. Lynch, and R. Hackett (eds.) *Expanding Peace Journalism: Comparative and Critical Approaches* (Sydney: Sydney University Press) pp. 345–373.

J. Curran (2011) *Media and Democracy* (London: Routledge).

R. Entman (1993) 'Framing: Towards Clarification of a Fractured Paradigm', *Journal of Communication*, 43(4), 51–58.

R. Entman (2004) *Projections of Power* (Chicago, IL: University of Chicago Press).

Daily Mail (2013) Eleven People Across UK Arrested for making 'Racist or Anti-Religious Comments on Facebook and Twitter about British soldier's death', 25 May 2013.

J. De Bonville (2000) *Analyse De Contenu des medias: de la problematique de traitment statistique* (Quebec, Canada. De Boek Universite).

I. Drury (2013) Every Faith, every Generation Joined in the Mourning *Daily Mail*, 28 May 2013.

N. Fairclough (1995) *Critical Discourse Analysis: The Critical Study of Language* (Harlow, UK: Longman).

B. Farmer (2013) Angry mob descends on Woolwich after EDL coaxing; RETALIATION'. *Daily Telegraph*.

J. Galtung (2004) Violence, War, and Their Impact: On Visible and Invisible Effects of Violence, them.polylog.org/5/fgj-en.htm, date accessed 27 May 2015.

S. Huntington (1996) *The Clash of Civilizations and the Remaking of the World Order* (London: Simon and Schuster).

G. Khiabany and M. Williamson (2012) 'Terror, Culture and Anti-Muslim Racism' in D. Freedman and D. K. Thussu (eds.) *Media and Terrorism: Global Perspectives* (London: Sage) pp. 134–150.

I. E. Klyukanov (2005) *Principles of Intercultural Communication* (Boston, MA: Pearson Education Inc).

J. Lynch and A. McGoldrick (2005) *Peace Journalism* (Stroud, UK: Hawthorn Press).

H. McCoubrey (1997) *International Humanitarian Law* (Aldershot, UK: Ashgate).

C. Ogan, L. Wilnat, R. Pennington, and M. Bashir (2014) 'The Rise of Anti-Muslim Prejudice: Media and Islamophobia in Europe and the United States', *The International Communication Gazette*, 76, 27–46.

E. Said (1997) *Covering Islam: How the Media and the Experts Determine How We See the Rest of the World* (New York: Vintage Books).

P. Seib (2004) 'The News Media and the Clash of Civilizations', *Parameters*, 34(4), 71–85.

I. S. Shaw (2012a) 'Stereotypical Representations of Muslims and Islam following the 7/7 Terrorist Attacks in London: Implications for Intercultural Communication and Terrorism Prevention', *International Communication Gazette*, 74, 509–524.

I. S. Shaw (2012b) 'The "War on Terror" Frame and the *Washington Post's* Linking of the Sierra Leone Civil War to 9/11 and Al Qaeda: Implications for US Foreign Policy in Africa', *Journal of African Media Studies*, 4, 27–44.

P. A. Thomas (2002) 'September 11th and Good Governance', *Northern Ireland Legal Quarterly*, 53, 360–390.

S. Titscher, M. Meyer, R. Wodak, and E. Vetter (2000) *Methods of Text and Discourse Analysis* (London: Sage).

T. A. Van Dijk (1993) 'Principles of Critical Discourse Analysis', *Discourse and Society*, 4, 249–283.

J. Van Ginneken (1998) *Understanding Global News: A Critical Introduction* (London: Sage).

N. Weerakkody (2009) *Research Methods: For Media and Communication* (London: Oxford University Press).

R. Wodak and M. Meyer (2001) *Methods of Critical Discourse Analysis: Introducing Qualitative Methods* (London: Sage).

4
Peacebuilding through Dialogue in Northern Ireland

John S. Caputo

This chapter describes a peacebuilding project that emerges from the context of intercultural and international communication using dialogic theory and practice in Derry, Northern Ireland. To begin with, even the name of the city is in dispute in this conflict situation. The Northern Irish city has been known by two names, Derry and Londonderry. There are historical resonances for both names. Unionists – who want to maintain a union with the United Kingdom – have a strong preference for Londonderry, which it was renamed in recognition of its connections with City of London livery companies during the Plantation of Ulster in the 1600s. Nationalists – who want Northern Ireland to become a part of the Republic of Ireland – want to retain their original name of Derry (*Doire*). The city's Visitor's Bureau calls it 'Legenderry'. *The Guardian* Style Guide states: 'Derry, Co Derry. Not Londonderry'. Speaking with a local in Derry, he says 'You ask why any "self-respecting" Irish person would only call it Derry when we're not talking about a city in Ireland?' Derry IS a city in Ireland, on the island of Ireland, with a history going back to the 6th century. For the purposes of this chapter, the name Derry will be used.

Background of the conflict

It is important to know some of the geography and history of Ireland and Northern Ireland to understand the 'peace process' and the role intercultural communication plays in this context. Northern Ireland is the smallest of the four areas that comprise the United Kingdom (UK), and is made up of the six northern counties on the island it shares with Ireland. These six counties, and three in Ireland, made up the historical province of Ulster. Ireland had been under the rule of Irish kings when the English began invading Ireland in the 12th century. The Irish revolted in 1603, and England's Protestant king forced Catholics in Ulster to give up their land to Protestant settlers from England and Scotland. Catholics were excluded from power and the Protestant parliaments of Ireland and Great Britain were able to pass the Act of Union in 1801, joining the two countries into one, the United Kingdom of Great Britain and Ireland. But Irish dissent continued after Ireland became part of the UK. In 1916, the Easter Rebellion against British rule took place in Ireland. The rebellion led to the 1921 division of the island into the Catholic-majority Irish Free State in the south and the Protestant-majority Northern Ireland in the northernmost six counties. In 1949, the Irish Free State became the Republic of Ireland and formally withdrew from the United Kingdom. The six northern counties remained part of the United Kingdom.

From the very beginning, Northern Ireland was torn by cultural differences in religious practices, socio-economic status, and political divisions. These divisions are part of what Martin Buber describes in his 1967 work Hope for This Hour:

> The human world is today, as never before, split into two camps, each of which understands the other as the embodiment of falsehood and itself as the embodiment of truth. ... Each side has assumed monopoly of the sunlight and has plunged its antagonist into night, and each side demands that you decide between day and night. ... Expressed in modern terminology, he believes that he has ideas, his opponents only has ideologies. This obsession feeds the mistrust that incites the two camps. (p. 307)

Although Catholics made up almost 40 percent of the population, they were excluded from the government. In the 1960s, a peaceful movement among Catholics seeking civil rights was soon overshadowed by the violent campaign of the Irish Republican Army (IRA). The primarily Catholic IRA used assassinations and bombings to try to force the whole island to be reunited while Protestant extremists like the Ulster Defense Union and Ulster Volunteer Force reacted with similarly brutal tactics. This violence continued for decades and came to be called *The Troubles* (1969–1998). Unfortunately, in the US *The Troubles* were described by mass-media as primarily a religious struggle between Catholics and Protestants, rather than a civil rights movement, based on cultural and economic differences. It is difficult to find in Northern Ireland a citizen who sees this struggle as a simple dichotomy of different religious beliefs and practices.

The causes and history of *The Troubles* as well as the tortuous peace process following the Belfast Agreement in 1998 are well documented. Based on that agreement, Northern Ireland's devolved government finally became reality in 2008. Although the period of peace in Northern Ireland gives many a sense of optimism, it nonetheless remains fragile. Part of the fragility comes from where power lies (politicians, unionists, loyalists, paramilitary groups) and who makes decisions. Governmental decisions made in London, Belfast, or Dublin and passed down to the local communities and neighborhoods do not necessarily carry with them any agreement at the 'grass-roots' level. In a blog post, a former combatant writes, 'As a segregated community, we felt stuck and were fixed on the beliefs of what we were fed by the government and the media' (Gonzaga-in-Derry, 2014).

Top-down communication tends to leave communities both frustrated and seemingly powerless. Unacknowledged past wrongs result in the absence of trust. Understanding and healing between groups does not just happen. No one person can tell the story of the conflict. What is required is to bring together the disparate narratives in order to better understand the impact of the conflict to those directly and indirectly involved. Local peacebuilding through dialogue is central to understanding how peace has been maintained. Dialogue can only happen when people are free to share their experiences – their stories – without fear of reprisal from others. This must happen at the local level where interpersonal and intercultural risk-taking can start to build trust among people who have suffered the trauma of conflict. Communication is the key to slowly allowing this process to emerge, when people receive an acknowledgement of their own experiences and begin to understand the experiences of 'the other'. To really move to a culture of peace in a post-conflict society, storytelling and dialogue provide a person-by-person opportunity of coming to understand each others' history, culture, politics, and humanity. Peacebuilding is heavy lifting and requires individuals to have a chance to meet 'the other' in authentic dialogue, and only here can healing come to both.

Dialogue requires responsiveness that is made possible by qualities of thought and talk, allowing transformation to take place: transformation in how people understand the self, the other, and the societies they inhabit. These qualities of thought and talk include a willingness to risk change in one's own perspective. This perspective is shaped by one's lived experience. In sharing our experiences we open up our world view. As a former combatant now engaged in peacebuilding and involved in storytelling and dialogue describes, 'I was touched at a deep level hearing other people's stories and relating my own experiences, some of which remain surprisingly raw', or as another says, 'I found it very harrowing, but also enlightening – I gained a better understanding about people's loss and suffering' (*Towards Understanding and Healing*, 2008). To develop empathy for the 'other's point of view requires us to surrender not our experiences, but our closed-mindedness regarding others' experiences, which *can* be equally legitimate. Wood (2004) writes that 'dialogue is emergent (rather than preformed), fluid (rather than static), keenly dependent on process (at least as much as content), performative (more than representational), and never fully finished (rather than completed)' (p. xvii).

Role of intercultural communication in peacemaking

In order to understand the role of intercultural communication in peacemaking, this project brought American students into this milieu in Northern Ireland, for the first two years to the city of Armagh, and then for the last two years to the city of Derry. Working collaboratively with a grass-roots organization called *The Junction: Community Relations and Peacebuilding in Derry*, the process of dialogue and ethical remembering and healing was utilized to facilitate working with former combatants to build a lasting peace. Additionally, the practice of storytelling was incorporated as the touchstone to open up the space for dialogue.

Theoretical underpinnings

The approach to dialogue incorporates many of the theorists on whom communication scholars base much of their work: Martin Buber (1958, 1965), who grounds his work in dialogic meeting, and places listening as a critical communication function. Buber believes that human experiences are grounded in meeting and relation and that authentic human life exists with dialogic meeting – for Buber, what makes us most human is the centrality of speech and dialogue; Hans-Georg Godamer's (1976, 1982) work regarding truth which emerges from an understanding of texts in the context of cultural history, language, and audiences – for Godamer, these texts then are formed in the human ability to read relationships; Jürgen Habermas (1971, 1975, 1979, 1984, 1987) offers a discourse-based ethic for social communication, and his 'ideal speech situation' has been very influential for theorists seeking ways to reconcile pluralistic viewpoints with possibilities for consensus – for Habermas, structuring situations for dialogue to take place has much relevancy to communication scholars, especially the need to invite people into dialogue who hold divergent opinions; Mikhail Bakhtin (1981, 1984, 1986), as a social critic, has pointed out the pervasiveness of dialogue in language and human history – Bakhtin believes that society is multivocal and unfinalizable, and hence dialogue is the space of this multivocality; Paolo Freire (1990), as philosopher of education and dialogue, insisted that liberation at the expense of others is an act of oppression and that personal freedom and individual development can only occur in mutuality with others. This mutuality develops a critical consciousness that allows us to be in dialogue with others. He calls this quality of contact 'dialogue', and for Freire, dialogue requires love, humility, and faith. Freire (1990) writes, 'Only dialogue, which requires critical thinking, is also capable of generating critical thinking. Without dialogue, there is no communication, and without communication there can be no true education' (p. 81). Each of these philosophers, for different reasons, has turned his attention to human communication and meaning-making which occurs in language and nonverbal behaviors.

While these philosophers did not directly talk about peacebuilding or Northern Ireland, their approach to dialogue has provided a practical theory for storytelling and dialogue to emerge as a methodology for peacebuilding. It is this practical utility that has provided the notion of meeting in relationship, of providing a structure for dialogue to take place, and that in dialogue, communication can take place which allows personal freedom and individual development in our mutuality with others.

What makes dialogue unique?

Dialogue theory emerges from several disciplines in the academy including literary theory, philosophy, linguistics, sociology, education, and communication. What is dialogue and why is it important in anchoring it in the writings of Buber and others? According to Yankelovich (1999), dialogue has three essential features: equality and the absence of coercive influences (outside the dialogue there may be huge differences but inside the dialogue equity must reign); listening with empathy; and bringing assumptions into the open (the point of dialogue is not consensus but human contact, communication that embodies respect and civility). Dialogue is not a panacea for the world's troubles but does have the power to transform many toxic human interactions. As such, dialogue labels a particular quality of communication.

Dialogue is not confined to conversations between two people. Some writers on the subject believe that dialogue is best carried on in groups ranging from about a dozen to two dozen people. Stan Deetz (2013) and Deetz and Simpson (2004) refer to these people as the primary stakeholders. The quality of dialogue has a both/and tension, meaning, participants are often pulled in opposite directions. One tension may be 'letting the other happen to me' and the other 'holding your own ground'.

Dialogue is based on the concept of mutuality but does not necessarily idealize or seek common ground. The search for (and belief in) common ground may thwart, rather than facilitate genuine dialogue, because from an intercultural point of view, almost inevitably the dominant culture defines what ground is common or legitimate. Instead, dialogue allows people to speak fully and be listened to while creating opportunities for the exploration of each other's ideology, perception, attitudes, and sense of history to develop strategies that enable individuals to access further support structures allowing them to move forward (*Towards understanding and healing*, 2008, p. 3). And a caveat that McNee and Shotter (2004, p. 99) add is that 'our dialogical actions are neither yours nor mine: they are truly *ours*' (Anderson et al., 2004, p. 99).

Dialogue can lead to ethical and shared remembering. Ethical remembering can lead to ethical doing (McMaster and Hetherington, 2012). Jonathan Sacks (2005) writes,

> If I defeat you, I win and you lose. But in truth, I also lose, because by diminishing you, I diminish myself. But if, in a moment of truth, I forgive you and you forgive me, then forgiveness leads to reconciliation. Reconciliation leads to friendship. And if in friendship, instead of fighting one another, we can fight together the problems we share: poverty, hunger, starvation, disease, violence, injustice, and all the other injuries that still scar the face of our world. You gain, I gain, and all those with whom we are associated gain as well. We gain economically, politically, but above all spiritually. My world has become bigger because it now includes you. Who is a hero? One who turns an enemy into a friend. (pp. 112–118)

The Gonzaga-in-Derry project

Into this milieu then, an experiential graduate course grounded in intercultural communication was planned in 2013 to be held in Derry and Belfast, Northern Ireland. Intercultural communication and cultural immersion are experiential cornerstones of such an experience (Caputo and Crandall, 2013, pp. 58–63). Understanding the principles of intercultural communication adds the unique aspect of recognizing culturally different backgrounds of interactants and all the variables this brings into play in communication encounters. Gudykunst and Kim (1992) conceptualize the common underlying process of communication with people who are unknown and unfamiliar as communication with 'strangers'.

The aim of this course was to introduce concepts from the field of communication that enable an understanding of how local peacebuilding can build bridges between conflicting groups in deeply divided societies. Communication and dialogue are closely intertwined and together act at the heart of establishing shared space and creating a common future. In the peacebuilding process in Northern Ireland, bringing together former combatants to share their stories and to move to dialogue becomes part of the intercultural uncertainty reduction process so necessary to productive engagement. Peacebuilding in Northern Ireland, with its multiple factions, is essentially intercultural in both scope and content. Where to an outsider, Northern Ireland and the Republic of Ireland may look monocultural, to an insider there are clear and specific concrete boundaries. As Barth (1969) writes, 'It is clear that boundaries persist despite a flow of personnel across them. In other words, categorical ethnic distinctions do not depend on the absence of mobility, contact and information' (p. 9). Anthropologist Edward Sapir has referred to culture as a 'seamless web' that is interconnected in many ways. It is both seen and unseen and yet exerts an undeniable influence in daily life. Because culture is both overt and covert, people often don't even recognize its influence. This seamless web of cultural influence in the daily lives of the Northern Irish emerges in storytelling, where many of these cultural similarities and differences become clear in the process of uncertainty reduction.

The course

The course is a hybrid in delivery, with both online and on-the-ground components combining fieldwork with classroom experiences. Students are provided with a series of readings and multi-media materials on the history of the Irish conflicts, on theories of intercultural communication, and on dialogic theory, before taking up a 14-day residency in Derry. The residency period includes a storytelling session with former combatants, an understanding and healing session facilitated with local peacebuilding experts at The Junction, and class sessions devoted to interviewing, rapport building, and ethnographic story-writing, which is then incorporated into fieldwork interviews with former combatants. Stories and photos are then created and placed in a blog format to share with both community members and the larger educational enterprise. The course culminates in a photo exhibition and celebrations of the work, and publication of the class blog site. On the last evening a dinner is held honoring all of the former combatants who were willing to share their stories and their involvement in the peacebuilding process. For many of the former combatants, this is the first time they would have heard these stories, and it becomes part of their ethical remembering of divergent points of view.

The goals of the course include:

- Explain the dimensions and the role of dialogue in communication.
- Analyse the causes and history of The Troubles and the post-1998 peace process.
- Recognize the development of shared community through storytelling.
- Interview and tell a story in a photojournalistic style of one of the citizens of Derry.
- Explain the potential role dialogue can play as an effective tool for peacebuilding.

A place for storytelling and learning

On the second day of the residency, a real change begins to take place in the student's learning experience. We hold a storytelling session with former combatants titled *Towards Understanding and Healing* – Local Peacebuilding through Storytelling and Dialogue. In this session, former combatants from opposite sides of the Troubles share their personal stories of this time period, how it impacted their existence, and why they now want to work toward peace. The storytelling session is facilitated by members of The Junction – a Derry-based peacebuilding effort with representatives of all sides of the issues and history of the region. This storytelling session is characterized by open, raw, and emotional communication. One such story comes from James: 'I stand before you a grandfather and a father. I stand before you a convicted terrorist. As much as you would like to change the past you can't but you can live with it and change the future'. While James is thankful to move beyond being a terrorist and to be seeking peace, he realizes what it has cost him.

> My people would believe I had turned my back on them as a traitor. They would see it as the ultimate betrayal of my people and my beliefs. But I know that what I am doing now is better than killing people. Of course it is.

Former combatant Charlie tells his story:

> For three days I was badly beaten. I had all my hair pulled all
> out. I had my ears slapped. I was made to stand a lot. Shouted at.
> Psychologically tortured. And on the first day, after about eight hours
> of torturing and interrogation – being told that I was accused of
> things I never did. I was taken to my cell for a break, which was the
> first break I had taken. I grabbed a screw from a radiator and tried to
> cut my wrist.

Katie, a student, listening to these stories writes, 'Stories evoke empathy.
They evoke compassion. You get engaged with them'.

In the afternoon, students are invited into the storytelling and dialogue activity as participants by taking part in using beads to make a
personal bracelet. Students select a different bead for various turning
points in their lives. When all the students who want to participate
have finished their bracelet, they are then asked to sit in a circle and
share what each bead on their bracelet represents. They can say as little or as much as they want in sharing their story. They are emulating
relatively new methodologies of storytelling and dialogue in Northern
Ireland based on international models. While the storytelling process
is not psychoanalytical or clinically therapeutic in nature, it can start
a process of healing among former combatants, and in the students'
case, help in their understanding of the personal complexity and risk-
taking involved in the process. The storytelling and bracelet-making
activity helps to reduce uncertainty and to see the humanity in others.
Storytelling for former combatants breaks the silence, fears, and mis-
conceptions fed by years of conflict. For our students, it helps develop
their empathic listening skills to understand the complexity of long-
term conflict and the difficulty of working toward peace.

With this newly developed and highly engaged sensitivity, students
visit the Falls and Shankhill Road areas of East Belfast, led by former
combatants, and the Bogside area of Derry, where Catholics were kept
outside the walls of the city of Derry. The Bogside is also the scene of
the Bloody Sunday violence in which many Catholics lost their lives to
local police and the English military.

Students learn how dialogue requires a responsiveness, which is made
possible by qualities of thought and talk that allow transformation to
take place: transformation in how people understand the self, the other,
and the societies they inhabit; and the students in this class conclude
with a profile-writing component using storytelling and photography

to tell the story of a local community member for the *Faces and Voices of Derry Project*. Additionally, this course examines elements of the past that continue to remind people on a daily basis about their life experiences.

Moving beyond *'The Troubles'*: Bloody Sunday and the Murals of Derry

When the residency period starts to draw to a close, many questions arise about what next in terms of the quest for peace. The community of Derry, like much of Northern Ireland, has been on a journey towards understanding and healing. Individual experience in the larger story of conflict requires a safe space for people to articulate personal stories, or 'truths', in a way that does not diminish their own experience. Because of Northern Ireland's diverse culture and history, no one person can tell the story of the conflict. One way the story is told is through visual murals that are scattered throughout the city of Derry. These murals are explored in terms of the stories they tell, to what degree they hinder or assist the peacebuilding process, and the role remembering ethically, remembering together, and remembering the future plays in the process. Is it possible that remembering together can lead to a liberating option? In the process of dialogue, can an ethical framework for peacebuilding be co-created?

Political murals and graffiti are visual public political expressions. These public symbols, born from political struggle, become personal to the communities. Students take many photos of the murals as part of their blogs on peacebuilding. The murals become part of the past but they remain in the present for the local community. Political murals and graffiti transfer history and meaning from generation to generation. Olson and colleagues (2008) describe remembering and memorializing as 'those public practices by which history is turned into memory' (p. 99). The students ask how people can work for peace when they are reminded every day of some of the images of violence and the calls for social justice of the past. One answer lies in this student blog post of a combatant's story:

> While Mr. Doherty does not see true peace and the final end of the conflict being achieved in his lifetime, he does see that progress can be made through storytelling and dialogue. Though dialogue is a slow process, he feels it is the only option for peace building in Northern Ireland. With storytelling and dialogue, the goal is, in his

own words, to 'decommission the current mindsets, not weapons'. This method allows the people to see each side differently and to see the struggle and pain their counterparts on the opposite side have lived through.

Another combatant, named Richard, was shot in the eye as a ten-year-old on his way home from school. He has been blind since that time. He says, 'I am a victim of the troubles and there is nothing I can do about that but I refuse to be a victim of anger and I do have control over that'. He questions why anyone would want to be angry and *live* anger. He believes that forgiveness is a gift for yourself; it's not for the other person. Forgiveness doesn't change the past, but it can change the future. Forgiveness is not about the perpetrator; instead it is first and foremost about your ability to let go. When you can do that anything is possible. Six years ago Richard met the soldier (Charles) who shot him. He rehearsed what he would say at that meeting because he wanted Charles to know he has no animosity towards him and that he forgives him. For Richard, forgiveness was easy, but he knows it isn't easy for everyone. Clearly victims never want to be victims but it doesn't mean they don't have the capacity to forgive. Richard is not saying that by forgiving others you say that what they did was okay. Forgiveness isn't about justice.

Richard hopes his story is an example of how forgiveness can have an impact on the future. He explained that emotions and feelings are like cells within the mind and each of us holds the key (Gonzaga-in-Derry, 2013).

From storytelling to building another story

Ideally, these global, concrete instances of political struggle and expression can build skills toward recognizing history, ethical communication, and ethical remembering in the service of future communicative action. Effective public memory involves ethical remembering, which is about recognizing what is and is not useful to a community's efforts in reconciliation or building a shared future. As McMaster and Hetherington (2012) explain, 'The total context in which we remember is complex. … Remembering requires an ethical framework and it needs to be shared … Ethical remembering is critical remembering' (pp. 4–7). In this critical remembering, another former combatant writes: 'The primary victim of conflict is truth'. 'Ethical and Shared Remembering' calls upon those seeking to understand their experiences to take a personal journey where they find themselves being confronted with questions around their assumptions. With Ethical and Shared Remembering, the effort is not about offering a definitive account of events. It is in developing an account that captures the multiplicity of narratives and perspectives. Combatant Seamus Farrell explains, 'We run the risk of repeating ourselves unless we can begin to come to an understanding of our multiple narratives and create a future that is different from the one that was completely overwhelmed by a sectarian version of what happened'.

In studying the dialogic peacebuilding process and Ethical and Shared Remembering, students eventually move into their home communities with this knowledge. A key idea resonating with all the students is how the presence of conflict and differences makes communicative interaction even more necessary. This communicative action – speaking and listening together – does not do away with the conflicts that arise from uncertainty, inequality, and identity. Rather, it enables political actors to decide democratically *how to* act in the face of conflict (Bickford, 1996, p. 2).

The roles of culture and communication are woven into the peacebuilding process in Derry. Intercultural communication allows us to reduce uncertainty through storytelling, and to open the doors to dialogue. The theoretical underpinnings of this work by Buber, Godamer, Habermas, Bakhtin, Freire, Yankelovich, Gudykunst, Kim, Deetz, and many others cited in this chapter all play a significant role. But it is the day-to-day grass-roots peacebuilding efforts by people like Johnston McMaster, Maureen Hetherington, the people at The Junction, and those former combatants who are willing to risk and tell their stories and engage in dialogue who are showing how to apply the theories without even knowing that they are. And it is the process of understanding the intercultural nature of dialogue and ethical remembering that is a cornerstone of the peacebuilding process in Derry, Northern Ireland.

References

R. Anderson, L. A. Baxter, and K. N. Cissna (eds) (2004) *Dialogue: Theorizing Differences in Communication* (Thousand Oaks, CA: Sage).

M. M. Bakhtin (1981) *The Dialogic Imagination: Four Essays.* (Michael Holquist, ed. & Caryl Emerson and Michael Holquist, trans.) (Austin and London: University of Texas Press).

M. M. Bakhtin (1984) *Problems of Dostoevsky's Poetics* (Caryl Emerson, ed. and trans.) (Minneapolis: University of Minnesota Press).

M. M. Bakhtin (1986) *Speech Genres and Other Late Essays* (Vern W. McGee, trans.) (Austin, TX: University of Texas Press).

F. Barth (1969) *Ethnic Groups and Boundaries: The Social Organization of Cultural Difference* (Boston, MA: Little, Brown and Company).

S. Bickford (1996) *The Dissonance of Democracy: Listening, Conflict, and Citizenship* (Ithaca, NY: Cornell University Press).

M. Buber (1958) *I and Thou*, 2 edn (R.G. Smith, trans.) (New York: Scribner).

M. Buber (1965) *Between Man and Man* (R. G. Smith, trans.) (New York: Macmillan).

M. Buber (1967) 'Hope for the Hour' in F. W. Matson and A. Montagu (eds) *The Human Dialogue: Perspectives on Communication* (New York: Free Press) pp. 306–312.

J. S. Caputo and H. M. Crandall (2013) 'The Intercultural Communication Cultural Immersion Experience: Preparing Leaders for a Global Future', *Journal of Leadership Studies*, 6, 58–63.

S. Deetz (2013) 'Critical Theory of Organizations' in E. M. Griffin, S. Ledbetter, and G. Sparks (eds) *A First Look at Communication Theory*, 9th edn (New York: McGraw-Hill) pp. 99–106.

S. Deetz and J. Simpson (2004) 'Critical Organizational Dialogue: Open Formation and the Demand for "Otherness"' in R. Anderson, L. A. Baxter, and K. N. Cissna (eds) *Dialogue: Theorizing Differences in Communication* (Thousand Oaks, CA: Sage) pp. 141–158.

P. Freire (1990) *Pedagogy of the Oppressed* (M. B. Ramos, trans.) (New York: Continuum).

H.-G. Godamer (1976) *Philosophical Hermeneutics* (D. E. Linge, ed. & trans.) (Berkeley: University of California Press).

H.-G. Godamer (1982) *Truth and Method*, 2nd edn (G. Barden & J. Cumming, trans.) (New York: Crossroad).

Gonzaga-in-Derry Blog (2013) http://gonzagainderry2013.blogspot.com/search/label/stories, accessed 27 May 2015.

Gonzaga-in-Derry Blog (2014) http://gonzagainderry2014.blogspot.co.uk, accessed 27 May 2015.

W. B. Gudykunst and Y. Y. Kim (1992) *Communicating with Strangers: An Approach to Intercultural Communication*, 2nd edn (New York: McGraw-Hill).

J. Habermas (1971) *Knowledge and Human Interests* (J. J. Shapiro, trans.) (Boston, MA: Beacon Press).

J. Habermas (1975) *Legitimation Crisis* (T. McCarthy, trans.) (Boston, MA: Beacon Press).

J. Habermas (1979) *Communication and the Evolution of Society* (T. McCarthy, trans.) (Boston: Beacon Press).

J. Habermas (1984) *Theory of Communicative Action: Vol. 1. Reason and the Rationalization of Society* (T. McCarthy, trans.) (Boston, MA: Beacon Press).

J. Habermas (1987) *Theory of Communicative Action: Vol. 2. Life World and System: A Critique of Functionalist Reason* (T. McCarthy, trans.) (Boston, MA: Beacon Press).

S. McNee and H. Shotter (2004) 'Dialogue, Creativity and Change' in R. Anderson, L. A. Baxter, and K. N. Cissna (eds) *Dialogue: Theorizing Differences in Communication* (Thousand Oaks, CA: Sage) p. 99.

J. McMaster and M. Hetherington (2012) *Ethical & Shared Remembering: Commemoration in a New Context – Remembering a Decade of Change and Violence in Ireland 1912–1922* (Derry Londonderry, Ireland: The Junction: Community Relations & Peacebuilding).

L. C. Olson, C. A. Finnegan, and D. S. Hope (2008) *Visual Rhetoric: A Reader in Communication and American Culture* (Thousand Oaks, CA: Sage).

Towards Understanding and Healing (2008) http://thejunction-ni.org/index.php/towards-understanding-and-healing, date accessed 27 May 2015.

J. Sacks (2005) 'Turning Enemies into Friends' in A. S. Ahmed and B. Forst (eds) *After Terror: Promoting Dialogue among Civilizations* (New York: John Wiley and Sons) pp. 112–118.

D. Yankelovich (1999) *The Magic of Dialogue: Transforming Conflict into Cooperation* (New York: Simon and Schuster).

J. Wood (2004) 'Forward, Entering into Dialogue' in R. Anderson, L. A. Baxter and K. N. Cissna (eds) *Dialogue: Theorizing Differences in Communication* (Thousand Oaks, CA: Sage) pp. xv–xxiii.

5
Ethnic Conflicts and Deleuzo-Guattarian Rhizomes of Cultural Affirmation

Mariam Betlemidze

Introduction

This chapter offers a Deleuzo-Guattarian and Badiouian ideas to challenge existing perspectives on South Caucasian conflicts; to examine how the application of a plateau of intensity to the Caucasian situation reveals multiple images of dynamism, desiring productions and states of endless becomings. The intention behind this endeavor is to bring to light factors of intercultural, interethnic, and international cooperation that are hidden under transcendent strategies of the conflicting Caucasian parties. The chapter hence argues that affirmative philosophy and, in particular, the way of thinking in terms of multiplicities unlocks enormous potential for paving the way of gradual conflict resolution in the region of South Caucasus.

The central advantage of employing affirmative cultural philosophy as a tool to explore potentials for conflict resolutions, is in its ontological grounds, referred to as pluralism and empiricism. Deleuze (1983), whose works are in this vein, analyses Nietzsche's philosophy and states that 'there is no event, no phenomenon, word or thought which does not have multiple sense' (p. 4). Truly, there is no event or notion that does not have multiple meanings in the Caucasus, but this is not why conflicts exist in the region. The reason for the conflict deadlock in the Caucasus is the growing potential for renewal of war and the negation of not only the idea of multiplicity, but even of any other, single, different understanding, belief, or ideology.

Deleuze (1983) says, 'a thing has as many senses as there are forces capable of taking possession of it' (p. 4). 'Forces' are something Caucasians claim to have fought against throughout centuries to survive numerous conquerors and those forces continue coming from East and West. On the basis of that, Caucasians claim to have significant understanding of 'forces' and continue to fight for the sake of surviving territorialization. However, that idea of 'forces' seems to be rather far from the Neitzcheian or Deleuzian thinking of forces as spectrums of potential. There is no acknowledgement of the 'lines of flight, movements of deterritorialization and destratification'. There is only particular, self-justifying 'lines of articulation or segmentarity, strata and territories' (Deleuze and Guattrari, 1987, p. 3).

According to Deleuze and Guattari (1987), 'binary logic and biunivocal relationships still dominate psychoanalysis, linguistics, structuralism, and even information science' (p. 5). People try to connect things that are not related to each other and, thus, create images of black and white pictures, polarized ideas, extreme ends that seem not to have anything in between and have no way to meet or co-exist. Badiou (2003) calls that phenomenon a 'profoundly illogical regime of communication' to which the whole world is submitted. In Neitzcheian (Deleuze, 1983) philosophy such a regime enslaves masters, and causes the negation of events and trends that do not justify one's own state and actions, thus transforming active forces into reactive ones.

Nietzsche and Deleuze (1983) would call such a despotic force an exhausted one as it 'does not have strength to affirm difference, a force which no longer acts but rather reacts to the forces which dominate it' (p. 9). For instance, the Georgian government affirms that Abkhazian authorities are not under the influence of Russia, and their desire to be independent from Georgia is based only on their desires and those of their civil society. Such neglect of the Abkhazian desire for independence does not imply any action. Thus, it is more a reaction, a reaction to the fear that it might not be able to act effectively. Such fear of action is similar to procrastination, but seems to be much more pessimistic than procrastination, as it is a 'genealogy taken up by slaves' (Deleuze, 1983, p. 55).

Calling people who are in charge of a country 'slaves' should not be surprising, as in Nietzscheian philosophy, reactive force that is related to negative will and is called slave, and affirmative will, sometimes with active force, is called master. The master versus slave juxtaposition is not highly metaphorical, because, at least based on the Georgian-Abkhazian or any other Caucasian conflict, there is little affirmation of difference, acknowledgement of one's counterpart's desires and, consequently, seems to have much less potential for reaching any kind of breakthrough. Thereby, these conflicts are slaves to their own fears. If one would surrender to forms of incorporeal transformation and affirm/acknowledge existence of differences in a dice-throw in a political game, one would have more control over the situation and thereby be a master.

There is an interesting phenomenon about slaves enslaving masters described in *Nietzsche and Philosophy* (Deleuze, 1983), which can easily be illustrated by contemporary situations. 'Reactive force, even when it obeys, limits active force, imposes limitations and partial restrictions on it and is already controlled by the spirit of negative' (Deleuze, 1983, p. 56). Again, going back to Caucasian conflicts and meetings of conflict resolution groups from the conflicting sides, one would easily notice how participants in those meetings surrender to incorporeal transformation of being equally biased and faulty in the conflict, and are willing to reach social change. However, when going back to their places of origin, and encountering the negative spirits of friends, co-workers, family, neighbors, and mainstream ideas, those 'masters' of affirmative will and active force turn into 'slaves' of dominant ideas. The reason for this is not only the influence of dominant ideas of negative will, but the conformist nature of people, the fact that perhaps it is easier to be nihilist and have 'bad consciousness' (Deleuze, 1983).

As Deleuze explains, based on his analysis of Nietzsche, the reactive force separates the active force from what it can do, thus turning it into a reactive force, a slave that does not want to stop being a slave. This kind of phenomenon could be similar to the relation of minus and plus in mathematics. Minus turns plus into minus, but in comparison to math, two or multiple negative wills, reactive forces, so called slaves, do not turn into masters as it happens in math when two or more even minuses turn into pluses. Deleuze (1983) says that we have the hierarchy we deserve. Hierarchy that 'also designates the triumph of reactive forces, the contagion of reactive forces and the complex organization which results—where the weak have conquered, where the strong are contaminated, where the slave who has not stopped being a slave prevails over the master who has stopped being one ...' (Deleuze, 1983, pp. 60–61).

When looking closer, such contamination of strong and noble, and its transformation into dialectic resentment, resembles the root systems of the absurd. Every enslaved mater becomes part of the arborescent root system, which has mystification, falsification, and absurdity as the main principles. From the point of view of contaminated affirmative will, none of the tree-like structure can be noble, because it is based on one main principle. But there cannot be one main principle, there can only be a multiplicity of principles that may form unity or go beyond unity.

More precisely, a multiplicity of truths could be better understood through the plane of consistency:

> Inscribed on the plane of consistency are haecceities (*thisness*), events, incorporeal transformations that are apprehended in themselves; nomadic essences, vague yet rigorous; continuums of intensities or continuous, variations, which go beyond constants and variables; becomings, which have neither culmination nor subject, but draw one another into zones of proximity or undecidability; smooth spaces, composed from within striated space. We will say that a body without organs, or bodies without organs (plateaus) comes into play in individuation by and haecceity, in the production of intensities beginning at a degree zero, in the matter of variation, in the medium of becoming or transformation, and in the smoothing of space. A powerful nonorganic life that escapes the strata, cuts across assemblages, and draws an abstract line without contour, a line of nomad art and itinerant metallurgy.
>
> (Deleuze and Guattari, 1987, p. 507)

This kind of philosophy, which deterritorializes discourses, could be rather useful and timely in the Caucasus where sharp lines are drawn between various territories, social layers, and ways of thinking, talking and acting. Haecceity could open up new possibilities for the deadlocked conflicts that too much adhere to lines of distinction and territorialization, literally and figuratively. To better understand how haecceity and intensities of multiple plateaus could create new opportunities, a more detailed analysis of the Caucasian conflicts should be provided. For that, the next section will focus on the idea of nomadic, active war machines appropriated by sedentary, reactive forces.

War machines and the need for interruption

Before examining Caucasian militarism, it is important to note that none of the South Caucasian nation-states or their breakaway territories officially consider themselves reactive, militarist forces. They rather accentuate their desire to solve ethnic and territorial conflicts peacefully. However, they never stop arming, training soldiers, or striving to get accepted into the North Atlantic Treaty Organization (NATO). They remain transcendent to the point where they will be winners in the conflicts because they are poised to take advantage of opportunities to succeed in war. Ongoing sedentary media coverage is well suited to ensuring the smoothness of the militarist process through the creation of war-machine-justifying sedentary contexts. In a simplified sense, that mostly means to maintain a 'frightened, confused and misinformed public' (Buchanan and Parr, 2006, p. 22).

Why do the nation-states remain on their roads of militarism and breed belligerence among their populations, if they claim they are willing to resolve conflicts peacefully but continue to spend billions of dollars from their own budgets and those of international organizations to support their preparations for war? This phenomenon, seemingly paradoxical at first glance, could be understood more thoroughly through the application of the war machine (Deleuze and Guattari, 1987) concept. It should be noted that even though the nation-states appropriate war machines, eventually they lose control over them. The reason is the nomadic nature of the war-machine, which makes it hard to regulate. As Deleuze and Guattari say:

> ... even though the nomadic trajectory may follow trails or customary routes, it does not fulfill the function of the sedentary road, which is to parcel out a closed space to people, assigning each person a share and regulating the communication between shares. The nomadic trajectory does the opposite: it distributes people (or animals) in an open space, one that is indefinite and noncommunicating.
>
> (Deleuze and Guattari, 1987, p. 380)

If applied to Caucasian conflicts, and perhaps to any other conflicts, war machines, once fights break out and injustices occur, pull in more and more people, ideas, and movements as parts of the war machine. This war machine moves in an open, indefinite space in tandem with the other, similar war machines on the other side of the conflict. It should be noted that neither of them are sedentary, territorialized state armies, but non-controllable and deterritorialized, a nomadic mix of guerrilla troops, civilian armed groups, mafiosi gangs, individual avengers, journalists, politicians, etc. The existence of a similar nomadic war machine on the other side of a conflict does not mean that these two are in a state of communication and information-sharing. People living in these divided societies follow news of their own side and see the opposing side through the dark lenses of one-sided, distorted media coverage. Thus, media coverage turns out to be in an informational vacuum, a space of noncommunicating, as Deleuze and Guattari say (1987).

For a closer look at the origins of the contemporary conflicts in the Caucasus and the functionality of the war machines in those lands, Merab Mamardashvili, a Georgian philosopher, provides a similar concept to that of the war machine—the mechanism, which should be helpful. During the pre-wars period of the early 1990s, Mamardashvili was ringing alarm bells, due to the fractioning among Georgian political parties and multi-ethnic populations that was taking place in the striated space, right after the break-up of the Soviet Union, in a hive of nationalistic pressures. With the major support of ethnic majorities, authorities of the newly-born nation-states of the South Caucasus helped compose a smooth space for the recently unleashed war machines, which they eventually proved to be incapable of controlling. That is because what was at first anticipated to be limited war morphed into *so-called 'total war'* and transformed the relation between aim and object (Deleuze & Guattari, 1987, p. 421). To translate that into Caucasian ontology, the war-machine's unleashers were thinking of ensuring territorial integrity and ethnic identity, before starting to build newly independent states, but then found themselves sinking in the rhizomatic roots of uncontrollable violence and injustices, which had war itself as their main principle. Again, going back to Deleuze and Guattari (1987), 'when total war becomes the object of the appropriated war machine, then at this level in the set of all possible conditions, the object and the aim enter into new relations that can reach the point of contradiction' (p. 421). This contradiction is between the initial goal which is ensuring territorial integrity/salvation of the ethnic identity, and the actual goal which is destruction; initial controller which is the state, and eventual ruler which is the war machine. As Buchanan says, 'it effectively subsumes the state, making it just one of its many moving parts' (Buchanan and Parr, 2006, p. 31). Governments of those Caucasian conflicting sides still remain hostages to the public opinion they helped create throughout history, and therefore prove to be one of the moving parts of the war machines.

Some may argue that war machines have now stopped, and bring up the fact that there are no armed conflicts or mass killings going on right now. But 'war does not necessarily have the battle as its object, and more importantly, the war machine does not necessarily have war as its object, although war and the battle may be its necessary result', as Deleuze and Guattari (1987) point out (p. 416). In response to that, others may even claim that there have never been war machines unleashed, only one-sided oppression, and claim that those who believe in war machines are anti-Georgian, anti-Armenian, anti-Azerbaijanian, etc. As it is rather unimaginable for Caucasians to accept someone's neutrality, 'you are either with us or against us' has been the dominant thinking in recent decades.

As a result, non-acknowledgement of one-sidedness, the win/lose approach and the dynamics of the nomadic war-machines prove that Mamardashvili's statements of the 1990s are still relevant today: 'the [war] mechanism is in full swing and is beating the hammer into our heads, we should do something to stop it before it causes more dramatic results'[1] (Tsiteli Zona [red zone], 12 March 2010). Unfortunately, Mamardashvili's words were not adhered to and the 'more dramatic results' he was warning about have already taken place. The August 2008 war between Georgia and Russia is one prominent example of the dramatic results of ongoing militarism and war-machine activity. Also, there will be more dramatic results in other parts of the South Caucasus because 'militarism creates problems it claims only militarism can solve, but its solutions are only so many more problems that, too, seem insoluble except to militarism' (Buchanan and Parr, 2006, p. 22).

Truly, 'media and official news services are only there to maintain the illusion of actuality, of the reality of the stakes, of the objectivity of the facts' (Baudrillard, 1994, p. 38). The same story archetypes are applied repeatedly to new events in Georgia. These archetypes are not hard to notice in news about Russia, breakaway territories, and North Atlantic Treaty Organization (NATO) summits, where the archetype of an evil country is applied to Russia. No matter the subject of the news story, the breakaway territories are introduced as measurable marionette secessionists and NATO officials as potential defenders and rescuers of Georgia from 'becoming limbo land to which', thanks to Russia and the breakaway territories, it is bound. Often reinforced and reproduced in the actual and virtual statements of the nation-state leaders, these archetypes crash into similarly one-sided claims of the other state or non-state actors. This dichotomy of conflicting narratives can be traced back to pre-soviet times, when there was no Internet or television, and it took much longer for a political statement or illusory, propagandistic news story to spread. However, finding the historic roots in this case does not provide the ultimate cure for these phenomena, which have expanded due to the development of information and communication technologies. 'We're moving toward

---

[1] My translation of Mamardashvili's speech that was broadcast in the retrospective TV show 'Red Zone'.

control societies that no longer operate by confining people but through continuous control and instant communication' (Deleuze, 1995, p. 174). There is a similar idea in Badiou's (2003) philosophy, where he talks about the danger of the peed by which our world is characterized:

> the speed of historical change; the speed of technical change; the speed of communications; of transmissions; and even the speed with which humans beings establish connections with one another ... It is because things, images and relations circulate so quickly that we do not even have time to measure the extent of this incoherency.
>
> (Badiou, 2003, p. 51)

When contemplating the same idea of speed in the Caucasus, there is even more danger of incoherency, because, there, more actors have submitted to the propaganda of the war machine. In such situations, one may not find it sufficient to revolt in real life, but seek to express protest via hacktivism.

Deleuze (1995) introduces the need for 'vacuoles of noncommunication, circuit breakers' (p. 175) as means of resisting the regimes of communication in control societies. 'It's true that, even before control societies are fully in place, forms of delinquency or resistance are also appearing. Computer piracy and viruses, for example, will replace strikes and what the nineteenth century called "sabotage" ("clogging" the machinery)' (Deleuze, 1995, p. 175). It could be proved that 'vacuoles of noncommunication' have been realized already. In the summer of 2008, weeks before the Russian troops marched into full-scale conventional war against Georgia, cyber attacks began on Georgian websites (Clarke, 2009). Based on the Shadowserver Foundation's comments, Danchev (2008) writes that the website of President Mikhail Saakashvili of Georgia was unavailable for over 24 hours due to a 'multi-pronged distributed denial of service (DDoS) attack' (Danchev, 2008). Later on, Hollis (2011) and others labeled these cyber attacks a 'dress rehearsal' for a Russian 'cyber war', synchronized with conventional warfare, less than a month before the physical assault began (Hollis, 2011, p. 4).

The DDoS attacks against Georgian cyberspace reached an unprecedented level on 8 August, the first day of Georgia's armed conflict with Russia over its breakaway territory of South Ossetia. Nearly all the most important Georgian media, finance, business, and government websites were successfully attacked. The website StopGeorgia.ru was established in the summer of 2008 and provided volunteer hackers with the list of targeted websites in Georgia and instructions on how to carry out those attacks:

> Any civilian, Russian-born or otherwise, aspiring to be a cyber warrior was able to visit pro-Russia websites to download the software and instructions necessary to launch denial-of-service attacks on Georgia. The only effort required by the user was to enter the Web address of a target and click a button labeled 'Start Flood'.
>
> (Kurtz, 2009, p. 6)

In fact, the rhizomatic networks of hacktivists, or cyber warriors as they call themselves, exemplify Deleuzian nomads, as they have virtually tactile relations with each other. Deleuze and Guattari (1987) describe this relation this way:

> The interlinkages do not imply an ambient space in which the multiplicity would be immersed and which would make distances invariant; rather, they are constituted according to ordered differences that give rise to intrinsic variations in the division of a single distance.
>
> (Deleuze and Guattari, 1987, p. 493)

Thus, I would argue that nomads, within their rhizomatic network, are creating 'vacuoles of noncommunication'. But before elaborating more on those, it is appropriate to unfold the concept of control societies, which is basically the enclosed environments that dominate the contemporary world. These structures and enclosed institutions are factories, hospitals, and schools, which are becoming prison-like systems and thereby morphing into bigger machines of control than their little moving parts. For Deleuze, 'instant communication' plays a major role in feeding the control societies, keeping them in a constant state of modulation (Buchanan and Parr, 2006). The process of constant modulation that is taking place in the Caucasus explains the existence of the archetypes in the public statements of government officials and news media. Thus, it is logical to agree with Deleuze and Guattari (1987) that subjectivity and collectivity are inseparable from a form of political communication that is characterized by resentment, and produces faces of evil (Ivie, 2007) for making the intentions of governmental and other reactive forces appear noble. Therefore, Deleuze's (1995) call—'we've got to hijack speech' (p. 175)—seems fair enough: 'The key thing is to create vacuoles of noncommunication, circuit breakers, so we can elude control' (Deleuze, 1995, p. 175).

Deleuzian (1995) 'vacuoles of noncommunication' (p. 175), the contemporary illustration of which would be cyber attacks aimed at disrupting war-machine workflow, are at the same time part of another war machine. Despite its liberating potential, the World Wide Web is still well permeated by money and efficiently serves propagandistic goals. Not all web content is commodifying, but hardly anyone would agree that a President's website is an objective and free source of information. Thus, if some choose to block the entrance of a television station and throw rotten vegetables and eggs against its windows, why would others not think of hacking a Presidential website, implementing denial of service attacks and replacing a President's photos with offensive images?

This kind of affirmation of the alternative view is painful for the Caucasian population, as it deterritorializes discourses, deprives countries' leaders of their illusory role of protector, and disrupts the belief that only the other is evil and we are innocent victims. However, such breaking away from modulation and the embracing of haecceity could open up new possibilities for the deadlocked conflicts, as those would draw abstract lines without contour, lines of 'nomad art' (Deleuze and Guattari, 1987, p. 507).

From the Deleuzo-Guattarian rhizome to new media

According to early researches, media is capable of both fomenting (Doob, 1935, Lasswell, 1928) and reducing prejudice and conflict (Cooper and Jahoda, 1947, Flowerman, 1949, Peterson and Thurstone, 1933). Unfortunately, the media's role in the reconciliation of ethnic conflicts has not yet been sufficiently realized. Most of the people in the South Caucasus are gatekept by mainstream media that some would call 'war journalism' (Webel and Galtung, 2007, p. 258). This kind of journalism mostly engages in framing events as if there were only one possible perspective, without implying that journalists are unwittingly serving as parts of a bigger war machine and pulling more and more people into adopting the mainstream perspective, thus increasing and/ or maintaining the number of war supporters. This is the type of communication Alain Badiou (2003) considers to be the principal obstacle for infinite thought; as he puts it, 'the world is submitted to the profoundly illogical regime of communication' (p. 41). The Caucasus is no exception.

The discussion of questions—how social change may happen in war-divided societies, and what the role of both traditional and new media in this process could be—would be more fruitfully discussed through the full spectrum of Badiou's (2003) list of principal obstacles for the infinite thought. Those are: 'the reign of merchandise, the reign of communication, the need for technical specialization and the necessity for realistic calculation of security' (Badiou, 2003, p. 42). Even though Badiou opposes the Deleuzo-Guattarian call for multiplicities and speed, he still makes a great contribution to the development of the Deleuzo-Guattarian idea of rhizome and new media. Application of Badiouean principles to Caucasian ontology helps classify the intensive multiplicity of dynamics.

After the Soviet Union broke up and a free market was introduced, the reign of governmental control of the media was replaced by the reign of merchandise. Newspapers started to self-censor to better and faster feed the needs of the war-traumatized population with the soviet mindset. Consequently, the newspapers with stories about the glorious nation of Georgia, and their evil neighbor Russia, who helped Abkhazia and South Ossetia to break away, were and still are selling best in Georgia. People are happily paying to become quickly satisfied with this kind of information, and at the same time, are having their interest in new ideas killed. The editors of those newspapers do not want to stop working in support of the war machine, as this will deprive them and their co-workers of their source of income. Fortunately, noncommercial newspapers supported by international organizations try to bring in different points of views, but find it hard to compete with the 'infinite glitter of merchandise' (Badiou, 2003, p. 40). For instance, a unique Georgian-Abkhazian newspaper, *Panorama*, which went through huge obstacles to put together the work of journalists from war-divided communities, providing balanced information, was less popular and in some cases was even called a Russian propaganda tool, for having information that was not well aligned with mainstream ideas. Thus, Badiou's principle of the reign of merchandise is logically intertwined with the reign of communication. In other words, communication is thoroughly permeated by the money, not only of big corporations, oligarchs, and governments, but also of the 'masses'.

Thus, media-reproduced and modulated transcendent and self-righteous policies in Georgia and the rest of the South Caucasus have already paved the way for further fracturing inside the region and are seeking emancipatory forces outside the region. This scenario begs the question, could new media be an optimal way to reach a social change in such conflict-swamped, locked, war-divided societies—and if yes, how? It would be helpful to go back to the ideas of Mamardashvili, regarding his analog to the Deleuzo-Guattarian war machine, which is the mechanism discussed in the previous section. According to Mamardashvili's logic, the mechanism should be stopped by those who helped put it into motion. Similar logic can be found in Deleuzo-Guattarian writing. 'The war machine is the invention of the nomads (insofar as it is exterior to the State apparatus and distinct from the military institution)', (Deleuze and Guattari, 1987, p. 380). It follows that, if a war machine is of a nomadic nature, it could never be influenced by something as sedentary as government or mainstream media. So, the nomadic multiplicity of people that helped put the war machine into motion should not wait to be represented via some supposedly emancipatory force, but speak up directly through creative media activism and thus challenge the militarist aspirations of the society. For that, it is extremely useful to employ the idea of the rhizome, proposed by Deleuze and Guattari, which has already been called 'the philosophical bible of the cyber-evangelists' (Spiller, 2002, p. 96). The rhizome, indeed, is a perfect model for the World Wide Web, which would multiply the nomadic nature of citizen journalists' activism.

Deleuzo-Gauttarian principles of rhizome, as applied to new media activism, represent the potential of those serving as catalysts of the conflicts to move towards the 'four dimensions of reconciliation' (Ramsbotham, Woodhouse, and Miall, 2005, p. 232). Principles of connection and heterogeneity would enable exchange of diverse points of views, which would gradually result in the acceptance of the status quo by the conflicting parties. That would mean that Azerbaijanians would accept Nagorno-Karabakh being broken away from their nation state; Armenians would have to admit that Azerbaijanians have the right to claim Nagorno-Karabakh, despite the fact that there is currently no Azerbijanian control over that region—it is their territory according to international borders; Georgians would have to accept that Abkhazians and South Ossetians do not recognize Georgian legitimacy on their territory; Abkhazians and South Ossetians would realize that international actors still consider Georgia as the official owner of the territory from which they are claiming to be independent.

The principle of multiplicity of the Deleuzo-Guattarian rhizome, i.e. new media, will help 'expose arborescent pseudomultiplicities for what they are' (Deleuze and Guattari, 1987, p. 8) and thus will question the objectivity and fairness of mainstream media coverage. Those multiple lines of new media networks would help find connecting threads for the conflicting accounts of war-divided communities and thus realize the second dimension of reconciliation—'correlation of accounts' (Ramsbotham, Woodhouse, and Miall, 2005, p. 232)—through blogging, commenting, sharing, tweeting, channeling, and foruming. In the Caucasus, a correlation of accounts, even between states such as Georgia and Armenia that do not have an official shared conflict zone, remains rather complex. Needless to say, the scale of complexity in correlating accounts related to the state borders would be much higher between the other state and non-state actors in the region, which do have official conflict zones. Therefore, from the point of view of current fractionation and self-centricity, bridging opposites seems rather problematic. It would be logical here to agree with Deleuze and Guattari on the fourth principle of the rhizome, regarding rupture: 'there is a rupture in the rhizome whenever segmentary lines explode into a line of flight, but the line of flight is part of the rhizome. These lines always tie back to one another' (Deleuze and Guattari, 1987, p. 9). Because of its openness to new ideas, sedentary, reactive forces might attempt to break the lines of connection between conflicting accounts, but a rhizome 'will start up again on one of its old lines, or on new lines' (Deleuze and Guattari, 1987, p. 9). The independence and nomadic nature of the lines of the rhizome are also due to the fifth and the sixth principles, which are cartography and decalcomania. These make new media activism 'not amenable to any structural or generative model' (Deleuze and Guattari, 1987, p. 12). Following the principles of rhizome, there would be all the conditions for the realization of the third and fourth dimensions of reconciliation, which are 'bridging opposites' and 'celebrating differences' (Ramsbotham et al., 2005, p. 232).

One of the most important advantages of the rhizome and new media activism, the call for immanence and distancing from the 'would be' reality of transcendence, is also what connects Deleuzo-Guattarian (1987) philosophy with Badiou's (2003) infinite thought. Badiou opposes multiplicity in forms of polyvalence, and says that 'thought must at least be able to extract itself from this circulation and take possession of itself once again as something other than an object of circulation' (Badiou, 2003, p. 49). However, if there is no circulation, there would not be anything to extract. Another similarity between Deleuze and Badiou, favoring new media, is the idea of needed interruption. 'If philosophy is to sustain its desire in such a world [the world of endless circulation], it must propose a principle of interruption' (Badiou, 2003, pp. 48–49). One of the types of interruption would be the 'cyber attack', or hacktivism, as discussed in the previous section. However, new media, or creative activism, would be more peaceful and constructive.

This is related to Deleuze's (1995) advocacy for the 'vacuoles of non-communication' (p. 175) as means of resisting the regimes of communication in control societies. Both types of interruptions are aimed at disrupting the reign of illogical communication. Provocative new media activism could be the best tool for the interruption Deleuze and Badiou are in favor of. Such surrender to nomadic infinite thought could well help Caucasians let go of their past grievances, focus on the present, and gain an immanent approach:

> a response to inequity and infringement designed for a singular set of circumstances promises to be better fitted to immanent political, economic, cultural, religious, and aesthetic conditions than does a response consisting in the discursive invocation of and reliance on abstracted categories of transcendent sets of universal principles.
> (Hawes, 2010, p. 263)

With such an immanent approach, Caucasians would ultimately switch their focus from narrow territorial claims to broader region-wide ambitions, which could also involve the fulfillment of their initial claims related to territorial integrity and the survival of ethnic identity.

It should also be noted that there are fantasies regarding the universality of the new media as catalyst. As Doug Schuler (2003) says, there is nothing inherently democratic about technology. An analysis of anti-Georgian and anti-Russian YouTube videos shows that technology is being used to spread propaganda and re-produce dominant ideology, which makes it a mere tool in the hands of ordinary people that are already 'gatekept' (Reese and Ballinger, 2001) by mainstream medias. Deleuze and Guattari also acknowledge the existence of 'micro black holes' and the lines of flight that 'always risk abandoning their creative potentialities and turning into a line of death, being turned into a line of destruction pure and simple (fascism)' (Deleuze and Guattari, p. 506). More concrete and material is Badiou's explanation of why there is no easy way for the realization of infinite thought. Here, going back to the discussion of Badiou's obstacles for infinite thought is timely. The last two obstacles, as he puts them, are the needs for technical specialization and calculation of security. The need for technical specialization not only breaks the circuit of the rhizome's universality by subjugating its lines to one or the other category; it also pulls the brightest minds into the arborescent fields of technical specializations, leaving the rhizomatic humanities insufficiently realized. On the other hand, the obsession with calculating security is already infringing on online privacy and militarizing some parts of the Internet.

Conclusion

This chapter tried to illustrate how belligerent one-sidedness of the war machine's media could be challenged by new media activism. The current findings add to a growing body of literature on Cultural Affirmative Philosophy and the role of media in conflict resolution through its transformative mediation. The findings in this study provide new insights into the reconciliatory potential of irrational and illogical South Caucasian conflicts without trying to centralize its problems around right- or wrong-doers.

The study ties existing literature to the Cultural Affirmative Philosophy and uses the scholarly and media works on Caucasus to illustrate war machines and potential development of their antidote that is the rhizome of media activism. The present study provides additional evidence with respect to the growing role of media production as the instrumental process of reaching "fusion of horizons" (Gadamerian concept as cited in Ramsbotham et al., 2005, p. 293).

This study confirms previous findings and contributes additional evidence that suggests that change is attainable through the empowerment of local actors. In other words, it confirms the importance of the immanent approach and argues that media activism could be the best way for the approach's realization. Whilst this study did not confirm that here have been significant changes already reached through media activism, it did partially substantiate the needs and transformative potential of the provocative, constructive, and creative media production. I argue that innovative, nomadic artful media activism can expose pseudo multiplicity of the reactive forces, interrupt transcendent circulations, help develop civil societies and reconcile divided communities.

References

A. Badiou (2003) *Infinite Thought* (New York: Continuum).

I. Buchanan and A. Parr (eds) (2006) *Deleuze and the Contemporary World* (Edinburgh: Edinburgh University Press).

E. Cooper and M. Jahoda (1947) 'The Evasion of Propaganda: How Prejudiced People Respond to Anti-Prejudice Propaganda', *Journal of Psychology*, 23, 15–25.

R. Clarke (2009) War From Cyberspace: The National Interest, http://www.nationalinterest.org/Article.aspx?id=22340, date accessed 27 May 2015.

D. Danchev (2008) Georgia President's Web Site under DDoS Attack from Russian Hackers, http://www.zdnet.com/blog/security/georgia-presidents-web-site-under-ddos-attack-from-russian-hackers/1533, date accessed 22 July 2008.

G. Deleuze (1983) *Nietzsche & Philosophy* (New York: Columbia University Press).

G. Deleuze (1995) *Negotiations: 1972–1990* (M. Joughin, trans.) (New York: Columbia University Press).

G. Deleuze and F. Guattari (1987) *A Thousand Plateaus: Capitalism and Schizophrenia* (B. Massumi, trans.) (Minneapolis: University of Minnesota Press).

L. W. Doob (1935) *Propaganda: Its Psychology and Technique* (New York: Henry Holt).

S. H. Flowerman (1949) 'The Use of Propaganda to Reduce Prejudice: A Refutation', *International Journal of Opinion and Attitude Research*, 3, 99–108.

L. C. Hawes (2010) 'Human Rights and an Ethic of Truths: Pragmatic Dilemmas and Discursive Interventions', *Communication and Critical/Cultural Studies*, 7, 261–279.

D. Hollis (2011) Cyberwar Case Study: Georgia 2008, http://smallwarsjournal.com/blog/2011/01/cyberwar-case-study-georgia-20/, date accessed 26 May 2015.

P. B. Kurtz (2009) Virtually Here: The Age of Cyber Warfare, http://img.en25.com/Web/McAfee/VCR_2009_EN_VIRTUAL_CRIMINOLOGY_RPT_NOREG.pdf, date accessed 26 May 2015.

H. D. Lasswell (1928) 'The Function of the Propagandist', *International Journal of Ethics*, 38, 258–268.

R. C. Peterson and L. L. Thurstone (1933) *Motion Pictures and the Social Attitudes of Children* (New York: Macmillan).

O. Ramsbotham, T. Woodhouse, and H. Miall (2005) *Contemporary Conflict Resolution* (Cambridge: Polity).

D. Schuler (2003) 'Reports of Close Relationship Between Democracy and Internet May Have Been Exaggerated' in H. Jenkins and D. Thorburn (eds) *Democracy and New Media* (Cambridge, MA and London, England: MIT Press), pp. 69–84.

N. Spiller (ed.) (2002) *Cyber-Reader: Critical Writing of the Digital Era* (New York: Phaidon).

C. Webel and J. Galtung (eds) (2007) *Handbook of Peace and Conflict Studies* (New York: Routedge).

Part II
From Local to Global: Mediated Identities in Conflicted Cultures

Continuing to demonstrate the scope of applicability of conflict contexts from the previous part, the current part highlights the ubiquity of media representations of a variety of identity conflicts around the world, starting from intimate ethnic identity conflicts and immigrant-host identity crises in a known context, to immigrant identity construction in a new context and the identity construction of two cultures at the opposite ends of Hofstede's cultural values spectrum. Roy's Chapter 6 delves into the types and quality of ethnic identity construction in Bollywood movies to show the power of discourse in mass, popular media in shaping stereotypes and the desirability of particular groups in India. She highlights the reasons why the localized Bollywood representations have global implications. Khrebtan-Hörhager, similarly, brings a global conflict to a local doorstep in Italy in Chapter 7. She discusses at length a film representation of the immigration crisis in the Mediterranean Sea. Lee and Choi demonstrate in Chapter 8 their global awareness of immigrant situations in countries such as the US, as they provide a consolidated analysis of the pros and cons of media representation of immigrant workers in South Korea. Wrapping up this part is Liu with Chapter 9, where she provides a theoretical and philosophical analysis of the US and Chinese Constitutions to offer alternative ways of conceptualizing American and Chinese identities through their views of human rights in modern society.

6
What's in a Name?: Examining Representation of Indian Ethnicities in Bollywood Movies in the New Millennium

Sudeshna Roy

Introduction

Popular Bollywood movies have long influenced the construction of identity of an Indian to a global audience. However, to the internal audience, an Indian, in all her/his diverse splendor, is not the sum of all ethnic parts of the country. The ubiquity of the ethnic identity in India cannot be overstated. Neither can the importance of Bollywood cinema in the cultural spectrum of the country be discounted.

The central question that then needs examination is the quality and extent to which these myriad ethnic identities find a space in modern Hindi cinema. If there is such a space, how then are they being portrayed and what underlying, discursive forces are at the core of such representations. The current study strives to deconstruct the politics of representation of the many Indian ethnicities in Bollywood movies in the new millennium.

With India's rise in importance in regional and global politics, the spectacular popularity of Bollywood movies all across South and South-East Asian countries, and the growing stature of India's economic clout, India's voice seems to be gaining momentum all across the world. What needs to be scrutinized, though, is its message to its internal stakeholders through the powerful depictions and storytelling in Bollywood movies.

At the helm of these depictions are the wealthy producers, directors, and actors who have considerable power to decide how the story will take shape. Considering Bhoopaty's (2003) assertion that 'cinema is widely considered a microcosm of the social, political, economic, and cultural life of a nation. It is the contested site where meanings are negotiated, traditions made and remade, identities affirmed or rejected'

(p. 505), it is imperative to assess the type of messages being constructed about ethnic identities in this pervasive form of mediated communication in the country today.

Literature review

The allure of Bollywood movies in India and for Indians living abroad has evolved in the last two decades in keeping with the changes the film industry and films have been naturally undergoing. Storylines, plots, contexts, formats, actors, and images of Bollywood films are in a state of constant adjustment and adaption to the changing times. These changes are part of the cycle any cultural artifact undergoes with the changes in the society within which it is embedded. Bollywood films are no different.

Films have long been constituted within the discourses generated in a particular society, reflecting and refracting contemporary issues, politics, and culture, as well as the historio-political realities of that culture. They are also constitutive of cultural trends and influence popular opinions amongst the masses. This chapter attempts to map the types and quality of Indian ethnic identities portrayed in contemporary Bollywood movies in order to identify the underlying power of discursive construction of identities considering the status of Bollywood movies as a crucial force of socialization in the lives of the diverse people of India. It explores whether Bollywood films perpetuate patterns of negative stereotyping of particular ethnicities with regard to their physical features, use of language, and professional classifications. The author conducts critical discourse analysis (CDA) of key scenes from ten of the highest grossing Bollywood movies released so far in the new millennium. The chapter also aims to contribute to the growth in discourse analysis of visual texts.

Ethnicities in India and Bollywood

Indian culture results from a combination of a complex mixing of micro and macro cultures for thousands of years. The identities of the people within this culture are equally complex and defy simplistic decoding and analysis. Moreover, those years of cultural evolution encompass deep political ambitions and moves by groups and individuals that have left indelible stamps on the construction and reification of certain cultures and ethnicities. The country boasts the kind of diversity that few other places in the world can begin to comprehend. People in India follow all the major religions of the world. Most prevalent amongst them are Hinduism, Christianity, Islam, Sikhism, Buddhism, and Jainism. The country is divided into 35 different states and union territories, giving rise to different ethnicities and regionalism (Ethnicity in India, 2010). The government of India recognizes 22 different languages, while designating Hindi as the official language of the country.

Georgiou (2001) provides a conceptual map of how ethnicities are formed and sustained in the media in multi-cultural societies such as India. She situates ethnicity development in places of habitat, but the eventual social crossings that ethnicities experience happen in the junction of domestic space, the media, and communication technologies. In India, this junction has been portrayed a multitude of times in Bollywood movies. 'Indeed popular Indian cinema in Hindi constitutes a particularly interesting area of study as much because of its history as because of its key role in the creation of the national identity and its place in the collective imagination' (Therwath, 2010, p. 2).

However, Bollywood film's representation of the diverse people of India also encompasses the national-level play of cultural homogenization and cultural heterogenization (Appadurai, 1996). Exactly which format particular representations take depends on the filmmakers, the writer, the interpretation of the story by the cast, and the director's vision. The national politics of ethnic identity construction through various mediated means is a powerful force that colors the making of such movies.

While many of the movies clearly try to provoke thoughts about social injustice and discrimination against various groups in India, there is an underlying 'idea of the nation as a continuous narrative of national progress, the narcissism of self-generation' (Bhaba, 1990, p. 1) that permeates the overall messages of the movies. Within that narrative, the beauty and diversity of the ethnicities are subsumed and the work of internal homogenization continues discursively. At the same time, cultural heterogeneity is maintained in order to create distinctions between groups, where some groups are privileged over others. As such, some ethnicities are considered model, and some not so desirable. Such media representations satisfy the convoluted politics of the country and keep alive the idea of India for an international audience.

Indian national identity and Bollywood

Prasad's (2001) influential work on the ideology of Hindi film traces the portrayal of Indian national identity as an antithesis to the Western ideals of national identity. Moreover, Prasad provides examples to prove that such portrayal falls within the coordinates of power of the dominant narrative form and do not just set up a binary opposition to Western conceptualization of national identities. Following the demands of modernity, an Indian national identity is at once a paradox to be portrayed on the screens of Bollywood. The juxtaposition of cultural lineages and traditional belief systems and the call for a more globalized, easily recognizable Indian, lead to a confusing palette from which filmmakers must create their movies. Add to that the language of economy and the game of national and global politics that the films must satisfy. As all these forces collide at the local and global level, what is revealed is the unique position of Bollywood movies that has created a commodified Indian national identity that specifically caters to North Indian, Hindu cultural leanings (Prasad, 2001).

The questions that then beg answers are: What then becomes of representation of the many different ethnicities that make up modern day India in Bollywood movies? What dynamics do they play out against each other and together as elements of Indian national identities in these movies? What are their unique functions in the making of national identity in the movies? What stereotypes are revealed as these functions are defined in the discourses of the movies? This chapter is an attempt to satisfy these questions about the treatment of ethnic identities in Bollywood movies of the new millennium.

Method

Fairclough's (1992, 1993) critical discourse analysis is used to understand how the discourses in the selected movies reproduce or challenge the ideologies embedded in the construction of disparate ethnic stereotypes. This method is particularly useful in finding out how the specific scenes in the movies reproduce subtle power relations and inequality, evident in broader social discourses, within and between ethnicities. This study is not only concerned with what is present in the key scenes, 'but also with the interactive process of meaning-making' (Fairclough, 2003). Fairclough (2003) outlines three elements in processes of meaning making: the production of the text, the text itself, and how the text is consumed. 'What is "said" in a text always rests upon "unsaid" assumptions, so part of the analysis of texts is trying to identify what is assumed' (p. 11).

In this analysis, the author focuses specifically on those scenes where multiple ethnicities share the same screen, analysing the plots, the character traits portrayed, the phenotypes of the characters' physical presence, the names and surnames of the characters, the people in the background and the professions of all involved. The author also ensures that the chosen scenes are pertinent to the larger storyline and, thus, are not lost in the clamor of projecting the overall goal and narrative flow of the movies. The choice of scenes for analysis is qualitative in nature and is a culmination of the author's experience in consuming Hindi, Bollywood movies for over three decades and deep study of critical discourse analysis and the implications of power.

In the spirit of providing the reader with at least a cursory context of the ten films analysed for this chapter, the following are, in alphabetical order, names of the films, their release year, gross earnings in Indian and US currency and short summaries of their plots.

Three Idiots (2009) – 300 crore INR – USD 50 million

Farhan Qureshi, Raju Rastogi, and 'Rancho' become unlikely but good friends at Delhi's Imperial College of Engineering but they go their own ways after they graduate. The movie plays out mostly in flashback when ten years after their graduation two of the friends, Farhan and Raju, embark on a journey to find 'Rancho'. The movie depicts the unpliable state of Indian higher education and those who abide by the necessity of antiquated means of imparting knowledge. The Dean of the engineering college, Viru Sahastrabudhe, and his daughter, Pia, play key roles in the movie, depicting the evolution of their own ideas about education and life with the help of unlikely life-lessons from 'Rancho' who, at the end of the movie, is revealed to have the name Phunsukh Wangdu.

Barfi (2012) – INR 175 crore – USD 27 million

Set in the 1970s, in the hilly city of Darjeeling, east India, *Barfi*'s story plays out as a love triangle between three unlikely people. Barfi, a hearing and speech impaired boy, falls in love with Shruti. In spite of her deep affection for Barfi, Shruti gives in to her parents' wishes and marries a 'normal' man, to lead a 'normal' life. Many years later their paths cross once again when Barfi, now in love with Jhilmil, an autistic but wealthy woman, is on the run from the police. He is being sought by the police because he tried to kidnap Jhilmil from other kidnappers employed by Jhilmil's own father so that he could get ransom money from her trust fund. Eventually, Barfi and Jhilmil are married and Shruti realizes that she is still in love with Barfi but has lost the chance to be with him.

Bhaag Milkha Bhaag (2013) – INR 164 crore – USD 26 million

Based on the true story of the life of the 'Flying Sikh' – world-champion runner and Olympian Milkha Singh – the movie depicts the trials and tribulations he endures to achieve success as an athlete during a time of social and political turmoil in post-independence India. Specifically, the movie shows how Milkha Singh overcame the massacre of his family during partition of India and Pakistan, civil war during the partition, homelessness, prejudice amongst peers, etc., to become one of India's most iconic athletes.

Dil Chahta Hai (2001) – INR 26 crore – USD 4.1 million

The movie depicts the journey of three young men, Akash, Sameer, and Siddharth, as they go from being close college friends, full of excesses and pranks, to mature and wise men within a span of five to six years. The story hinges on a rift that develops between Akash and Siddharth as the later falls in love with a much older woman who is a divorcee and alcoholic. Akash feels that life should be lived to the fullest without getting bogged down by feelings of love and pain. He tries to counsel Siddharth on the benefits of living life skimming only the top of what life has to offer. But, Siddharth wants to live life deeply, and feel love and pain as they come his way. The friends do manage to work through their differences, as Akash himself falls in love and feels the gamut of emotion he has been trying to protect himself from all his life.

Gangs of Wasseypur – Part 1 (2012) – INR 27.8 crore – USD 4.4 million

The movie revolves around the life of Sardar Khan, whose feelings of revenge color not only his own actions but the actions of his children throughout the movie. His father, Shahid Khan, was exiled and slighted by the powerful Qureshis for impersonating the legendary Sultana Daku (who was one of the Qureshis) in order to rob British trains. Once outcast, Shahid becomes a worker at Ramadhir Singh's colliery, only to be assassinated by Ramadhir's men as his ambition for taking over the colliery comes to light. His son, Sardar, crafts his entire life to get his father's honor back, becoming the most feared man in Wasseypur in the process.

Lagaan (2001) – INR 58 crore – USD 9 million

This is the story about the resilience shown by the Indians in the form of winning an epic cricket match played against the British Raj's Jack Russell and team, with the wager being that the British will not tax the small village for three years. Cruel tax laws brutally implemented by Russell and his cronies bring about this unequal duel of a cricket match, help the villagers unite together despite differences, and, ultimately, provides the viewers with a David versus Goliath story about how the Indians win this very English sport of a cricket match from right under the noses of the British.

Munna Bhai MBBS (2003) – 30 crore INR – USD 4.7 million

In India, gangsters are called Bhai (brothers). One such Bhai is Munna, who is feared by everyone in Mumbai, a big city in India. However, he cons his village-based parents into believing that he is a doctor. When he finds out that his parents have decided to come and visit him, he transforms his shanty house into a makeshift hospital, populated by patients, people he beats up. His parents are happy for his success but also want him to get married to a doctor's daughter. The movie takes a turn for humorous when the doctor's daughter he is set to marry finds out about Munna's true identity, setting up Munna to try to get a real degree in medicine in order to rectify the hurt he has caused his parents and to marry the woman he loves.

Rang De Basanti (2012) – INR 93 crore – USD 14.5 million

A young, idealistic English filmmaker, Sue, arrives in India to make a film on Indian revolutionaries Bhagat Singh, Chandrashekhar Azad, and their contemporaries and their fight for freedom from the British Raj. Owing to a lack of funds, she recruits students from Delhi University to act in her docu-drama. She finds DJ (Daljeet), who graduated five years ago but still wants to be a part of the University; Karan, the son of industrialist Rajnath Singhania, who shares an uncomfortable relationship with his father, but continues to live off him; Aslam, a middle class Muslim boy, who lives in the by-lanes near Jama Masjid – poet, philosopher, and guide to his friends; Sukhi, the group's baby, innocent, vulnerable, and with a weakness for only one thing – girls; Laxman Pandey, the fundamentalist in the group, the only one who still believes that politics can make the world a better place; and Sonia – the sole girl in the group, tomboy and vivacious spirit, engaged to Ajay – the dashing air pilot. As Sue's docu-drama progresses, the students begin the see the problems facing modern India. The death of Ajay serves as a catalyst for the friends to take matters into their own hands to rectify at least one such problem, in the style of the very leaders and fighters they have been enacting in Sue's docu-drama.

Swades (2004) – INR 34.2 crore – USD 5.4 million

Set in modern day India, Swades is a film that tackles the issues that development throws up on a grass-roots level. It is to this India, which is colorful, heterogeneous, and complex, that Mohan Bhargava (Shah Rukh Khan), a bright young scientist working as a project manager in NASA, returns on a quest to find his childhood nanny. The film uses the contrast between the highly developed world of NASA, which has been at the forefront of advances in space research, and this world back home in India, which is at the crossroads of development. Mohan's simple quest becomes the journey that every one of us goes through in search of that metaphysical and elusive place called 'home'.

Taare Zameen Par (2012) – INR 89 crore – USD 14 million

Ishaan Awasthi is an eight-year-old whose world is filled with wonders that no-one else seems to appreciate. He frequently gets in trouble in his school and his parents become more and more strict with him as he does not bring the desirable grades from school. When he gets into far more trouble than his parents can handle, he is packed off to a boarding school to 'be disciplined'. Things are no different at his new school, and Ishaan has to contend with the added trauma of separation from his family. One day a new art teacher bursts onto the scene, Ram Shankar Nikumbh, who infects the students with joy and optimism. He realizes that Ishaan is dyslexic and holds Ishaan's hand throughout, bringing out the best in him through methods that are non-traditional and frowned-upon.

Findings

This part is divided into three distinct themes that emerged as a result of the analysis of the key scenes from the ten movies identified in the Method section. The themes are titled Gradation, Reification, and Segregation, and together speak to the discursive means of communicating the differences between the Indian ethnic identities portrayed in the top grossing movies till date of the new millennium. The themes are also a testament to the power of the hegemonic discourses which can be found embedded in the choice of stories, lead characters, their names, their facial features, the choice of bit parts, their portrayal, the back stories, and the plots themselves.

Gradation

One of the most consistent themes that emerged from the analysis of the key moments of the movies was the emergence of a system of social gradation tied with assigning certain social classes to particular ethnicities. The ongoing gradation process occurs whenever particular trades and socio-economic backgrounds are assigned to predetermined ethnicities identifiable through facial features, last names, and other physical characteristics. Blue collar jobs and white collar jobs were systematically reserved for particular ethnicities. If a socially-determined, aspirational job, such as that of a CEO or a highly successful entrepreneur, was assigned to a member of an ethnicity not socially recognized for such a job, it was portrayed as an exception and not a norm. Thus, discursively, the films were able to portray a kind of social hierarchy through job-assignment that privileged a few ethnicities over and over again.

For example, in all the movies analysed, almost all the bit parts and the background personnel specifically show people from particular ethnicities in professions of servitude. The household maids, the people providing services such as taxi drivers, barbers, cooks, and roadside restaurant owners reflect certain ethnicities. Small grocery-store owners or people selling in the marketplace are portrayed as Biharis or Rajasthanis. Maids and cooks are portrayed as Marathis or Gujratis. Taxi drivers have been portrayed as Punjabis or UP-ites (from Uttar Pradesh), and roadside restaurant owners as Punjabis.

Most of the lead characters in the movies are from these very states but shown as protagonists who are fighting against antagonists, literally and figuratively. Literally in the form of characters having opposing qualities or viewpoints. Figuratively in the form of exemplifying binary oppositional signifiers in facial features, clothing, accent, dialect, facial expressions, and the trades and professions they are involved in. The lead characters embody socially acceptable and desirable qualities from select ethnicities while the antagonists and bit-part characters are representative of the undesirable qualities so frequently found in people existing in the sordid underbelly of society. For example, in *Swades*, the lead character's name is Mohan Bhargava and he is portrayed as a Brahmin, the most desirable caste, who is intelligent, suave, and has made a name for himself as a successful aeronautical engineer in NASA, Houston.

However, in *Rang De Basanti*, the lead character's name is Daljeet, and it is indicated that he is a Punjabi from New Delhi. But, his college-educated, English accent is shown as cosmopolitan and not the thick Punjabi-accented English one might hear from a lot of other Punjabis in Delhi. Similarly, his actions are shown as intelligent, and as such, different from how Punjabis are viewed generally – as hardworking but lacking intellect, and thus the butt of a million jokes. Daljeet may share his ethnicity with those of roadside restaurant owners, but he is given qualities of the upper class in order to make him a more agreeable lead character who can take the responsibility of carrying the film on his shoulders in a manner that will garner more acceptance by the film's viewers. These types of characterizations are shown to be exceptions and not rules, thus sustaining the discursive process of grading ethnicity without raising alarms.

The burden of ordinariness in *Rang De Basanti* is carried by the small *dhaba* (roadside restaurant) owner shown in the movie, who speaks exaggerated Punjabi around Daljeet and his equally cosmopolitan friends when they venture outside the mega-city New Delhi and eat at such places on a whim. The juxtaposition of the lead characters showing up at the *dhaba* and eating, seen more as a largesse on their part, and the happiness of the Punjabi *dhaba* owner as the recipient of such customers, only work to drive a deeper wedge between 'normality' and the ethnic stereotype being portrayed.

Similarly, in *Taare Zameen Par*, the lead character is named Ram Shankar Nikumbh, originally a Rajput, member of one of the patrilineal clans of western, central, and northern India who were once very powerful in leading India's princely state of Rajasthan. He is depicted as an intelligent and compassionate teacher with alternative teaching style in modern India's stifling, competitive education environment. However, the teacher who delivers the traditional and the undesirable aspects of Indian school education, such as expectation of rote memorizations of course work, severe disciplinary approach, etc., is portrayed by a Bihari, a state and ethnicity frequently stereotyped as backwards and uneducated in the Indian psyche.

While the depiction of equivalence between social classes and particular ethnicities may seem innocuous enough, it certainly begs the question of how deep the entrenched belief systems are that enable these depictions to be received by millions of people without questioning the premises of the relationships between class and ethnicity. Filmmakers bear the responsibility of bringing to the fore social injustices and discrimination, as well as providing entertainment to the masses. However, the irony that this analysis reveals is that the very same film that purports to unearth social injustice and forward alternative ways of thinking and social change, uses a form of social injustice – and equating certain classes with particular ethnicities to do it.

Reification

A key form of discursive identity construction in the movies happen through the process of reification, as characters over-exaggerate certain stereotypical characteristics associated with particular ethnicities.

As a result, these stereotypes are given lives of their own that are permanently connected to the idea of being a particular ethnicity in India. The process entails already-existing stereotypes assigned to particular ethnicities being enacted with added drama, fervor, and exaggeration so as to indelibly etch the association of these stereotypes with these ethnicities. Most of these stereotypes are negative to neutral in terms of the portrayal. Sometimes, the portrayal is intended to highlight the problems of stereotyping these ethnicities, which create conditions of unequal treatment in modern Indian society.

These characterizations are a reflection of the historical naturalization of certain stereotypes with certain ethnicities. On the part of the filmmakers, it seems that the choice of stereotypical characterizations does not require nuanced thinking or consciousness because the stereotypes are very deeply entrenched in the fabric of society. Since stereotypes in many instances lead to discriminatory practices, the next section highlights forms of discrimination depicted in the movies analysed that exacerbate the ethnic differences.

In the movie *Gangs of Wasseypur – Part 1*, the violence shown as a character plot for the revenge-seeking Sardar Khan, the protagonist, is already deeply associated with the state where the plot unfolds – Jharkhand (formerly part of the Indian state of Bihar). The key moments of the movie that were part of the analysis for this chapter all portray some form of extreme violence, incredibly offensive language, and lustful sexual encounters. For years, the state of Bihar was stereotypically associated with being a festering gangland with local goons with political ties terrorizing normal people who dared to stand up to their excesses. Moreover, a Naxalite-Maoist insurgency is also rife in the states of Bihar and Jharkhand. This insurgency is a result of what the Naxalites claim is a strategy of rural rebellion similar to a protracted people's war against the government, and involves frequent assassinations and other violent methods. Biharis, especially male members, are thus stereotyped as violent, lacking culture and sensitivity, corrupt, impulsive, and misogynist.

Gangs of Wasseypur – Part 1 solidifies the connection between the stereotypes of the Bihari male with the characters of the film. The violent turns in the movie are reminiscent of the Hollywood-esque attempts to immortalize hyper-real takes on gore and violence depicted in movies such as *Pulp Fiction* (1994) and *Inglorious Basterds* (2009). However, the cultural contexts are very different in this movie compared to those in Hollywood productions. Most importantly, the audience is very different for the analysed movie. In the Indian context, the movie over-emphasizes the very qualities that are used to stereotype and discriminate against Biharis in society. As a result, the stereotypes take on larger-than-life roles in shaping public opinion about who Biharis are and how to interact with them.

Similarly, in *Bhaag Milkha Bhaag*, the characteristics and conduct of the Sikh athlete Milkha are shown as highly simplistic, bordering on foolishness. In key scenes, the athlete is shown to be easily fooled but mostly to be lauded for hard work and determination. Milkha is shown to give in to temptations and be gullible, as he is unable to make the right call at the crucial time before his race. As a result, he is unable to get the result he was looking for in the Olympic 400-metre event. While such a treatment of the main character comes partly from the setting of the story in post-independence-era India, and the village background of the athlete in general, the dramatization of the stereotypes renders them quite potent in characterizing all Sikhs as empty-headed and only capable of manual labor. Sikhs, who are mostly understood as sword-bearing, simple-minded people with agriculture as their main trade, can then be reduced to just that and nothing more when blockbuster films like *Bhaag Milkha Bhaag* portray them as the cumulation of these stereotypes.

In *Munna Bhai MBBS*, the everyday Marathi (from the state of Maharashtra) women are shown as highly sexualized, wearing cleavage-baring blouses in provocative poses. These are women doing everyday jobs such as household cleaning, laundry, etc. Moreover, the men are even more comical in the role of the *Bhais* (or gangster brothers), with exaggerated comments, crass, expletive-filled language, and general disregard for the well-being of people around them. Specifically, the striking acceptance of the existence of *Bhais* amongst the common people depicted in this movie along, with their willingness to help Munna con the medical school to acknowledge him as a student of medicine, provides the viewers with a portrayal of a lifestyle that is devoid of integrity and honesty. While the film ultimately shows a reformed Munna who wants to follow the path of education and help people, the majority of the movie is dedicated in prolonging the stereotypes of Marathis as people willing to take short-cuts to get to the top, working hard on conning people rather than actually getting the job done.

In *Lagaan* and *Barfi* as well, stereotypes of particular ethnicities are highly dramatized and exaggerated. In *Laagan*, the lower castes and tribe members are shown to exhibit particular characteristics that provide justification for the village-folks keeping them at an arm's length at the beginning of the movie. The main character, Bhuvan, who leads the charge towards getting them all ready for the cricket match to be played against the British, does provide ample opportunity for the viewer to see the harm in associating certain stereotypes with certain ethnicities. However, the fact that the characters are made to hyper-project the stereotypes in order to bring attention to them, can work in ways that are detrimental to the overall goal of reducing discrimination against particular ethnicities. In *Barfi*, the exaggeration and association of particular stereotypes does not involve ethnicities but the representations of physically and mentally disabled instead.

These stereotypes are entrenched in the minds of people who watch these movies about the members of the ethnicities portrayed. In fact, as these stereotypes are repeated over and over again in popular movies, they are difficult to dislodge, setting up pre-determined expectations about fellow countrymen. The identity conflicts are exacerbated with these constant reminders of stereotypes. The more exaggerated the stereotypes are, the more humorous and popular the movies get. Little attention is given to the positive and enduring qualities of members of ethnicities. The hope for the chasm between negative stereotypes and respect for all ethnicities to become narrower rather than wider does not seem to be reflected in the portrayals of people of India in the movies analysed for this chapter.

Segregation

The final theme to be described in this chapter is titled segregation mainly because it shows a pattern of providing nuanced and embedded binaries in the key moments of the movies that highlights pros and cons of what it means to belong to a particular ethnicity in modern India. The binaries help a sort of automatic segregation between characteristically different ethnicities, pitting them against each other in an already chaotic and diverse country full of economic and cultural disparities between people.

In *Dil Chahta Hai*, the most significant characters of the movie, the three friends Sameer, Akash, and Siddharth, are shown to belong to a more-or-less similar socio-economic class. This class is further emphasized by the many scenes where the lifestyle of the three friends is shown to be full of choices and apparent wealth. The ethnicity of Akash Malhotra is that of Khatri caste base, originating from the North-Western part of India including Delhi, Punjab, Haryana, etc. The Khatris, today, play a significant role in the Indian economy, serving as businessmen, civic and government administrators, landlords, and military officials. The ethnicity of Siddharth Sinha is difficult to identify, as people from different parts of the country have the same surname. However, the surname is important in this case for *what it is not* rather what it is. It is not a surname commonly and clearly associated with lower castes and tribes or undesirable ethnicities. In this case, the commonness of the surname serves as a way to shield this character from exposure to any negative stereotypes associated with other surnames with distinct relationships to certain castes, ethnicities, and tribes. The third friend, Sameer, does not even have a surname revealed in the movie. He is always referred to as Sameer. The absence of the need to announce his ethnicity along with the presence of the defining characteristics of the high socio-economic class and company he obviously belongs to, provides the viewer with a vague, but clearly underlying, sense of approval of this character. This character is already able to segregate himself from the rest of the ethnicities that are undesirable by associating with the other two friends. Since the other two friends belong to desirable ethnicities, Sameer, by dint of his friendship with them, is able to remain of nameless but be viewed positively, in terms of his ethnicity, by the audience.

In *Three Idiots*, the segregation factor is brought about by the fact that the main characters, hailing from different ethnicities of India, are intellectually capable of erasing the stigmas and stereotypes attached to their respective ethnicities. The film is meant to be a critique of the ways in which certain forms of education in India are privileged at the cost of physical, mental, and emotional stress to the students and their families. However, the same students who critique the system, are shown to benefit from it. They all become successful professionals and entrepreneurs by applying their considerable intellect post-graduation. The intellectual bar is shown to be the demarcating factor between social mobility and ignominy. Thus, identification with ethnic identity is foregone in this case to establish the features necessary to rise above ethnicity and caste – intellectual superiority, economic strength, familial name and fame, and street smarts. Only with the combination of one or more of these features can the ethnic identity be relieved of the shackles of stereotypes.

In sum, there are processes of segregation shown in all the movies analysed. In each case, the processes are embedded in discursive ways and need discerning and trained eyes to distinguish them and understand the implications of such segregation that seems naturalized in all these movies. The segregation works either to promote the virtues of certain ethnicities, to provide insights which crucify others, or to justify neutrality towards characters who are shown to embody the characteristics of desirable ethnicities.

The movies are rife with innuendoes and significations that work to privilege certain ethnicities while downplaying others. Through the systematic, thematic processes identified in this section, namely, gradation, reification, and segregation, the movies provide many examples of how discourses are sustained to reflect and maintain social attitudes about ethnic identities. They, in turn, inform viewers about how to perceive ethnic identities and how the viewers are either similar or different to those exemplified in the movies. Public opinion about ethnic identities is formulated, challenged, solidified, and re-imagined within the confines of these highly popular movies, seen by millions of people in the country. The conflicts between Indian ethnic identities are played out within and beyond the stories told in these movies.

Discussion and conclusion

The author conducts a critical discourse analysis of the ten highest grossing Bollywood Hindi movies of the current century to unearth discourses of marginalization, extreme stereotypes, and disenfranchisement embedded in the ideological 'othering' of particular ethnicities in these movies. Some ethnicities are portrayed as more powerful and more desirable than others, leading to the construction of a model ethnic stereotype. These types of representations parallel social and political conditions in the country's complex class, ethnic, racial, and religious hierarchies. The potential for such representations to influence the social attitudes and perceptions of groups of people is enormous and has far-reaching implications in a heavily fractured and chaotic political scenario. Such representations have the power to drive people into deeper crises about who they are and what their place/space is in the national and international imagination.

This study sheds light on the types of discourses, the strategies used and the power moves employed to provide a substantive but unequal position for and narrative about the different ethnicities within the larger social milieu of entertainment and cultural economics in India. The discourse analysis allows the author to provide a historical and political context for the treatment and subject positions of the different ethnicities in the movies analysed. These movies are powerful tools in their ability to identify and portray negative influences and stereotypes with regard to particular ethnicities. Moreover, the movies are also undeniable forms of socialization for a local and global audience, about what it means to be a particular ethnicity in India.

The movies portray the normative limitations of the Indian culture as well as oversimplifications and stereotypes of ethnicities based on several assumptions that come through. First, they portray an ideology of social mobility based mainly on educational/economic success as primary. Second, the economic successes are tied to particular, desirable professions at the expense of scores of legitimate trades and professions that are vital to the livelihood of multiple geographies and ethnicities of India. Third, the striking naturalization of particular roles and functions of particular ethnicities speaks to the hegemonic, discursive devices entrenched in the art of making Bollywood movies. Fourth, the idea of Indian national identity is being constructed not as opposed to a Western notion of national identity but, rather, as opposed to certain internal, local, undesirable qualities portrayed through the acts of particular ethnicities.

Many of the Bollywood films analysed in this study have positive messages in their conclusions but the rampant use of stereotypes, the closing ranks through discursive segregation, and the assignment of certain professions to certain ethnicities to create a system of gradation, together reflect historical and material structures that benefit the status quo and support the dominant ideology of the social movers and shakers. Classism is alive and well in these movies, and now it is also connected to particular ethnicities.

Bollywood filmmakers need to consider carefully their choices of character portrayals, the choosing of names for their protagonists, the physical attributes of the actors portraying the characters and the use of stereotypes to elicit interest or humor. As long as they continue to make movies without regard to the social and cultural costs at which they come, they will continue to create class, race, and ethnic hierarchies that reinforce the status quo and negate the efforts of members of particular ethnicities who are working hard to dispel stereotypical conceptualizations of their groups.

References

A. Appadurai (1996) 'Disjuncture and Difference in the Global Cultural Economy' in M. Featherstone (ed.) *Global Culture: Nationalism, Globalization and Modernity* (London: Sage) p. 295–310.
Barfi, 2012, Motion Picture, Ishana Movies, India.
Bhaag Milkha Bhaag, 2013, Motion Picture, ROMP Pictures, India.
H. Bhabha (ed.) (1990) *Nation and Narration* (London, New York: Routledge).

D. Bhoopaty (2003) 'Cinema and Politics in India' in K. Prasad (ed.) *Political Communication: The Indian Experience* (Delhi: B. R. Publishing Corporation) p. 507–517.

Dil Chahta Hai, 2001, Motion Picture, Excel Entertainment, India.

Ethnicity of India (2010) http://www.archive.india.gov.in/knowindia/culture_heritage.php?id=70, accessed 27 May 2015.

N. Fairclough (1992) 'Discourse and Text: Linguistic Intertextual Analysis within Discourse Analysis', *Discourse & Society*, 3, 193–217.

N. Fairclough (1993) 'Critical Discourse Analysis and the Marketisation of Public Discourse: The Universities', *Discourse & Society*, 4, 133–168.

N. Fairclough (2003) *Analysing Discourse: Textual Analysis for Social Research* (New York: Routledge).

Gangs of Wasseypur – Part 1, 2012, Motion Picture, Anurag Kashyap Films and Jai Pictures, India.

M. Georgiou (2001) 'Crossing the Boundaries of the Ethnic Home: Media Consumption and Ethnic Identity Construction in the Public Space: The Case of the Cypriot Community Centre in North London', *International Communication Gazette*, 63: 311–329.

Lagaan, 2001, Motion Picture, Aamir Khan Productions, India.

Munna Bhai M.B.B.S., 2003, Motion Picture, Vinod Chopra Productions and Entertainment One, India.

M. M. Prasad (2001) *Ideology of the Hindi Film: A Historical Construction* (Oxford: Oxford University Press).

Rang De Basanti, 2006, Motion Picture, Rakeysh Omprakash Mehra Pictures, India.

Swades, 2004, Motion Picture, Ashutosh Gowariker Productions, India.

Taare Zameen Par, 2007, Motion Picture, Aamir Khan Productions, India.

Three Idiots, 2009, Motion Picture, Vinod Chopra Productions, India.

I. Therwath (2010) '"Shining Indians": Diaspora and Exemplarity in Bollywood', *South Asia Multidisciplinary Academic Journal* [Online], 4, http://samaj.revues.org/3000, date accessed 27 May 2015.

7
A Mediterranean Clandestine: A Friend or a Foe?

Julia Khrebtan-Hörhager

The immigrant crisis in the Mediterranean: facts, fiction, and fallacies

A large and growing number of immigrant tragedies in the Mediterranean have increased the salience of intercultural tensions in the European Union and the urgency of pro-active and effective strategies of conflict resolution at the so-called 'gates of Europe'. In October 2013, multiple deaths of illegal immigrants occurred in a failed attempt at reaching the European continent. Incidents such as these have turned the media's attention towards the crises, and issues surrounding immigration have come to occupy a central position in the cultural and political discussions of both the Italian national and the European transnational consciousness. Similar tragedies recurred in 2014 and 2015. As recently reported in *The Guardian* by Beaumont (2014), 'Migrants trying to reach more prosperous countries have died at a rate of eight every day for the past 14 years, the majority of them trying to get to Europe'. In accordance with the estimates provided by the International Organization for Migration (2014), almost 40,000 people have died on various migrant routes worldwide, and at least 22,000 of the same have perished trying to get to Europe. IOM also emphasize that, most likely, the true number of fatalities is even higher than the figures in its report.

Curiously, in reaction to the tragic events in the region, the Parliamentary Assembly of the Council of Europe (*PACE*, 2013) reported that 'Italy has shown itself, once again, ill-prepared for what appears to be a new surge of mixed migration flows, and appears to have learnt few, if any, lessons from its experiences in 2011'. Placing the majority of the blame on the Italians, the European Union is effectively increasing the pressures being felt by the country dealing with increasing influx of helpless and hopeless immigrants from Africa and the Middle East. The conflicting perspectives of various European Union members on the responsibilities and immigration/refugee policies of the European Union member states in the immigrant crisis further complicate the situation. For example, while the *PACE* report indicates serious flaws in the Italian national policies and concerns about the 'spillover' of migration flows to other European Union member states, it does not offer any plausible solutions to the current crisis, affecting the 'European Fortress' (Khrebtan-Hörhager, 2014). Nor does it address the overall status of European immigration and the *status quo* of European multiculturalism, which, under such circumstances, has historically demonstrated a chronic lack of effective interdisciplinary peacebuilding approaches. Taking into consideration the large (and growing) number of the clandestine immigrants who seek hope and find death in the mighty Mediterranean, urgent and creative theoretical/policy level thought and practical action is required to adapt to this situation.

Peacebuilding and conflict resolution can be approached from a variety of multifaceted and interdisciplinary perspectives with awareness of the intercultural communication concepts of 'self' and 'other' being at the heart of potential and current conflict negotiation around the globe. Generally focused on the role of intercultural communication in conflict resolution, this chapter also analyses intercultural cinematography as a potential methodological tool for peacebuilding by means of creating intercultural awareness and political engagement of the audiences in a dialogical discourse with the on-screen narrative. The intercultural approach to analysing cinematography was specifically chosen because of its significant impact and growing outreach to the vast majority of the population; an impact and an outreach that typically extend far beyond the walls of the academy or legal institutions. Most importantly, cinema frequently assumes a pedagogical role in the lives of various audiences and serves as an actual means of teaching culture, intercultural tensions, and various conflicts to people from all walks of life. Since viewing of cinema is still an affordable way to experience storytelling that involves many of our five senses, it is really an effective means of communicating the tensions and conflicts afflicting different communities in the world. Finally, intercultural cinematography focuses on the dynamics between the 'self' and the 'other', and by doing so, provides a solid on-screen foundation for learning and understanding typical immigration dynamics and complexities; the latter being the scholarly emphasis of this inquiry. As suggested by hooks (1996):

> Movies remain the perfect vehicles for the introduction of certain ritual rites of passage that come to stand for the quintessential experience of cultural border crossing for everyone who wants to take a look at difference and the different without having to experientially engage with 'the other'. (p. 12)

From this perspective, movies serve as cultural journeys with limited risks for those who expose themselves to the challenges of world travel to the unknown side of the 'other': cinematography provides the necessary platform for a critical display and negotiation of identities, their struggles, and their cultural transformation. In her work with visual rhetoric, Sonja Foss (1988) argues that for members of marginalized groups, artwork creates a new forum for participation in non-discriminatory public dialogue. Foss further explains that the display of identity in a public, aesthetic way creates a place for that group's discourse in the web of social relations.

In the current century of economic and political crises and consequent on-going migration, creating safe spaces for immensely diverse and differently empowered groups to engage in dialogues and gain visibility has become pivotal. Intercultural films serve as a suitable arena for such spaces. Using the award-winning film *Quando sei nato non puoi più nasconderti* (2005) as a cultural and political on-screen text, representative of the current immigrant crisis in the Mediterranean, this research project explores and advocates intercultural cinematography as an unconventional methodology and epistemology in the process of pro-active and holistic conflict negotiation. It addresses particularities and possibilities of communication dynamics between the local European population and the incoming immigrant population from different parts of the globe; problematizes the 'push/pull' factors of the migration dynamics; suggests concrete examples of complex strategies of approaching the challenging relationships between the European 'self' and the non-European 'other'; and examines its impact on the multicultural dynamics in the European Union.

Intercultural dialogues from *reel* to *real*

In parallel with the tragic and largely alarming reality of immigration, *Quando sei nato non puoi più nasconderti* (2005) (which translates as 'Once you're born you can no longer hide')[1] offers an honest, moving

---

[1] Translation from Italian by the author.

and endlessly sad fictional journey to the turbulent Mediterranean, the space that encapsulates both human hope and human despair, that ultimately challenges the existing paradigms of 'selves' and 'others', extends beyond the traditional conceptualizations of identity politics, and largely problematizes the concepts of social marginalities, inclusion, belonging, morality, and humanity.

The story is remarkable in its dualistic symbolism, representative of haves and have-nots in a country that has gradually become known as the 'unsafe harbour' of the Mediterranean: Italy. In the affluent Italian north (the city of Brescia), we see a wealthy Italian industrial tycoon in a sizeable factory, giving orders to a large group of his subordinates, embodied by multi-ethnic Italian 'others', many of them former clandestine immigrants. Shortly afterwards, the tycoon invites his teenage son, Sandro, to travel south and join him and his friend on what promises to be a great adventure on his fancy yacht. While yachting at twilight, Sandro, the main protagonist of the film, accidently falls overboard and is about to drown. Although the father eventually notices the absence of his son, he does not manage to save or even spot him during that tragic night at sea. The desperation and devastation of the father and the pain of his tragic loss set the initial atmosphere of the cinematographic journey.

As the story unfolds, the audience finds out that the boy did not drown that night but was rescued by a boatload of clandestine migrants: i.e., undocumented immigrants in a desperate attempt to reach Europe by sailing across the Mediterranean from north Africa. Paradoxically, the most prominent symbol is once again a boat, only this time, it represents exactly the opposite social class and serves as a space where countless ethnically and nationally diverse human beings are united in their misery, paired in their risky search for a better life and, ultimately, survival. The viewer is invited – in fact, forced to watch a great multitude of tired human faces, co-existing in a space, marked by inhumane living conditions, and treated more like animals than human beings. The particularity of the film is in its narrative perspective: a phenomenological lens of interpretation through the eyes of Sandro.

Immediately upon his rescue, the audience is confronted with the nautical reality, opposite to the initial anticipation of a yacht adventure: we see how corpses of the less resistant are thrown overboard; how people starve and die of thirst; how a young Romanian girl is sexually molested by the owners of the boat but chooses to surrender to them in exchange for drinking water; and we ultimately overhear the actual plans of the boat owners – human traffickers in fact – to abandon the ship. Sandro, who grew up with multiple social privileges and was never really exposed to the clandestine reality reigning in the Mediterranean, has to adjust and adapt, as his own life is at stake. And he owes his life to a Romanian youth – a criminal, as we find out later – who not only drags him out of the water but also covers up for him in a life-threatening interaction with the human traffickers. Naturally, Sandro befriends the young Romanian and his teenage sister and strives to help them once they reach the Italian shore.

Although the film problematizes a great number of extremely urgent issues – child prostitution, human trafficking, illegal immigration, social class tensions in Italy, human rights, citizenship, refugee rights and limitations, as well as cheap labour and an increasingly diverse Italian labour market – it is the simple human interaction between these two boys – one Italian and one Romanian – that is pivotal for understanding the conflicting perspectives of European haves and clandestine 'others'. This complex and often paradoxical interaction is symbolic of the reality of dynamics in the Mediterranean. As Italian Sandro is about to drown, Romanian Radu risks his own life to save him, and he does it again in front of the criminal boat owners. Initially, this particular scene in *Quando sei nato non puoi più nasconderti* (2005) suggests humanity *ad infinitum:* humanity that values not a European, not a Romanian, but primarily a *human* life at risk. And a few moments later, Radu warns Sandro not to trust anyone – not even Radu himself.

As the story continues in Italy, Sandro – who stubbornly chooses to identify with the clandestine group even upon his return to Italy – gradually understands why trust is such a salient and quite illusionary value in the interaction: the 13-year-old Sandro gradually finds out that nothing about the story of his Romanian friend is true – from his claimed teenage age to his actual relationship to his 'sister' Alina. Having robbed Sandro's family after the family gratefully offers to adopt the Romanian 'siblings', they flee – knowing that their cover story will not be plausible for long. In the end, Sandro manages to find Alina – an underage prostitute in the Italian underworld – whose 'brother' happens to be her pimp. Sandro's helpless and too-mature-for-his-age tears of despair in the final scene of the movie leave the audience as frustrated and hopeless as the protagonist himself. 'And now what?' manifests itself not only as a natural question at the end of the tragic fictional story, but also transcends it as an overwhelming and urgent question for the real, factual, tragic dynamics in the Mediterranean. 'And now what?' Where does Europe go from here? Will it protect itself from the persistent Mediterranean 'others'? Will it allow for a peaceful coexistence? Will it welcome and integrate them? And – what does any of this entail for the perceived 'promised land', and for the illegal immigrants? A conflict of interests, a clash of civilizations, a bloom of human trafficking, child labour and prostitution, abuse of human rights, combined with piracy and crime – or a new beginning? Ultimately, is the – obviously unavoidable – Mediterranean clandestine a friend, or a foe?

In his famous work *The philosophy of literary form,* Burke (1941) suggests that various art forms (such as, tragedy, comedy, or epic) function as equipment for living. Today, media in general and inter-cultural cinematography in particular play a major role in equip-ping their audiences with a specific epistemological framework as participants in global economies. In other words, as stated in the 2011 documentary success *Miss Representation* (2011), 'you cannot be what you can not see', and *vice versa. Quando sei nato non puoi più nasconderti* (2005) is an example of a vehicle of new consciousness, of a long-overdue cultural transformation into global citizens. This is not to suggest that the film offers a perfect solution to the less than imperfect reality. Yet, the film manifests the transformative power of human connections and genuine care: its price, its consequences, and its risks. It also suggests an invitation to a cross-cultural dialogue that succeeds only if all parties involved know first hand the bit-ter meaning of cultural *othering.* Sandro, whose destiny and cultural positionality are 'flipped' several times within the narrative – from the social class of 'othering haves' to the 'othered and have nots', and then back – serves as a cultural bridge with a unique political and communicative agency. As a political and cultural text, *Quando sei nato non puoi più nasconderti* (2005) offers a dialogical platform that forces the audience to undertake. virtually, a risky, frustrating, and at times life-threatening journey to the 'parallel' universe of the clandestine 'other', whose fast-growing presence in the European multicultural society cannot be denied.

Communication, peacebuilding and multiculturalism in action: state, art, and public consciousness

Arguably an inclusive but undeniably a multicultural society, Europe has always needed its historically created fixed borders that distinguished and separated it from the culturally different 'others'. At the same time, those borders enabled Europe's strong political, economic, and cultural position-ality, its Western dominance, otherwise known as Eurocentricity (Bhabha, 1994, 1996; Lorde, 1984; Mohanty, 2003). Lorde (1984) explains:

> Much of western European history conditions us to see human differ-ences in simplistic opposition to each other: dominant/subordinate, good/bad, up/down, superior/inferior. In a society where the good is

defined in terms of profit rather than in terms of human need, there must always be some group of people who, through systematized oppression, can be made to feel surplus, to occupy the place of dehumanized inferior. (p. 114)

Lorde continues, suggesting that typically the dominant civilizations (such as Western Europe) deliberately treat those differences as 'insurmountable barriers'; and any human *difference* as a human *deviance*. As a result, as a society, we do not develop the tools necessary for considering and utilizing human difference as a catalyst for creative change within our lives. And the globalized and globalizing reality of Western societies, such as Italy in particular and the European Union in general, both prove and remind us that as a global community, we can no longer afford living without these critical tools for enabling a major social change.

Robins (1996) specifies:

Cultural experience is always experience of the others; the others, the real others, are the indispensable transformational objects in historical change. [...] Non-Europe could now play a critical role in re-historicizing European culture. Europe must become open to cultural interruption. (p. 82)

Such disturbing cultural interactions and interruptions of European 'selves' and Mediterranean clandestine 'others' as those in *Quando sei nato non puoi più nasconderti* (2005) perfectly exemplify how challenging yet transformative multiculturalism can be as enacted on screen. Such portrayals serve as powerful depictions of social change. This is not to suggest that an intercultural film praising transnational and transracial humanity can solve the entire immigration crisis caused by, among other factors, the lack of such humanity; but as a cultural and political text, it certainly contributes to the multitude of interdisciplinary peace-building methodologies and epistemologies.

There are multiple ways to approach the phenomena of globalization, immigration, conflict, and inclusive multiculturalism within the framework of intercultural communication alone. Diverse approaches extend from the macro-level of state and its institutions, including media and cinematography in particular, to the micro-level of the state of mind, or individual consciousness. On the level of the Italian state, or of most of the European Union, certain institutional policies should be revisited and many improved in order to better integrate the constantly growing cultural diversity: such as, for example, national immigration laws. Many political analysts and critical scholars call for the debureaucratization and liberalization of naturalization laws in the European Union as necessary for peacebuilding. Harnisch et al. (1998) specifically argue that:

> Different models for an inclusive multicultural society cannot be discussed until foreigners have attained the same legal status as all other citizens. In the absence of such a policy, racial and ethnic differences as the ground for differences in legal status will continue to undermine any multicultural model. (p. 9)

And indeed, legalizing the status of foreigners might create the necessary premise for an inclusive model of peaceful, multicultural European society. However, mobilization of European institutions alone will certainly not produce the same outcomes if not embedded within a bigger social change – on the level of public consciousness – with regard to the complexity of dynamics between the European 'selves' and the non-European 'others'. To enable such change, intercultural films serve as powerful vehicles for such new consciousness. Visuality, as demonstrated in *Quando sei nato non puoi più nasconderti* (2005), has the power to influence our minds, to create certain images of 'selves', 'others', and our relationships with people and cultures different from our own. Jensen (2002) conceptualizes the arts as representative of the social reality around us and capable of changing it:

> If we want to change the world, we need to do it directly. The arts aren't good for us; they are us – expressions of us. We can't look to the arts to transform us, or make the world a better place. To make things better, we need to dispense with instrumental logic and intervening variables, and find democratic ways to identity and engage in right action. It's up to us, not art. (p. 206)

Quando sei nato non puoi più nasconderti's (2005) cinematographic imagery, instead of discursively fortifying the boundaries between the European 'selves' and the non-European 'others', suggests creative ways towards a peacebuilding cross-cultural contact on screen: challenging, frustrating, yet unavoidable and thus necessary. The audience can see how a contact with the 'other' takes place in virtual reality and profoundly affects both parties involved, culturally transforms their identities, and mutually enriches and simultaneously troubles their concepts of 'selves', and their relations to 'others'. As suggested by Robins (1996):

> We must consider identities in terms of the experience of relationships: what can happen through relationships, and what happens to relationships. In this way, we can take up again the question of dynamism versus closure in identity. Ideally, cultural relationship and interaction will be open to new experience. It will be possible to confront and modify more basic cultural emotions (fears and anxieties) and to recognize the other as a culture apart, not as a projection or extension of one's own culture. On this basis, reciprocity becomes feasible, and it will be possible to display empathy, concern and responsibility in the cultural relationship. (p. 79)

Contemporary intercultural cinematography plays an educational role in lives of many people. The images we see and interpret, together with the cultural interactions we observe in films, have the power to create certain visions of the world. They also have the power to either confirm or challenge our values, our attitudes, and our relations with different people and cultures. Through an open, non-judgmental visual contact with the 'other', will the film audiences involved be able to liberate themselves from existing anxieties and fears of cultural difference in their minds? This liberation is transformative because it allows for a reciprocal dialogue with the 'other' in everyday non-fictional interactions: a dialogue that reaches beyond 'irreconcilable differences' and creates awareness, necessary for adjusting to the multicultural community the European Union is and will be, and – in many cases – practising cross-cultural solidarity. Bhabha (1994) writes:

> Political empowerment, and the enlargement of the multicultural cause, comes from posing questions of solidarity and community. Social differences are not simply given to experience through an already authenticated cultural tradition; they are the signs of emergence of community envisaged as a project – at once a vision and a construction – that takes you 'beyond' yourself in order to return, is a spirit of revision and reconstruction of the present. (p. 4)

Creating images of solidarity and community in intercultural cinematographic works is certainly a further milestone in the institutional approach towards inclusive multiculturalism. With certain multicultural imagery Europe might show how such inclusion looks like, and what risk but also what potential for transformation it entails. The unique ability of cinematography to extend beyond existing cultural limitations and create an alternative reality on screen contains a reservoir of possibilities for cultural interactions that, instead of fear and anxiety, might be based on tolerance, solidarity, and empathy – the defining criteria of a new, inclusive consciousness with regard to the immigration dynamics happening in the European Union every day. Mohanty (2003) suggests that 'consciousness is simultaneously singular and plural, located in a theorization of being "on the border"' (p. 55). Intercultural cinematography enables such plurality. A universal change of consciousness means the start of a long overdue discussion of repressed identity problems and fear of contact with foreigners (Şenocak and Tulay, 1998), a process that contains a reservoir of possibilities of cultural transformation. This change starts with deconstructing the rigidity of the concepts of 'self' and the 'other'. In other words, the change of consciousness is in many way what is often defined as 'decolonization of the mind', an alternative perspective on the specificities of intercultural communication. hooks (2000) specifies:

> Living consciously means we think critically about ourselves and the world we live in. We dare to ask ourselves the basic questions who, what, when, where, and why. Answering these questions usually provides us with a level of awareness that enlightens. (p. 55)

In the 21st century, the era of globalization and migration, contemporary European society has to reflect on the fact that its population and its borders are constantly changing and shifting. Under such circumstances, promoting inclusive multiculturalism and learning how to accept and tolerate people's differences is no longer a matter of choice but a matter of necessity.

Using its multifaceted institutionalized power, Europe might have erected physical and metaphorical walls, redefined borders, and established (often via media) a legitimate justification of its choices with regard to the clandestine 'others' ... However, individual boundaries of intercultural tolerance, non-selective humanity, and the overall morality of democratic European citizens are still subject to their own, personal choices; or their own consciousness. Based on this perspective, *Quando sei nato non puoi più nasconderti* (2005) serves as a key space for the negotiation of a humanity that reaches beyond cross-cultural conflicts and functions as an important epistemological facilitator of the debate on multiculturalism and political activism.

References

P. Beaumont (2014, September 29) 'Eight Migrants Die Every Day Trying to Reach Richer Countries, Study Reveals', *The Guardian*, http://www.theguardian.com/global-development/2014/sep/29/europe-deadliest-destination-migrants-report, date accessed 3 September 2015.

H. K. Bhabha (1994) *The Location of Culture* (London and New York: Routledge Classics).

H. K. Bhabha (1996) 'Culture's In-between', in S. Hall and P. du Gay (eds) *Questions of Cultural Identity* (Thousand Oaks, CA: Sage), pp. 53–60.

K. Burke (1941) *The Philosophy of Literary Form: Studies in Symbolic Action* (Baton Rouge: Louisiana State University Press).

S. K. Foss (1988) 'Judy Chicago's "The Dinner Party": Empowering of Women's Voice in Visual Art', in B. Bate and A. Taylor (eds) *Women Communicating: Studies of Women's Talk* (Norwood, NJ: Ablex Publishing Corporation), pp. 9–26.

A. Harnisch, A. M. Stokes and F. J. Weidauer (1998) *Fringe Voices: An Anthology of Minority Writing in the Federal Republic of Germany* (Oxford: Berg Publishers).

b. hooks (1996) *Reel to Real: Race, Sex, and Class at the Movies* (New York: Psychology Press).

b. hooks (2000) *All About Love* (New York: Harper Perennial).

International Organization for Migration (2014) 'Fatal Journeys: Tracking Lives Lost during Migration', http://publications.iom.int/bookstore/free/FatalJourneys_CountingtheUncounted.pdf, date accessed 3 September 2015.

J. Jensen (2002) *Is Art Good for Us?: Beliefs about High Culture in American Life* (Lanham, MD: Rowman & Littlefield).

J. Khrebtan-Hörhager (2014) 'Italia–la Terra Promessa? Lampedusa and the Immigrant Crisis of the European Union', *Journal of Multicultural Discourses*, 10(1), 85–99.

A. Lorde (1984) *Sister Outsider: Essays and Speeches by Audre Lorde* (Freedom, CA: Crossing).

C. T. Mohanty (2003) *Feminism without Borders: Decolonizing Theory, Practicing Solidarity* (Durham, NC: Duke University Press).

Miss Representation (2011) Motion Picture, Jennifer Siebel Newsom, USA.

PACE (2013) 'Parliamentary Assembly of Council of Europe PACE', http://www.assembly.coe.int/nw/Home-EN.asp, date accessed 3 September 2015.

Quando sei nato non puoi più nasconderti (2005) Motion Picture, Rai Cinema and Cattleya, Italy.

K. Robins (1996) 'Interrupting Identities: Turkey/Europe' in S. Hall and P. du Gay (eds) *Questions of Cultural Identity* (Thousand Oaks, CA: Sage), pp. 61–86.

Z. Şenocak and B. Tulay (1998) 'Germany – A Heimat for Turks?' in A. Harnisch, A. M. Stokes and F. J. Weidauer (eds) *Fringe Voices: An Anthology of Minority Writing in the Federal Republic of Germany* (Oxford: Berg Publishers), pp. 256–63.

8
Peace or Conflict Maker: The Role of News Media in South Korea's Multicultural Society

MiSun Lee and Jinbong Choi

Introduction: characteristics of South Korean multiculturalism

South Korea today is well on its way to joining the list of countries all over the world dealing with the impact of immigration and immigrant communities. In order to build a peaceful society, South Korea must seek lessons from countries well-versed in encounters with immigrants in their histories; countries such as the United States and Canada, and regions such as the European Union. These countries and regions have come a long way towards building multicultural, peaceful societies: some of their efforts are evaluated as successful while some others are not. However, the process of Korean multicultural transformation differs from other traditional immigrant countries; it is therefore impossible to apply their findings entirely to the South Korean experience. This paper thus introduces the idea of Korean multiculturalism through analysis of its media representation of immigrant issues. It takes the global immigrant experiences of countries from the West and applies parts of that learning to the local South Korean immigrant scenario, particularly with regard to media reportage of immigrants.

It is a long-held belief, locally and globally, that Korea is a one-race country. However, globalization and international migration have changed the homogeneous demographic of Korean society into a multicultural society. Since the late 1990s, there has been an influx of migrant workers in the country. Moreover, marriages between women of other South Asian countries and Korean men have soared during the same time period. As of 2011, more than 100,000 immigrants have become naturalized Koreans. In the last ten years alone, the rise of the immigrant population in Korea has necessitated new policies in the Korean national and local governments. Social integration is now among the most urgent tasks of the South Korean government in that 2.8% of the whole population are immigrant citizens (Korean Statistical Information Service, 2013).

This percentage may not seem significant when compared to Western countries such as the United States, Canada, and Australia, known for large immigrant populations. As those countries were founded on the strength of multiracial and multicultural people, their residents are accustomed to being with foreign people. In fact, about 34% of the New York population and 30% of London population were born outside the respective countries, while only 4% of the Seoul population is from outside of South Korea. Unlike the Western countries referenced above, multiculturalism is an unfamiliar phenomenon being experienced by the Koreans.

The rapid transition from a homogeneous Korean community to a multicultural community is very strange to most Koreans, and some even feel uncomfortable facing this sudden and prevailing social demographic change. When the foreign population escalates, citizens tend to feel uneasy, as if strangers are invading the resident culture. As the demographic make-up of the community changes abruptly, negative impressions about the foreign population are amplified. In fact, when mass immigration occurred in Western Europe after the oil crisis in the 1970s, their fears turned to xenophobia (Wolfer & Vientiane, 1975). This even led to ultra-nationalist political parties in Europe in the 1980s. Although in Korea, unlike Europe, racial discrimination is not prevalent, the United Nations Committee on Elimination of Racial Discrimination (CERD) sent Korea a letter of advice regarding racial discrimination in 2007, drawing attention to the fact that Korea's pride in the country's ethnic homogeneity could result in future conflicts.

Key to the discussion about South Korea's demographic changes of late is the pace at which these changes have occurred. As a solution to problems such as a negative population growth and lack of labor force, the South Korean government has promoted immigration since the late 1980s. In addition, as a result of promoting immigration, many foreign women married Korean farmers, and numerous laborers from other South Asian countries started working in factories in outlying areas. Although the number of immigrants exceeds 1.5 million, the large majority of Koreans have no direct experience with immigrants, since most foreign residents live in suburban areas. In that sense, most Koreans have no understanding of these social changes. For the general public with no direct experience, multiculturalism is merely a policy rather than a reality. However, the long-term implications of multi-culturalism and ignorance about social change by the majority of the population could lead to the social conflict invariably experienced by countries who have had similar immigrant situations to the one being faced by South Korea now.

Followed by the growth of interracial marriage and its resulting chil-dren, the Korean government initiated the construction of multicultural policies and developed them as a social agenda for the Korean commu-nity (*Pressian*, 4 April 2006). From 2006 to 2013, every year, the Korean government legislated policies and established departments or programs supporting immigrant families and workers. In the beginning, immigrant married women who stayed permanently and nurtured 'Korean' children formed the main group of interest to the government. Later, due to criticism and requests from NGOs involved in foreign labor, the Korean government finally provided programs for the rest of the immigrant populations in Korea. However, illegal laborers are strictly excluded from all governmental protection, while at the same time, the South Korean economy is benefitting from the labor of such illegal immigrants. Such unequal treatment, based on different residential qualifications, could again be the cause of conflict among immigrants and between immigrants and resident Koreans in the near future. Thus, it has become necessary thoroughly to analyse how the immigrants are being portrayed in the national media and how that facilitates or challenges knowledge about immigrants amongst the greater population of the country.

Importance of news media

Whether Korea is ready for multicultural transformation or not, the immigrant population is increasing and playing various important roles as members of modern Korean society. It is clear that Korean society has undergone a transformation that is diverse, permanent and can no longer be undone; immigrants are no longer strange laborers, but friends, teachers, relatives, neighbors, and so on. As the society has transformed into a multicultural society, perceptions of and attitudes toward people from different cultural backgrounds should also be exam-ined, evolve and, at the very least, be formed on the basis of free and fair information about the immigrant population. To achieve this change, it is necessary for Koreans to embrace differences. Since Korea has been a one-race country for a long time, the idea of 'pure blood' is widespread: most Koreans take for granted that 'Korean' means those who have genetically Korean parents. In order to cope with cultural transformation and build an integrated multicultural society, immigrants and their children should be treated as eligible members of the same society, rather than substitute labor or substitute brides.

Negative attitudes and conflicts between immigrants and residents have put the emphasis on accommodating cultural diversity. To resolve conflicts and build social integration in a multicultural era, it is important to explore elements affecting conflicts between new and existing members of society. Various historical, social, political, economic, and cultural elements may influence the perceptions about immigrants. However, among these, there is one factor that encompasses key information from all of these aspects of society – the news media. Especially for this study, the researchers narrow their focus on how Korean newspapers represent immigrants.

Scholars have long established that news media have authoritative power in society. News media are important socialization tools for immigrants and also for the resident population (Croteau & Hoynes, 2006). In this chapter, we examine how newspapers represent immigrants and whether this representation accurately portrays the social transformation Korea has undergone in the last decade. Public perceptions about important issues are invariably influenced by news media reportage: what varies is the extent of the influence. Specifically in cases where people have little to no direct experience with the issue/culture/community in question, people tend to rely on indirect narratives and information available through news media. Therefore, press coverage is worth reviewing, especially for Korea, which has undergone its very first multicultural social change. The role of news media in establishing discourses about cultural communities in Korea has not been investigated before.

For immigrants, the way news media represent them affects their attitude toward their new society and their sense of social belonging (Clement et al., 2001; Erjavec, 2003). Korean multiculturalism is paradoxical to say the least. Immigrants have practically no voice, or act as mere reactors in articles although they are the main subjects at issue (Yang, 2007). It is a means of discrimination as well. Although immigrants use media to learn about a new society, such news reporting lowers a sense of social belongingness. For residents, it is convenient to adopt the media's portrayal of immigrants (Croteau & Hoynes, 2003; Golding & Murdick, 1991). Thus, misunderstanding leads to dissent or conflict due to the media framing of immigrants. Conflicts often occur when people have different expectations of 'others' not from the same culture. On the other hand, the media can establish multicultural values through fair and free reporting and representation of cultural groups. In order to examine the press reports of immigrants in Korea in changing times, this paper thus analyses South Korean news articles about immigrants in 2005 and 2011.

Previous analyses of Korean newspapers

For those who have no real-life experience, news media provides them with an opportunity to experience multiculturalism indirectly. Since interacting with immigrants is still infrequent in Korea, media representation can create stereotypes among the resident audiences. Media portrayals have an impact not only on the resident public's understanding of immigrants, but also on the immigrants' recognition of self-identity in the new place (Croteau & Hoynes, 2003; Golding & Murdick, 1991). However, there is still a lack of scholarly interest in Korean news media. Since the history of Korean multi-culturalization is short, few analyses exist regarding news reports on immigrants or immigration issues.

First, Yang (2007) investigated Korean newspaper coverage of interracial married women for a three-year period. According to her analysis, the news actively constructs the identity of the females only in relation to the Korean community. Interracial married women, especially, are represented as helpless, and needing to adjust to the values and lifestyle of the mainstream Korean community. Yang pointed out that these media representations tend to ignore the women's diverse ethnic and cultural identity and background and, thus, negatively influence the multicultural social environment. Also, according to her analysis, the news articles focus on solutions rather than the fundamental reasons for the problems being experienced by the immigrants. Furthermore, most of the solutions involve the assimilation of immigrant women. For example, to resolve these problems, the news media illustrate education programs supported by the Korean government as the solution to these women's troubles and sufferings. Moreover, although these women are subject to the conflicts or problems, their voices are not heard in most of the news coverage.

Based on the inflowing foreign population and interracial marriages in Korea, there is rising concern about racially mixed second generations. Jung and Lee (2007) compared news coverage before and after the visit of a successful Korean American athlete, Hines Ward. The story of his success made Korean media pay attention and represent racially mixed people, hidden or underrepresented in media discourse until that point. The researchers analysed one online, one conservative, and one liberal newspaper. As a finding of the study, they reported a high occurrence of the spectacle news frame, which tends to lead a collective frame of perception and interpretation. According to the content analysis, even those newspapers that are typically identified as having an opposite ideological approaches, shared a similar reporting attitude toward racially mixed Koreans. Regarding this issue, newspaper journalists construct news discourse in a similar frame due to a shared mainstream journalistic custom, while online news discourse displayed a context-based frame because of the influence of internet-based, alternative civic journalism.

Chae's (2007) study explored a different aspect of the media representations of the immigrants living in Korea – 'the otherness' aspect. He suggested that the coverage plays an important role that reflects and heightens the process of racial domination of the major culture. 'The otherness' is the dominant news frame in reporting on foreign residents in Korea through which foreign residents are differentiated from 'us' to uphold the racial superiority: 'that their identities tend to be reconstructed to be fragmented as well as obsolete characteristics being subordinate to that of native population' (Chae, 2007, 240). By comparing the diverse patterns of the otherness in conservative and liberal newspapers, his study examined how ideologically different newspapers frame immigrants employing five unique 'otherness' frames, including 'Paternalism frame, Criminalization frame, Nationalism frame, Discrimination frame, Action frame' (Chae, 2007, 241). According to the analysis, a liberal newspaper is likely to use the paternalist frame and actively participate in creating the image, while a conservative newspaper is likely to use a nationalist frame. Nevertheless, 'otherness' is the dominant frame found in both types of newspapers.

From a feminist point of view, Hong (2010) investigated how Korean mainstream newspapers covered interracial married migrant women in terms of the power relations they shared within the family. In her results, migrant women (mainly from South Asian countries) are portrayed as performers of strict patriarchal virtues. Based on analysis of four newspapers over ten years, she suggested that Koreans' nationalism is based on a pure-blood ideology, in that the main characteristics of their representation are victim, beneficiary, and patriarchal housewife: 'better-Koreanism by accepting the poor and inferior married migrant women and their children into Korean workforce [is] another way to enforce the pure bloodism by focusing [on] their inferiority' (Hong, 2010: 678). She pointed out that in the newspapers, immigrants face both racial and gender discrimination. According to her results, compared to conservative papers, liberal newspapers are more likely to depict women as active participants who solve the workforce troubles of the country rather than portray them in positive roles of housewives or mothers as examples of successful family settlements.

The way newspapers represent immigrants in the Korean community demonstrates well how they construct the meaning of the 'other'. Their meanings are formed from the viewpoint of the mainstream Korean community. Regardless of where immigrants are from, in Korean newspapers they are treated collectively as 'others' who differ from residents in significant matters and need help from their government.

Research questions

This research was aimed at identifying the attitude of the Korean news media toward immigrants. Because news media play an important role in socialization, this study was conducted under the hypothesis that news stories relating to immigrants influence the ideas or attitudes of the general public toward immigrants. The researchers compared news stories between 2005 and 2011, when the government worked to support policies for immigrants. Longitudinal analysis was conducted between 2005 and 2011. During the ensuing years, social and political interest in the immigrant issue has increased in Korea. Since 2005, every year, the Korean government has legislated various policies to support immigrants. As the government established various immigrant policies, multiculturalism began to grab residents' attention. This paper identifies how the news media reflected social change and covered immigrants in the meantime, to determine whether the news media's representation of immigrants changed as governmental efforts and social interest grew.

Furthermore, news media play an important role in influencing the public, especially members of the public without direct experience of immigrants. Unlike in fictional media platforms, people generally trust the news media and trust the information as facts about all immigrants.

For these purposes, the study attempts to answer the following research questions:

RQ 1: How did the news media represent the images of immigrants during the period 2005 to 2011?
RQ 2: What changes in the media's attitude towards immigrants during this time period can be identified through this representation?

Method

Materials

The data was collected from 2005 to 2011 because during this time, due to the inflow of the foreign population and an increase in interracial marriages and families, the Korean government initiated the construction of a multicultural social system and developed it as a Korean social agenda. For that purpose, every year from 2006 to 2013 the Korean government created supporting policies, established respective departments, and allocated programs for the successful adjustment of immigrant families and workers. Therefore, the researchers hypothesized that social concern about immigrants would differ before 2006 and that it would differ progressively between 2005 and 2011.

Procedure

Data were analysed using content analysis for four daily newspapers in 2005 and 2011. Four representative Korean national newspapers were selected for the study: *Hankyoureh Shinmoon*, *KyungHang Ilbo*, *DongAh Ilbo*, and *Chosun Ilbo*. News articles were selected through KINDS, a search engine, by using keywords such as 'immigrants', 'internationally married women', 'immigrant women', 'Kosian', 'foreign resident', and 'Korean Chinese'. Foreigners and tourists were excluded from the analysis; the results were analysed using SPSS+ 20.0.

Two coders coded the same 50 stories to test for intercoder reliability. After 50 stories were selected randomly, the news stories were coded independently. The overall Scott's Pi calculated to access intercoder reliability was 89.5%; since this is above the standard of Kassarjian (1977), the Scott's Pi was sufficient.

Results

The volume of news coverage and the content tend to influence audience attitudes toward the subject or issue. Therefore, the numbers of news articles regarding immigrants was counted. As seen in Table 8.1, all newspapers increased coverage regarding immigrants during the time period. Overall increase rate of *Hankyoureh Shinmoon*, *KyungHang Ilbo*, *DongAh Ilbo*, and *Chosun Ilbo* was 56.7%: a total of 120 stories in 2005 and 188 stories in 2011.

Regarding immigrants, the most frequently covered topic was the trouble or difficulty they undergo; in 2005 and 2011, respectively, 23.3% (28 stories) and 24.5% (46 stories) appeared. As shown in Table 8.1,

Table 8.1 Topics of news story

	Gov. measure	Social climate	Volunteer	Support program	Active participant	Crime	Problem	Statistic	Total
2005	23	18	13	8	12	3	28	15	120
	(19.2%)	(14.2%)	(11.7%)	(6.7%)	(10%)	(2%)	(23.3%)	(12.5%)	(100%)
vs.2011	52.3%	34.6%	31.7%	27.6%	27.3%	50%	37.8%	83.3%	38.9%
2011	21	34	28	21	32	3	46	3	188
	(11.2%)	(18.1%)	(14.9%)	(11.2%)	(17%)	(1.6%)	(24.5%)	(1.6%)	(100%)
vs.2005	47.7%	65.4%	68.3%	72.4%	72.7%	50%	62.2%	16.7%	61.1%
Total	44	52	41	29	44	6	74	18	308

Note: vs.2011: rate of 2005 compared to the total of 2005 and 2011.
vs.2005: rate of 2011 compared to the total of 2005 and 2011.

the requests for adequate government measures for immigrants increased with the progress of time. The media asked the government to come up with solutions to help immigrants: in 2005 and 2011, respectively, 19.2% (23 stories) and 11.2% (21 stories) appeared. The decrease in related news stories was the result of government work from 2006.

In contrast, news about requests for an improved social climate increased from 14.2% (18 stories) in 2005 to 18.1% (34 stories) in 2011. This means that although social systems were being developed by government work, changes in public attitude were still required. In addition to asserting multiculturalism as an appropriate social wave, stories about Korean volunteer workers helping immigrants increased from 11.7% to 14.9%. Also, coverage of supporting programs or events by the government increased from 6.7% to 11.2%. The analysis of these news stories suggests that they focused on the image of the beneficiary. This reporting attitude influences readers to consider immigrants as a passive group of people who are definitely in need of help to settle into their country.

Table 8.2 summarizes the images of immigrants in newspapers. As shown in Table 8.2, researchers found the following six images: victim, beneficiary, marginal man, large population, active participator, and invisible/hidden volunteers. News depicting immigrants as beneficiaries create a passive image. In addition, mentioning immigrants as a large population provided daunting mental imagery while some news did not even mention immigrants, but rather assigned them the term 'Korean volunteers'.

Among the four newspapers, the most frequently found image in news coverage was that of the marginal man who is having difficulty living in a new society (25.8% in 2005, 34% in 2011); the beneficiary image was also frequently found (22% in 2005, 23% in 2011). These two images represented almost half of the immigrant images used in the newspapers (48% in 2005, 57% in 2011). This result implies that although immigrants increased in number and took on various roles, the view of the news media did not change, and even deepened.

On the other hand, immigrants' image as active increased from 10% (12 stories) to 21% (40 stories). In the news articles, immigrants were portrayed as actively participating in mainstream society, and Koreanized. In a way, such praiseworthy anecdotes encourage readers to consider immigrants as friendly rather than strange. However, if used as a role model, the anecdotes seem to imply that immigrants should be assimilated to live successful lives in Korea.

Table 8.2 Image of immigrants

	Victim	Beneficiary	Outsider	Population	Hidden	Active	Total
2005	19	26	31	23	9	12	120
	(15.8%)	(21.6%)	(25.8%)	(19.1%)	(7.5%)	(10%)	(100%)
vs. 2011	70%	37%	33%	64%	32%	23%	39%
2011	8	44	63	13	20	40	188
	(4%)	(23%)	(34%)	(7%)	(11%)	(21%)	(100%)
vs. 2005	30%	63%	67%	36%	71%	77%	61%
Total	27	70	94	36	29	52	308

Note: vs.2011: rate of 2005 compared to the total of 2005 and 2011.
vs.2005: rate of 2011 compared to the total of 2005 and 2011.

Another change between 2005 and 2011 was the statistical image; 19.1% (23 stories) of news stories in 2005 treated immigrants as a population statistic, while the rate was reduced to 7% (13 stories) in 2011. Figure 8.1 helps visualize this change. This means that the media focused on the population phenomenon more in 2005, but when the population actually increased in 2011, the media were interested in their actual stories and not just their demographic statistics. In fact, news stories referring to an active life increased from 10% (12 stories) in 2005 to 21% (40 stories) in 2011. This result implies that although the media emphasized the beneficiary or outsider image, they did start to capture other aspects of the immigrant community.

In addition to this, the news sources also influenced images of news subjects, as depicted in Table 8.3. According to the data, the government is most frequently quoted (33.3% in 2005 and 36.2% in 2011). After the government, the most often cited source was non-governmental organizations (NGOs) (25.8% in 2005 and 27.1% in 2011). After this, media and experts such as professors and administrators were quoted most often. However, although the news content involved immigrants' problems and conflicts, immigrants were not the ones who suggested opinion or solutions for their own issues (11.7%, 36 stories in total).

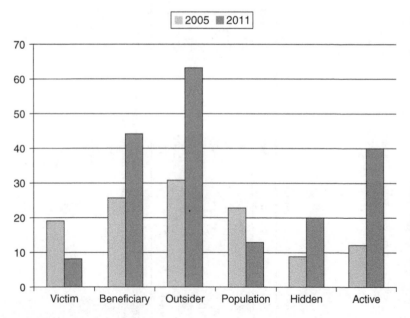

Figure 8.1 Image of immigrants

127

Table 8.3 Source

	Gov.	NGO	Expert	Resident	Media	Immigrant	Total
2005	40	31	12	7	21	9	120
	(33.3%)	(25.8%)	(10%)	(5.9%)	(17.5%)	(7.5%)	(100%)
vs.2011	37.4%	37.8%	42.9%	41.7%	53.8%	25%	
2011	67	51	18	7	18	27	188
	(35.6%)	(27.1%)	(9.6%)	(3.7%)	(9.6%)	(14.4%)	(100%)
vs.2005	62.6%	62.2%	57.1%	58.3%	46.2%	75%	
Total	107	82	30	14	39	36	308

Note: vs.2011: rate of 2005 compared to the total of 2005 and 2011.
vs.2005: rate of 2011 compared to total of 2005 and 2011.

This tendency implies that even though news articles are about immigrants, other people's opinions or judgments are more influential than immigrants' views. Such media attitudes can help readers suppose that immigrants have no ability to resolve their own troubles independently.

Discussion

To understand the multicultural social climate in South Korea, this study investigated the attitude of news media toward immigrants in South Korea. Conducting longitudinal analyses of news coverage about immigrants, we explored how newspapers view immigrants and whether the attitude of the news representation of them changed after the social transformation in the late 2000s.

According to the analysis results, along with an increase in the immigrant population in Korea, the number of news items regarding immigrants or immigration has increased. However, although the society has transformed into a multicultural society, the attitudes of news media have not responded appropriately.

In the results, the same framing, sharing similar views on immigrant-related issues, was found in all newspapers. During the social transformation, not only did the immigrant population increase, but immigrants also assumed various roles in society; however, news media still focused on negative images such as the helpless marginal man or beneficiary. While portraying images of active immigrants increased somewhat, the image of the marginal man was depicted more often. In news stories about the troubles immigrants face, emphasizing the sympathy frame, the media indicated that Koreans should help immigrants.

Analysis of news sources also shows that the most often used sources were the Korean government and NGOs rather than immigrants. Immigrants' voices were not heard – they were rather 'reactors' to troubles or benefits from the government or NGOs. Thus, in constructing a passive image, the news media might impress upon readers the idea that the government and private organizations are the main forces working for immigrants. Since they are not only a numerical, but also a social minority, they need help. Nevertheless, such reporting attitudes might portray immigrants as incompetents who cannot act independently to resolve their own problems. It is problematic because such news structures can influence interpretations of cause and solution through perceptions (Entman, 1993).

In addition, newspapers imply that to live a prosperous life in Korea, immigrants should be Koreanized. The Koreanized image might construct a friendly impression, but assimilation is always the solution to being welcomed. This also implies that immigrants should abandon their original culture; without assimilation, they are 'others'. It seems that because Korea has been proud of being a homogeneous nation, it tries to construct a 'culturally homogeneous' multicultural nation. However, such an attitude negatively stimulates social belongingness and is an obstacle to the development of a peaceful multicultural society.

This is problematic because the lack of change even after six years implies that the images have been stereotyped as the general images of immigrants. Thus, the news media and journalists should understand how important their role is for stable social transformation. Since media are one of the strong socialization tools, media coverage can influence multicultural society positively or negatively; and when it is in a transitional period, media representation is even more powerful. By selecting and emphasizing certain aspects, news frames implant certain images in the resident public. Because this news media attitude is influential, when news media concentrate on negative aspects of immigrants, residents have bad impressions of or look down upon immigrants, and immigrants can neither form a positive self-identity nor create a healthy sense of social belongingness (Clement et al., 2001; Erjavec, 2003). This study not only explores images of immigrants in the Korean media, but it also sheds light on how news media frame social issue interplay with audience knowledge (Entman, 1993; Gitlin, 1980). It implies that news coverage helps the audience to understand issues in a certain way. Also, the way in which news texts are interpreted determines emotional response (Roseman, 1991). According to Roseman, emotion is derived not from special mental processes, but from cognitive processes. In sum, news coverage can influence people's knowledge and even emotions. As a result, skewed views can cause conflict making it difficult for a peaceful and integrated society and coexistence of multiple communities. In this sense, journalists ought to take responsibility for their roles and have a vision for building an integrated society rather than revealing its negative aspects. To build a peaceful society, journalists should be careful with their approach to social transformation and try to assist by contributing to reportage that develops new social values.

References

Y-G. Chae (2007). Media's the Otherness Frames in Korea: Comparative Time Series Analysis of The Otherness Frames between Hankyoureh Shinmoon and Chosun Ilbo. *Korean Journalism Studies*, Vol. 14 No. 2, 205–241.

R. Clément, K. A. Noels & B. Deneault (2001). Interethnic Contact, Identity, and Psychological Adjustment: The Mediating and Moderating Roles of Communication. *Journal of Social Issues*, Vol. 57 No. 3, 559–577.

D. Croteau & W. Hoynes (2006). *The Business of Media*. Thousand Oaks, CA: Pine Forge Press.

R. M. Entman (1993). Framing: Toward Clarification of a Fractured Paradigm. *Journal of Communication*. Vol. 43 No. 4, 51–58.

K. Erjavec (2003). Media Construction of Identity through Moral Panics: Discourses of Immigration in Slovenia. *Journal of Ethnic and Migration Studies*, Vol. 29 No. 1, 83–101.

T. Gitlin (1980). *The Whole World Is Watching: Mass Media in the making and Unmaking of the New Left*. LA: University of California Press.

P. Golding & G. Murdock (1991). Culture, communications and political economy. Mass media and society, 2, 15–32.

Ji-A. Hong (2010). Multiculturalism of Korean Newspapers in the Gender Perspective: The Analysis of Kyunghyang, Dong-A, Chosun, Hankyoreh. *Korean Regional Communication Research Association*, Vol. 10 No. 4, 644–678.

E. Jung & C. Lee (2007). Analysis of Media Coverage of Racially Mixed People: Before and After Hines Ward's Success Story. *Korean Journalism and Communications Studies*, Vol. 51 No. 6, 84–110.

H. H. Kassarjian (1977). Content Analysis in Consumer Research. *Journal of Consumer Research*, Vol. 4 No. 2, 8–18.

K-S. Oh (2007). *Multiculturalism for Whom?: A Critical Review of Multiculturalism in Ansan*. Seoul: HanWul.

I. J. Roseman (1991). Appraisal Determinants of Discrete Emotions. *Cognition and Emotion*, Vol. 5 No. 3, 161–200.

Korean Statistical Information Service (2013). *Resident and Foreign Population of 2012*. Seoul.

J. A. Wolfer & M. A. Visintainer (1975). Pediatric Surgical Patients' and Parents' Stress Responses and Adjustment as a Function of Psychological Preparation and Stress-Point Nursing Care. *Nursing Research*, Vol. 24 No. 4, 244–255.

J. H. Yang (2007). Representation of Migrating Women: News Depiction of Inter-racially Married Asian Women to Korean Men. *Media, Gender & Culture*, Vol. 7, 47–77.

9
The Construction of Human Rights in US and Chinese Philosophical Discourse

Yanqin Liu

When exploring the origin and development of human rights, scholars tend to focus their attention on philosophical foundations. The concept of human rights comes from the West. The early conceptualization of human rights is associated with the ideas of natural law and natural rights in the West. How people understand the meaning of human rights influences their understanding of which specific human rights should be prioritized and which should be considered less essential. This chapter analyses the construction of human rights in the US and China and explores the possibility of sharing common values for human rights dialogue between the US and China.

Natural law, natural rights, and human rights in US discourse

A focus on the relations between natural law, natural rights, and human rights has been prevalent throughout US scholarship. Some scholars believe that in the West, natural law influences the emergence of natural rights and human rights, and that natural law is one source of human rights (Donald, n.d.; Hamburger, 1993; Porter, 1999; Shestack, 1998). According to the *Encyclopedia Britannica*, natural law is "a system of rights or justice held to be common to all humans and derived from nature rather than from the rules of society or positive law." Similarly, Kim (1981) defines natural law as "the law to which men are obliged to conform [under] the dictates of God, or of Nature, or of Reason" (p. 33). Natural law and natural rights are central concepts in John Locke's political philosophy (Tuckness, 2010). According to Shestack (1998), Locke characterized human beings as being in a state of nature. In this state, natural rights can ensure people's basic freedom, which affects their life, liberty, and property, and everyone has the freedom to self-determination. Setting up a body politic can contribute to the protection of natural rights of life, liberty, and property. In Chapter II of *the Second Treatise of Government*, Locke (1988) emphasized that all men in the state of nature are free, equal, and independent. People have the rights to do as they wish, but their behaviors should be situated "within the bounds of the law of nature" (p. 269). Men ought not to invade others' rights or do harm to one another, even in the state of nature. However, Locke's view of respecting other's rights is applicable when an individual's "own preservation comes not in competition" (p. 271). That means if a person cannot guarantee his or her life and freedom, there is no need to respect others' rights. Despite the connection between natural law and natural rights, natural rights play a primary role in Locke's philosophy. Similar to Locke, Jefferson developed his idea of duty (Jayne, 1998). Jefferson maintained that the right to liberty is restricted by a duty to respect others' rights. In the letter to Isaac H. Tiffany on 4 April 1819, Jefferson characterized liberty as "unobstructed action according to our will; but rightful liberty is the unobstructed action according to our will, within the limits drawn around us by the equal rights of others" (Jefferson, 1999, p. 224). However, he also contended that he did not "add 'within the limits of the law', because law is often but the tyrant's will" (p. 224).

Natural rights are "rooted in a natural condition of personal freedom" and seen as "the inborn and inalienable possession of every human being" (Zagorin, 2009, p. 21). In a letter to John Trumbull on 15 February 1789, Jefferson considered Locke as well as Bacon and Newton as "the three greatest men that have ever lived, without any exception, and as having laid the foundation of those superstructures which have been raised in the Physical & Moral sciences" (Jefferson, 1789). Based mainly on John Locke's concept of natural rights, that "people logically have rights to protection from others in their life, liberty, and property" (Weatherley, p. 17), Jefferson transformed the concept of natural rights into the concept of human rights. When it comes to American human rights discourse, Jefferson's views are crucial. As Koch and Peden (1944) contend, in the period of American Enlightenment, there was no leader as articulate, wise, and aware of the implications of free society as Jefferson. His human rights thinking has been highly influential in the configuration of US society.

When drafting the Declaration of Independence, Jefferson emphasized that "we hold these truths to be self-evident, that all men are created equal, that they are endowed by their creator with certain unalienable rights, that among these are life, liberty and the pursuit of happiness" (*Ushistory.org*, 1995). Natural rights theory is a significant philosophical inspiration for the United States Declaration of Independence.

Jefferson considered the right to life, the right to liberty, and the right to the pursuit of happiness to be basic human rights. He gave priority to the right to life, a right to what is our own. The right to liberty emphasizes that nobody has a right to obstruct others. As well as life and liberty, the pursuit of happiness is an unalienable right, which cannot be given up or taken away (Jayne, 1998; Zuckert, 1996). As Jayne says, "nothing then is unchangeable but the inherent and unalienable rights of man" (1998, p. 117). In this sense, Jefferson represents the affirmation of the inherent value of individuals.

The influence of Confucian language in Chinese discourse

In terms of Chinese human rights discourse, recent studies use Confucianism to analyse Chinese contexts and compare them to Western human rights discourses. De Bary (1998) believed that Confucius focuses on moral cultivation and consensual social rites rather than laws. In the *Analects*, Confucius says "Lead them by means of regulations and keep order among them through punishments, and the people will evade them and will lack any sense of shame. Lead them through moral force (*de*) and keep order among them through rites (*li*), and they will have a sense of shame and will also correct themselves" (De Bary et al., 1999, p. 46). The West sees constitutional law as the fundamental support for human rights protection (De Bary, 1998). However, Confucius prefers that human beings are more responsible for social development than the rule of law. Chinese traditions do not have faith in law.

In some situations when state power and human rights are in conflict, these traditions give priority to state power rather than law. In China's history, the weakness of rights consciousness, which comes primarily from Chinese traditions and language, plays a profound role in contemporary Chinese human rights practice. Different from the tendency to depend on the law for human rights protection, as is the case in the West, Confucianism emphasizes the application of consensual values in human behavior, such as respecting elders and taking responsibility for community. These traditions, as well as language, contribute to the weakness of human rights consciousness.

Some Confucian elements are incompatible with the concept of human rights, making it difficult to advocate human rights consciousness.

Confucianism characterizes imbalanced ethical relationships between parents and children, men and women, elder and younger generations, and rulers and subjects. On the one hand, the traditions of having loyalty to elders and complying with the dominant motivate the Chinese to become responsible for others. On the other hand, these traditions also advocate a vertical hierarchy in Chinese society and increasingly justify paternalism by prioritizing common demands and limiting individual values. For the authorities, Confucian hierarchy can relatively easily help them govern the "familistic state" characterized by Max Weber (as cited in Fairbank, 1983, p. 24). Furthermore, in Confucian hierarchy, people live in their networking, which means they have to fulfill responsibilities for their communities before seeking their personal goals and values. A Confucian point "Tianxia weigong" (all-under-Heaven as shared in common) implies that people seek their own desires at others' expense, and they should act in the common interest. If a person can benefit others, then they will benefit this person as well. It is hard to tell whether Confucianism is compatible with the concept of human rights, but some elements in Confucianism are incompatible with the concept of human rights, thus limiting Chinese human rights consciousness.

As well as Confucianism, language plays an import role in constructing the concept of human rights in China. Wittgenstein (2012) argues that the limits of human language mean the limits of how we understand the world. According to Gergen (2009), language is the central vehicle through which people construct the real and the good. People inherit lasting rules of language and these rules and traditions enable people to communicate with others in proper ways. Language serves not only as a communication tool, but also a representation of perception and thinking, because the way people think is provided by the language that they utilize (Burr, 2003). As scholars focus on the importance of language in sociocultural construction processes (Leeds-Hurwitz, 1995), language influences the social construction of human rights thought. The limit of language defines the limit of Chinese human rights discourse. According to Angle and Svensson (2001), there was no Chinese term which corresponded to the English term "rights" until the 19th century. Compared with a 5,000-year-long civilizational history, China has a short history of talking about rights. Although China has prominent philosophical ideas, which could have helped the construction of human rights concepts, lacking words for rights prevents people from developing the idea of human rights.

Human rights, called "renquan/人权" in Mandarin, is a translation word from the West. "Renquan" is the compound of "ren" (human) and "quan" (right). Consider the word "ren" firstly. "Ren," referring to "human/ren/人," can be understood as an individual or a group of individuals. It is the synonym of "min/民." "Min" can be understood as "people/ren min/人民" or "citizen/gong min/公民." These two words have two semantic differences in Chinese. The first difference is defini-tion. "People/ren min/人民" refers to those who can help the develop-ment of a society, and support socialism and national unification, while "citizen/gong min/公民" refers to a person who has a nationality, is enti-tled to have rights and fulfill duties according to the Constitution and other laws. These two definitions show that "people/ren min/人民" is a political concept and "citizen/gong min/公民" is a legal concept. The second difference is that "people/ren min/人民" is a collective concept and emphasizes a general group in a society, while "citizen/gong min/公民" is an individual concept and emphasizes an individual in a society. The Chinese government is inclined to follow a collectivist perspective in understanding human rights. Therefore, governmental documents construct the meaning of group rights through the concept of human rights. In the term "human right/ren quan/人权," the second word "quan" comes to mean power within many Chinese social contexts, but here "quan" can be understood as two words "quanli/权力(power)" and "quanli/权利(right)," which have the same pronunciation but different characters. The first "li/力" means force and the second "li/利" means benefit. The meaning of the second "quanli" is most similar to that of the word "right." However, in Chinese human rights discourse, the second "quanli" is often related to another Chinese word "yiwu/义务," which refers to duty or obligation. The Chinese constitution says that Chinese citizens have the rights that the constitution and other laws allow, and at the same time, they must fulfill obligations that the con-stitution and other laws require (*Xinhua News Agency*, 2004). Duties entail other people's rights and rights entail other people's duties. In this regard, in the collective context, although China protects human rights, the implementation of human rights is conditional, and depends largely on whether individuals perform their duties and contribute to society. According to Feinberg (1970), a claim asks for a right and a right is a valid claim. Valid claiming plays an important role in understand-ing what rights are in China. As noted above, China does not have a tradition of rights. If people do not know about rights, then "they do not have a notion of what is their due; hence they do not claim before they take" (p. 249). Even in contemporary China, when people become increasingly conscious of their rights, they may not be able to claim a right unless someone violates their rights.

The role of Taoism in human rights discourse

Although China does not have a tradition of discussing rights, some
philosophical ideas are representations of Chinese natural law. Scholars
think that the ideas of Lao Zi on Taoism reflect the origin of natural law
in China (Cheng, 2000; Kim, 1981; Zhang, 1991). Lao Zi's work, the *Tao
Te Ching* (1985), is the most distinguished work on Taoism. It began as
a discussion between the sixth century BC and the fourth century BC,
in ancient China. This was the period of social transformation from
slavery to feudalism. At that time, people were concerned with ideas
of peace and nonviolence. The *Tao Te Ching* does not conceptualize
human rights, natural rights, or natural law *per se*, but probably as a
reaction to the concerns of the time, it relies on words and concepts
close to natural law. According to the *Tao Te Ching*, in managing human
affairs as well as in ruling a nation, it is necessary for the authorities to
follow the concepts and principles of Tao. "Man models himself after
the Earth; The Earth models itself after Heaven; The Heaven models
itself after Tao; Tao models itself after Nature" (Lin, pp. 145–146). The
concept of Tao, signifying the way or principle of nature, is a key word
to both Taoism and Confucianism. While Confucius interpreted Tao as
ethical principles of society, Lao Zi extended the concept of Tao to the
level of nature and the universe. Tao can be the law of how the universe
works, or a principle which helps govern a country and guide people to
take action. From the perspective of Lao Zi, the essence of Tao is nature.
Tao is self-existent and intangible, but its use is inexhaustible.

The Tao of Taoism, the Way of Heaven, which goes beyond the
Tao of Confucianism, the Way of Man, is implicitly represented in
the thoughts of Feng Youlan (2012), one of the most prominent philosophers in modern China. Feng posits four realms of human life: the
natural realm (to behave instinctively), the utilitarian realm (to behave
for individual benefit), the moral realm (to work for the development
of society), and the universal realm (to work for the development of
universal benefit). He maintains that in natural and utilitarian realms,
people are what they are currently, and in moral and universal realms,
people are what they should be. The first and second realms are typical states of people in a society; moral and universal realms are ideal
human states and higher life goals. He does not relate Confucianism
or Taoism to his concept of the four realms of human life. However,
according to Feng, Confucianism complies with values in the moral
realm. In the highest realm, the universal realm, people take actions
willingly in order to serve the universal benefit. Meanwhile, they are

aware of the value of their actions. The universal realm is similar to the goal of Lao Zi.

Taoism is the origin of Chinese natural law and the concept of Tao can be compared with the concept of natural law in the West. Confucianism is the most dominant philosophy in Chinese society. However, this philosophy cannot be the only representative of the wealth of social and cultural traditions in China. In terms of the compatibility between human rights and Chinese traditions, Lao Zi cannot be ignored. His ideas on Taoism encompass the wisdom of peace (Mindell, 1995). Mindell describes the *Tao Te Ching* as "one of the oldest books on earth" and insists that it "discusses many of the abilities necessary to facilitate groups and get along with people and nature" (p. 188). Following natural law does not mean being truly passive. It means "using the energy of what is happening" instead of pushing things further than they can go now (p. 189).

When analysing the *Tao Te Ching*, it is noted that some of the ideas can be compared to the values of the Declaration of Independence in terms of life, liberty, pursuit of happiness, and equality. Theoretically, the similar ideas between the *Tao Te Ching* and the Declaration of Independence can be regarded as commonly accepted values by the US and China when they participate in a constructive dialogue.

Life

As well as Jefferson, Lao Zi expressed his care for life. "Soldiers are weapons of evil. They are not the weapons of the gentleman. When the use of soldiers cannot be helped, the best policy is calm restraint" (Lin, 1948, p. 167). Lao Zi did not specifically define the Tao, but from his description that "soldiers are instruments and weapons of evil" (p. 167), we can think of military action as a violation of Tao. Soldiers and weapons symbolize violent power. According to this idea, because violent power can deprive one of the right to life, a gentleman should not resort to it in daily life. The deprivation of life is not a harmonious behavior. A disrespect for life goes against nature. In order to attain a state of harmony between man and nature, people should strengthen their propensity for self-restraint and work with nature rather than against it.

Additionally, Lao Zi described the pattern of an ideal society as "(let there be) a small country with a small population, where the supply of goods is tenfold or hundredfold, more than they can use. Let the people value their lives and not migrate far. Though there be boats and carriages, none be there to ride them. Though there be armor and weapons, no occasion to display them" (Lin, p. 310). Here "not migrate far" speaks to the principle that people do not have to suffer hardships caused by lasting warfare and move from one place to another. In an ideal society, people can liberate themselves from poverty, hunger, and homelessness. If they cherish the value of lives, they will never use weapons for murder. Furthermore, Lao Zi insisted that the avoidance of tension relies largely on the maintenance of softness, which is the representation of enduring life-giving force. "When man is born, he is tender and weak; at death, he is hard and stiff. When the things and plants are alive, they are soft and supple; when they are dead, they are brittle and dry. Therefore hardness and stiffness are the companions of death, and softness and gentleness are the companions of life" (Lin, p. 305). To promote the value of life, softness and gentleness cannot be neglected; "the more sharp weapons there are, the greater the chaos in the state" (p. 265).

Liberty

Another similarity between Jefferson and Lao Zi is value of liberty. Consider Lao Zi's famous saying, "Man models himself after the Earth; The Earth models itself after Heaven; The Heaven models itself after Tao; Tao models itself after Nature" (Lin, pp. 145–46). Lao Zi described the blueprint of an ideal world: everything is created naturally; harmony is reached as a consequence. "By doing nothing, everything is done" (Lin, p. 229). This quotation, also translated into "action without deeds," means that respecting the principles of nature and the state of freedom can help the achievement of harmony rather than taking action intentionally.

The concept of noncontention (a translation of buzheng/不争) is one of Lao Zi's most important principles. Noncontention is associated with softness. Lao Zi advocated the value of softness, gentleness, and weakness. As the phrase "gentleness is the function of Tao" (Lin, p. 207) reveals, the purpose of being soft and gentle is to put Tao into practice. In Chapter 43 of the *Tao Te Ching*, "the softest substances of the world go through the hardest. That-which-is-without-form penetrates that-which-has-no-crevice" (p. 216). Here the softest substance can be referred to as water, which reflects the nature of gentleness but can overcome the hardest substances, like stone. "There is nothing weaker than water, but none is superior to it in overcoming the hard, for which there is no substitute" (p. 306). In the *Tao Te Ching*, the image of water is used to convey the meaning of softness and flexibility. "The highest benevolence is like water. The benevolence of water is to benefit all beings without strife" (Lao Tzu, p. 48). Just as water runs everywhere without exertion, it is difficult for human forces to control water.

In Chinese culture, people prefer using the mild and benevolent image of water at a spiritual level in order to analogize femininity, peace, or gentility. The approach of being like water can be considered a way to overcome hardness. The physical image of water is tangible, but its spiritual image is hidden in a cultural context as a symbol. As water functions without striving in the natural world, the concept of noncontention can play a profound and indirect role in an ideal society. An ideal society should allow people to have the freedom (i.e., liberty) to make a choice and to take action, and "the more prohibitions there are, the poorer the people become" (p. 265). Noncontention is essential for the progress of a society. The goal of noncontention is to maintain liberty. Without governors, people are free to do as they wish. Lao Zi focused on a natural state and his focus implies a spiritual freedom of liberty.

Hartz (1991) understands the US as a liberal community. He says that "America was settled by men who fled from the feudal and clerical oppressions of the Old World. If there is anything in this view, as old as the national folklore itself, then the outstanding thing about the American community in Western history ought to be the nonexistence of those oppressions" (p. 3). Based on the liberal tradition in the US, Jefferson described in the Declaration of Independence that "a prince whose character is thus marked by every act which may define a tyrant is unfit to be the ruler of a free people" (*Ushistory.org*, 1995). In *A Summary View of the Rights of British America*, he wrote that "the God who gave us life gave us liberty at the same time; the hand of force may destroy, but cannot disjoin them" (Jefferson, 1944, p. 310). In Jefferson's view, freedom is inherent and unchangeable. Jefferson is not the creator of America's liberal tradition, but he integrates liberal tradition into his idea of human rights. Further, he attempted to situate liberal values in civil and political settings. In the letter to James Madison in 1787, he said:

I will now tell you what I do not like. First, the omission of a bill of rights, providing clearly, and without the aid of sophism, for freedom of religion, freedom of the press, protection against standing armies, restriction of monopolies, the eternal and unremitting force of the *habeas corpus* laws, and trials by jury in all matters of fact triable by the laws of the land, and not by the laws of nations.

(Thorpe, 1901, p. 212)

The focus on civil and political liberty of citizens has become a fundamental value in the U.S.

The pursuit of happiness

In the Declaration of Independence, Jefferson substituted the pursuit
of happiness for property. He did not provide an explanation for this
substitution. However, in his letter to DuPont, Jefferson mentioned that
the right to property is a right to the external world rather than a right
to what is our own (Zuckert, 1996, p. 80). The rights to life and liberty
are unalienable "even though external coercion or duress could cause
an individual to renounce these rights externally or to lose the physical manifestation of them" (Jayne, 1998, p. 122). Therefore, he used an
inherent right, the right to pursuit of happiness, to replace property
rights. The pursuit of happiness is an inalienable right, which was developed in Locke's *An Essay Concerning Human Understanding* (1836). Locke
focused on the constant pursuit of happiness instead of the temporary
achievement of happiness, because seeking happiness "consists in the
enjoyment of pleasure, without any considerable mixture of uneasi-
ness" (p. 171). Therefore, when addressing the pursuit of happiness
rather than the achievement of happiness, Jefferson believed that seeking happiness can liberate people from being obsessed with temporary
individual desires.

In the *Tao Te Ching*, Lao Zi did not specify seeking happiness, but he
explained how an individual and a society could achieve their happiness. At the individual level, he insisted that "there is no greater curse
than the lack of contentment. No greater sin than the desire for possession. Therefore he who is contented with contentment shall be always
content" (Lin, p. 225). Rather than struggle for material desires, he
advocated complying with nature for the achievement of happiness. At
the societal level, Lao Zi described "a small country with a small population" as an ideal society. He hoped to "let the people again tie ropes for
reckoning, let them enjoy their food, beautifying their clothing, be satisfied with their homes, delight in their customs" (Lin, p. 310). Without
poverty, hunger, or disaster, people can maintain the state of nature and
enjoy the freedom to have a stable life.

Equality

In the Declaration of Independence, Jefferson did not identify equality
as a right. However, Jefferson and his colleagues proclaim that all men
are created equal, which has been used to understand universal human

rights in other parts of the world. For example, in 1789, the fundamental document in the French Revolution, the Declaration of the Rights of Man and of the Citizen, asserted that "men are born and remain free and equal in rights" (Manent, 2006, p. 103).

Similarly, Lao Zi mentioned the spirit of equality. Consider Lao Zi's famous saying, "Nature is unkind: It treats the creation like sacrificial straw-dogs. The Sage is unkind: He treats the people like sacrificial straw-dogs" (Lin, p. 63), for example. Here "unkind" is a translation of "bu ren/不仁." "Bu" means without and "ren" means benevolence. If a person treats others without benevolence, it illustrates that the person does not have any personal preference and treats others equally. Straw-dogs were regarded as sacrificial offerings in a ritual in ancient China. Without like or dislike, people treated straw-dogs as a ritual tool. Before the ritual, people attached importance to straw-dogs, which does not demonstrate that people liked them. In the same way, after the ritual, they threw straw-dogs away without any personal preference. In other words, they chose sacrificial offerings without love or hate and treated straw-dogs as they treated any other objects. Without love or hate, everything is equal.

When comparing the *Tao Te Ching* and the Declaration of Independence as important assertions of human rights, life, liberty, the pursuit of happiness, and equality are expressed in both Chinese and American values. These similar values provide a possibility of constructing a new human rights dialogue between the two countries. On 3 July 1943, the day before US Independence Day, *Xinhua Daily*, the mouthpiece of the Chinese Communist Party, published an editorial that spoke highly of the spirit of democracy and freedom introduced by Thomas Jefferson. This example demonstrates that, although China has a different understanding of human rights, it can be open-minded enough to absorb positive aspects of US values.

In a similar way, the US could learn from Chinese philosophical values to advance the development of its society. Some scholars argue that Chinese thinkers emphasize the roles of persuading, cajoling, and manipulating others in order to seek harmony (Peerenboom, 1998). As a consequence, they argue that human rights and Chinese traditions are not compatible. In fact, the compatibility between human rights and Chinese traditions depends largely on the understanding of harmony. In the eyes of Lao Zi, an ideal society can maintain a harmonious state of nature through the achievement of values such as life, liberty, pursuit of happiness, and equality. Harmony cannot be equated with uniformity or sameness. Lao Zi said "Rule a big country as you would fry small fish" (Lin, p. 177). When cooking small fish, a chef may use different flavors of sauces. Rather than combining the same amount of flavors, the chef would keep the blending of different flavors proportionate for a balanced delicious dish. This balanced connectedness between things is what Lao Zi advocated and what Jeffersonian followers can learn from the wisdom of the *Tao Te Ching*.

Theoretical implications

As the texts above indicate, although different countries construct human rights issues within different historical, philosophical, and cultural contexts, they can still learn from each other to achieve positive transformations. Although such transformations take time, appropriate learning and changes may reduce conflicts. With the help of shared philosophical foundations, the US and China can work together to reconsider human rights dialogue by using a constructionist perspective. According to Gergen (2009), people understand the world through their own experience of the world emerging from relationships, and constructions gain their importance based on their social utility. Exploring similarities and differences of philosophical discourses and the construction of human rights not only helps maintain traditions, but also develops ways of framing new possibilities of social reality and conceiving of a more viable future regarding human rights dialogue between the US and China.

Limitations

China could develop the idea of natural law based on Taosim. However, the construction of Lao Zi's ideas about natural law was based on the specific reality in which Lao Zi was engaged, and these ideas might not be applicable in the context of other periods, because of their academic abstraction. In Lao Zi's works, the concept of Tao is too general and inclusive to be understood. In Chinese, people can understand Tao as way/principle/path/road/order/truth/track. In order to understand the nuances of these abstract words, people have to relate them to social contexts. The understanding of social contexts may result in different interpretations of Tao.

Conclusion

The *Tao Te Ching* and the Declaration of Independence share similar values theoretically, it is possible for China and the US to learn from each other. Rather than assess human rights grievances in their own isolated contexts, they can move from these contexts to the point at which human rights issues emerge. Farrell (2013) mentions that "China, which remains a closed society in many ways, has an open mind, whereas the US is an open society with a closed mind" (Wake up America: Asia will soon be 5 times bigger, more powerful, para. 1). Here Farrell's idea demonstrates that a conservative China attempts to learn from advanced civilizations and a liberal US maintains its ethnocentric values. When both China and the US address their communication dilemma, both sides might coordinate their current misunderstandings by seeking common principles in human rights discourse. Instead of both countries disseminating differences, dialogue may be initiated and facilitated so that issues of human rights can be appropriately and effectively discussed.

References

S. C. Angle and M. Svensson (2001). General introduction. In S. C. Angle & M. Svensson (eds), *The Chinese human rights reader: Documents and commentary 1900–2000* (pp. xiii–xxx). New York: M. E. Sharpe, Inc.

V. Burr (2003) *Social constructionism*, Second Edition. Hove: Routledge.

W. R. Cheng (2000). *Taoism and Chinese legal culture* (道家与中国法文化). Shanghai, China: Shanghai Jiaotong University Press.

W. T. De Bary (1998). *Asian values and human rights.* Cambridge: Harvard University Press.

W. T. De Bary, I. Bloom & J. Adler (1999). *Sources of Chinese tradition* (Vol. 1, 2nd ed). New York: Columbia University Press.

J. A. Donald (n.d.). *Natural law and natural rights.* Retrieved from http://jim.com/rights.html

P. B. Farrell (3 June 2013). *U.S. losing economic war and Asia loves it.* Retrieved from http://www.marketwatch.com/story/america-the-quitter-getting-whipped-by-china-2013-06-01?pagenumber=2

J. Feinberg (1970). The nature and value of rights. *The Journal of Value Inquiry*, 4, 243–257.

Y. L. Feng (2012). *Realm: Feng Youlan talks about life* (境界：冯友兰谈人生). Beijing, China: Zhongxin Press.

K. J. Gergen (2009). *An invitation to social construction.* Los Angeles: Sage.

P. A. Hamburger (1993). Natural rights, natural law, and American Constitutions. *The Yale Law Journal*, 102(4), 907–960.

L. Hartz (1991). *The liberal tradition in America* (2nd ed.). New York: Harcourt, Brace & World.

A. Jayne (1998). *Jefferson's Declaration of Independence: Origins, philosophy, and theology.* Lexington, KY: University Press of Kentucky.

T. Jefferson (15 February 1789). *Thomas Jefferson to John Trumbull.* Retrieved from http://www.loc.gov/exhibits/jefferson/18.html

T. Jefferson (1944). *The life and selected writings of Thomas Jefferson.* A. Koch & W. Peden (eds). New York: The Modern Library.

T. Jefferson (1999). *Jefferson: Political writings.* J. Appleby & T. Ball (eds). Cambridge, UK: Cambridge University Press.

H. I. Kim (1981). *Fundamental legal concepts of China and the West: a. comparative study.* Port Washington, NY: Kennikat Press.

A. Koch and W. Peden (1944) *The life and selected writings of Thomas Jefferson.* New York: Random House.

W. Leeds-Hurwitz (1995). Introducing social approaches. In. W. Leeds-Hurwitz (eds), *Social approaches to communication* (pp. 3–20). New York: The Guilford Press.

Y. Lin (1948). *The wisdom of Lao Tse.* New York: The Modern Library.

J. Locke (1836). *An Essay Concerning Human Understanding.* Retrieved from http://books.google.com/books?id=vjYIAAAAQAAJ&printsec=frontcover&hl=es&source=gbs_ge_summary_r&cad=0#v=onepage&q&f=false

J. Locke (1988). *Two treatises of government.* Cambridge, UK: Cambridge University Press.

P. Manent (2006) *A world beyond politics: A defense of the nation-state.* Princeton: Princeton University Press.

A. Mindell (1995) *Metaskills: The spiritual art of therapy.* Tempe, AZ: New Falcon Publications.

National Archives and Records Administration. (n.d.). *The U.S. Bill of Rights.* Retrieved from http://www.archives.gov/exhibits/charters/bill_of_rights.html

Natural law. (n.d.). In *Encyclopedia Britannica online.* Retrieved from http://www.britannica.com/EBchecked/topic/406283/natural-law

R. Peerenboom (1998). *Lawyers in China: Obstacles to independence and the defense of rights.* New York: Lawyer's Committee on Human Rights.

J. Porter (1999) From natural law to human rights: Or, why rights talk matters. *Journal of Law and Religion,* 14(1), 77–96.

J. J. Shestack (1998). The philosophical foundations of human rights. *Human Rights Quarterly,* 20(2), 201–234.

F. N. Thorpe (1901). *The constitutional history of the United States: 1788–1861.* Chicago: Callaghan & Company.

A. Tuckness (29 July 2010). *Locke's political philosophy.* Retrieved from http://plato.stanford.edu/entries/locke-political/

L. Tzu (1985). *Tao Te Ching.* (H. G. Ostwald, Trans.). Boston: Arkana.

The United Nations. (n.d.). *The universal declaration of human rights.* Retrieved from http://www.un.org/en/documents/udhr/drafters.shtml

"United States Declaration of Independence." (4 July 1995). *Ushistory.org.* Retrieved from http://www.ushistory.org/declaration/document.

L. Wittgenstein (2012). *Tractatus Logico-Philosophicus.* Retrieved from http://people.umass.edu/phil335-klement-2/tlp/tlp-ebook.pdf

P. Zagorin (2009). *Hobbes and the law of nature.* Princeton, NJ: Princeton University Press.

Z. Q. Zhang (1991). *Comparative studies between Chinese and Western legal cultures* (中法律文化比较研究). Nanjing, China: Nanjing University Press.

M. P. Zuckert (1996). *The natural rights republic: Studies in the foundation of the American political tradition.* Notre Dame, IN: University of Notre Dame Press.

Part III
From Deconstruction to Reconstruction: Rebooting Frameworks of Education on Culture, Conflict, and Peace

After focusing on macro, micro, local, and global level conflicts and the media's powerful role in representing different identities, this part takes a turn towards a thorough explanation of approaches to peace through education. Belanger's Chapter 10 takes the reader through the intricacies of Canada's Truth and Reconciliation Commission (TRC), and what we can learn from it. His minute deconstruction of the TRC process reveals some inherent strengths and weaknesses and provides a clearer picture of what works and what doesn't when dealing with institutional, culturally embedded violence against a particular group in society. Merkin picks up the thread in her Chapter 11, highlighting the importance of deconstructing ideological barriers to paths to peacebuilding. She then reconstructs parts of the ideologies to promote a positive outcome for the fight for education for girls in Pakistan and Afghanistan. Moving away from global concerns, Ruminshki's Chapter 12 successfully examines a particular local outcome of the Sustaining Campus and Community Dialogue Series project to better understand how it demonstrates the dialogic process and contributes to the ongoing construction of a community's narrative identity in times of violence and tragedy experienced by students. Finally, Lin, Edwards, and Khamis's Chapter 13 drives home the theme of this part as they describe a working project that truly utilizes reconstruction of antiquated educational approaches for sustainable peacebuilding between members of groups with historic conflict issues.

Part III
Using Decomposition to Reconstruct Reading: Children's Reading Evaluation and Literacy Constructionalism

10
Narrative, Decolonial Education, and Societal Transformation

Patrick Belanger

Introduction

In 1857, the (then) Province of Canada passed the Gradual Civilization Act with the explicit purpose of assimilating Native peoples into British colonial society. The Act stemmed from an assumption that Indigenous persons were inferior in both spirit and culture, a sentiment exemplified in empire enthusiast Rudyard Kipling's (1899) depiction of colonized peoples worldwide: 'Your new-caught, sullen peoples,/ Half-devil and half-child'. By 1920, federal government policy mandated residential school attendance for all Native children aged seven to 15. Children were often forcibly removed from their communities and compelled to reside for ten months a year in institutions wherein Indigenous languages, traditions, and cultural practices were discouraged or suppressed. Living conditions were substandard and students endured physical and emotional abuse. Notably, many Indigenous groups actively sought schooling for their children as part of a cogent strategy for weathering the changes the Europeans brought. However, the schools were orchestrated following Euro-Canadian racist assumptions. Approximately 150,000 Indigenous children attended Canada's 130 residential schools before 1996 when the last federally run school closed in Saskatchewan (Miller, 1996; International Center, 2014).

Nearly a century later, the Truth and Reconciliation Commission (TRC) of Canada (2010) organized its first national event in Winnipeg, Manitoba. The occasion was publicized as an opportunity to advance national reconciliation through public education. Individuals affected by the Indian Residential School (IRS) system had an opportunity talk about their experiences and envisage a path towards mutual respect between Indigenous and non-Indigenous Canadians. The TRC is not a criminal tribunal and does not have subpoena powers; its mandate is to collect stories, create public forums for marginalized Indigenous voices and histories, and advance education about the country's colonial foundation.

The following explores the idea that education alone is not a sufficient counterweight to colonial legacies. I make two central claims. First, substantive restitution for long-standing injustices mandates broad public support. Within the context of a colonial democracy such as Canada, public argument plays a critical role in securing non-Indigenous backing for Indigenous political autonomy and land rights. Second, enhanced knowledge of a country's past may not be a sufficient catalyst to bridge the gap between ideas and action. Truth and reconciliation are not concomitant; one does not necessarily lead to the other. Rather, some catalyst (for instance, justice, healing, or restitution) must intervene. Rather than assume that knowledge of 'truth' will stimulate a voluntary realignment of social and power relations, I examine one communicative model for motivating both conceptual *and* material evolutions: the theory of interest-convergence. To be clear, I whole-heartedly support the idea that understanding generates respect (both self and mutual). Education *is* a vital component of decolonization efforts. It is crucial to challenge racism in school curricula as well as in broader media discourse. But society can do more, and advocates can be more strategic in their efforts. A rigorous communication strategy will cover multiple bases and not rely on sanguine assessments of audience motivations.

I first provide background on the Canadian TRC and then offer several samples of TRC Chairperson, The Honourable Justice Murray Sinclair's (2010) rhetorical framing of the Commission's work. I look primarily at two important speeches from the TRC's third year of operation: one to the Canadian Senate, and one to the United Nations Permanent Forum on Indigenous Issues. This short chapter provides a necessarily partial overview of the Commission's operations. In July 2015, the TRC released a sweeping final report that summarizes its findings. I do not intend to simplify this complex and vital work. Although by no means fully representative of the Commission's comprehensive approach to cross-generational trauma and healing, the two examined speeches indicate a significant rhetorical pattern. The chapter's second half outlines the theory of interest convergence and offers several illustrative examples of the theory in action.

Canada's Truth and Reconciliation Commission

Broad Canadian awareness about the disenfranchised status of Indigenous peoples can be traced to the 1990 so-called Oka Crisis in

Oka, Québec, an event that coincided with the beginnings of 24-hour television news. That summer, the country's attention was focused on a 77-day standoff between Mohawk protestors, and provincial police and Canadian armed forces. The event catalysed First Nations across the country, and the federal government made efforts to appease First Nations communities by promising to create a Royal Commission on Aboriginal People that would investigate federal Aboriginal policies and their recurrent negative impacts. In 1998, the federal government issued a 'Statement of Reconciliation', an acknowledgement of the problems created by government policies over multiple generations. Above all, the document spotlighted the official policy of assimilation, premised upon racist attitudes of cultural superiority. In addition, Indian and Northern Affairs Canada provided a $350 million grant to found the Aboriginal Healing Foundation (2010), an organization tasked with assisting those affected by the residential schools.

These moves did not pacify Indigenous demands for restitution, reparations, and justice; the federal government and churches faced 12,000 individual abuse claims, and several class-action lawsuits representing approximately 70,000 former Indian Residential School students. Media coverage of survivors' accounts of abuse focused the country's attention on disreputable elements of federal policy towards Indigenous peoples. As a legal exigency, and following negotiations with churches, the Assembly of First Nations, and other Indigenous groups, the federal government agreed to a $1.9 billion settlement that included common experience payments to survivors, and the creation of healing and commemoration funds and a Truth and Reconciliation Commission. By doing so, the Government of Canada shifted away from a policy of dealing with lawsuits on individual bases, and conceded its role in the systematic and racially-motivated attack on Indigenous collectivities over the country's full history.

The TRC, imagined as a 'cornerstone of the settlement agreement' (Harper, 2008), is tasked with a set of substantial responsibilities. Its mandate is both to create 'an accurate and public historical record of the past', and to document the residential schools' ongoing legacy (TRC, 2010), thereby linking past and present. Striving to promote public awareness about the IRS system and its repercussions, the Commission ultimately aims to 'Guide and inspire Indigenous peoples and Canadians in a process of truth and healing that will lead toward reconciliation and renewed relationships' (TRC, 2010).

Since the 1970s, over 20 countries have established truth commissions in efforts to address violent and conflicted histories (examples include South Africa, Sierra Leone, Argentina, Chile, the Philippines, East Timor, the Solomon Islands). Such bodies aim to create a permanent public record of past injustices, and provide discursive space for victims' stories. Critics of such commissions question whether a focus on repentance, forgiveness, and healing, sacrifices goals of justice and the rule of law. One can argue that a focus on violent pasts risks dividing communities, neglecting the present, imposing contemporary moral codes onto historical actors, inappropriately assuaging responsibility, or averting attention from the more serious work of legal and political negotiation regarding material restitution and redistribution (Barkan and Alexander, 2006, p. 6). These are valid concerns. Indeed, the promises of truth commissions are somewhat spectral. Both 'truth' and 'reconciliation' are famously contested ideas. I define reconciliation as *a series of acts that create willingness to anticipate a shared future*. My focus is the national scale; the following emphasize issues of intra-national political and economic justice. Others have defined the term as the act of 'building or rebuilding relationships today that are not haunted by the conflicts and hatreds of yesterday' (Hayner, 2001, p. 161), a *'departure from violence'* (Borneman, 2002, p. 282), a voluntary process of addressing fractured relationships (Hamber and Kelly, 2004, p. 27), and as 'the point of encounter where concerns about both the past and the future can meet' (Lederach, 1997, p. 27). Although each definition focuses attention on a unique locus, there is broad agreement on several key features. First, truth and reconciliation are not synonymous, and may, indeed, prove incompatible. More important (in certain contexts) might be an end to violent threat, a reparations programme, an end to structural inequalities (and thus supply of basic material needs), and/or the bringing together of formerly opposed groups. Second, truth commissions are a starting point – they should not attempt to finalize/close episodes of historical injustice. Minow (1999) claims that truth commissions proceed with 'the assumption that it helps individuals to tell their stories and to have them acknowledged officially' (p. 61). Public acknowledgement of these previously silenced narratives can serve as the grounds for future discussion about social reconfigurations. Yet Hayner (2001) cautions that 'expectations for truth commissions are almost always greater than what these bodies can ever reasonably hope to achieve' (p. 8).

Without question, public knowledge about Canada's racially motivated and discriminatory policies towards the country's first inhabitants is deficient. As noted by Ladner (2009), 'For Indigenous peoples, the

story of Canada is one of myth, magic, deceit, occupation, and genocide. For Canadians, the story is one of discovery, lawful acquisition,
and the establishment of peace, order, and good governance' (p. 279).
Plainly articulating the government's aggressive assimilation policy,
Duncan Campbell Scott, head of the Department of Indian Affairs from
1913 to 1932, once wrote:

> I want to get rid of the Indian problem. I do not think as a matter of
> fact, that the country ought to continuously protect a class of people
> who are able to stand alone ... Our objective is to continue until
> there is not a single Indian in Canada that has not been absorbed
> into the body politic and there is no Indian question, and no Indian
> Department, that is the whole object of this Bill
>
> (As cited in Leslie, 1978, p. 114)

This history has for decades been silenced in mainstream media
and educational curricula. The result is that most Canadians are
mis-educated – ignorant about crucial elements of the country's history.
Following a generous reading of non-Indigenous Canadians' ethical
principles, one might therefore assume that ongoing discrimination
and socio-economic inequality are the consequences of imperfect
information. Given accurate knowledge, citizens would support social
programs directed towards socio-economic justice. Within this framework, an educational campaign might employ a range of rhetorical
tactics to address this exigency: foreground and personalize Indigenous
success stories (achieved despite difficult circumstances), move beyond
stereotypes, depict hard-working families with two parents striving to
raise healthy children, and highlight youth experiences and hopes.
Such tactics are precisely what Kinew (2012) foregrounds in the CBC
documentary series *8th Fire*. This is a charitable model. Without doubt,
efforts to challenge stereotypes are crucial, as are narratives that link
historical practice to the present by articulating the continued expression of underlying racist values. However, a communication strategy
aimed at maximizing its chances for success will take many forms, and
not restrict itself to sanguine understandings of non-Indigenous motivations, nor speak only to those individuals prone to respond favour-
ably to Indigenous political and territorial aspirations. In the current
colonial environment, enhanced historical education is a vital, but not
necessarily sufficient counterweight to that history's legacy: widespread
socio-economic inequity, broken communities, animosity, and a fractured relationship.

I wish to affirm that my position is sympathetic to the (at least occasional) optimism of rhetorical critics Farrell and McPhail (2005) who argue: 'there always exists the possibility that justice might become something more than the interests of the stronger or the protection of privilege' (p. 249). Humans have the capacity for identification and compassion, and communication may articulate needs and identities, and cultivate solidarity and integration. This hopeful narrative lies at the heart of TRC Chairperson, the Honourable Justice Murray Sinclair's (2010) public statements.

TRC Chairperson, the Honourable Justice Murray Sinclair

In a speech to the Canadian Senate, Sinclair (2010) outlines key elements of the Commission's mandate:

> To tell Canadians about the history of the residential schools, to give [those] affected by the schools the opportunity to participate in the telling of that history through national and community events and statement gathering, to collect all records relevant to that history and impact, [and] to help commemorate this history ... In this way, the Commission is intended to play an important role in truth-telling, as well as in healing and reconciliation within Aboriginal families and between Aboriginal and non-Aboriginal people, churches, governments and Canadians generally. ('Presentation' 3)

The above offers a succinct overview of the Commission's crucial objectives. Noticeably absent, however, is clarification of the relationship between 'truth-telling' and 'healing and reconciliation'. The connotation is that educating mainstream Canadians about a transparent undercurrent throughout the country's history will foster improved relations between Indigenous and non-Indigenous citizens.

This reconciliation model is openly premised upon a hopeful (perhaps generous) assessment of Canadian society:

> Most Canadians do not realize ... that for there to be true reconciliation, they must be part of the solution. Education, delivered through residential schools, was the tool for assimilation. It was education that helped to perpetuate the situation we see today for Indigenous Peoples in Canada. We at the TRC believe that it will be education, again, that will be the tool that best addresses all of that, for education will create knowledge and from knowledge will come understanding. From understanding will come respect – both

self-respect for Indigenous people and mutual respect for all. ('For the Child Taken' p. 9)

Sinclair here affirms education's central role in reconciliation efforts. The reference to mainstream Canadians' 'false belief in their own supe-riority' (the consequence of faulty educational practices) suggests that generations have grown up with a partial understanding of their coun-try's history, and have been deprived of the opportunity to learn from the land's original inhabitants.

Continuing a hopeful reading of non-Indigenous society, Sinclair stresses the importance of education to both assimilationist policy, and efforts to address/challenge that system's legacy:

Education, or what passed for it, got us into this situation, and education is what will lead us out. Schools seem to us to be one of the best vehicles to create and sustain a change in the attitude of all Canadians. ('Presentation' p. 6)

In a presentation to the United Nations, he provides a still fuller indict-ment of Canada's failed education system. Because the speech clearly articulates the presumed sequence of, and relation between, flawed edu-cational programmes and racial discrimination, I quote at length:

The history of residential schools is likely the least known dimension of Canadian history. It is not taught in our schools. It is not com-memorated anywhere in our country or in our national capital. The 150-year history of residential schools has not been made a part of our national memory. It has been ignored or, worse, dismissed. What is known however to most Canadians is the present legacy: that Indigenous Peoples in Canada do not have the same standard of life that is enjoyed by mainstream Canada. They easily fall into the trap of blaming Indigenous people for the conditions in which they live and for failing to address their problems adequately. That blaming leads inevitably to disrespect. That disrespect however also comes from the many generations of public policy founded on the view that white Euro-Canadians were superior, a view supported by law and taught in schools to Indigenous and non-Indigenous students alike. ('For the Child Taken' p. 8)

Implicit herein is an argument that settler Canadians, and specifi-cally those of European heritage, can be effectively re-educated about Indigenous nations and the historical, racist origins of contemporary socio-economic disparities. Such education will require both critical listening and a genuine willingness to change. But the (implied) result might be a transformation of Canadian identity and the establishment of more just social relations.

Again, the passages above do not represent the totality of the Canadian TRC's complex work. Nonetheless, the recurrent correlation of education and social change therein constitutes an important narrative pattern. Education *is* a crucial dimension of battles for justice. But it is part of a larger picture. Questions remain as to whether substantive institutional reform will accompany the TRC's accomplishments. Some suggest that public recognition of historical injustice is consequential only when supplemented by material reparations. For instance, Wilson (2004) has emphasized the structural dimensions of US racial inequity and argued that even an official federal apology for slavery 'would not add much to the configuration of race relations, because it [would] not challenge the systems that structure those relations' (p. 375). Canada did pay $1.9 billion in reparations to survivors of the Indian Residential School system. But even if the federal government was willing to meet First Nations' demands for substantial land rights (a viable option, as Crown lands could be relinquished), this would likely require extensive support from the voting public.

It's worth emphasizing that the Canadian TRC operates in a context very different from that of the more famous South African example. In the latter instance, the group seeking reconciliation and redress was the large majority. By contrast, Indigenous peoples constitute just four percent of Canada's population and therefore do not possess the capacity to pressure governments solely through traditional political channels (specifically, voting). There are of course exceptions to this general rule, and First Nations have proven extraordinarily adept at fighting for sovereignty through legal channels. Nonetheless, with respect to democratic processes, public argument plays a critical role in the pragmatics of securing non-Indigenous support for Indigenous political autonomy and land rights. In the following I outline one theoretical approach for motivating substantive political and economic change: the idea of interest convergence.

Interest convergence: the challenge of motivation

I have suggested that in Canada's colonial context, widespread historical knowledge may not be sufficient to spark a realignment of power bases and material resources. The Indigenous population is small, and it is easy for non-Indigenous Canadians to say, 'I did not commit these aggressive acts against their culture; that happened before I was born'. Indeed, Blackburn (2007) observes a broad recalcitrance towards reparations in the Canadian context: 'Even when nonaboriginal people are sympathetic to aboriginal claims, they often recoil when it comes down to the redistribution of entitlements' (p. 633).

Rational argument has limited capacity to motivate change; it is only when passion and understanding are brought together that will is kindled. Writing in the late eighteenth century, philosopher George Campbell (1990) proposed a formula for motivating action. First, gain attention via imagination. Second, gain understanding. Third, excite the passions in order to achieve the ultimate objective: move the will. The question is therefore: what is required to foster political mobilization? Media campaigns and mass publicity hold promise. Yet guilt is an imperfect motivator. Audiences have attention limits and repetition may lead to fatigue.

Communication theorist Larry Gross once warned me that neither wishful thinking nor complaints constitute solid research. This advice aligns with millennia of rhetorical theory that emphasizes the importance of addressing concrete practicalities. Writing in Toronto's *Globe and Mail*, Coates and Poelzer (2012) have noted that much commentary on Indigenous problems in Canada locates blame with one of two camps: the federal government, or First Nations themselves. They suggest, rather, that 'Canadians as a whole have to take ownership of the challenges facing first-nations communities'. A laudable proposition, this solution nonetheless neglects to address the challenge of motivation. 'Canadians as a whole' may not voluntarily reach out towards, and support the political efforts of, their Indigenous fellow citizens. Such actions often require a push.

Humans accept socio-political and economic systems because they think them beneficial to their interests, cannot imagine an alternative, or believe the current status quo is natural (Hall, 1982, p. 65). Emphasizing the need for non-Indigenous education, Canada's TRC foregrounds the last (and related second) of these reasons. Others have focused, rather, on the first. In such cases, more information may never be enough to prompt those who benefit from the current status quo to relinquish their advantage. Wilson (2004), for instance, argues that efforts to dismantle systems of privilege require more than appeals to ethics or justice – they require a perception of interest convergence. I agree and thus propose that education alone is an insufficient counterweight to colonial legacies (at least within the short-term).

Non-Indigenous Canadians are more likely to support substantive restitution to First Nations if doing so can be framed as an economic, as well as ethical, imperative.

In some instances, early relations between settlers and Indigenous peoples in what became Canada were based upon trade and mutual benefit. It is when numbers shifted towards a European majority that settlers entrenched unjust and discriminatory practices (Lutz, 2009, p. 275). This history aligns with the insights of critical race theory. Much popular discussion about reconciliation builds upon the tacit premise that education about past injustices and/or atrocities ensures that such events will 'never again' reoccur. Critical race theory highlights the habitual failure of this promise. Its theorists break from a tradition of thinking summarized by Myrdal (1944): racial advance takes place as a result of expanding white self-awareness (in other words, gradual understanding of the moral dissonance between national mythology and lived practice). The new argument rather, can be traced back to Carmichael and Hamilton's (1967) assertion that:

> [P]olitical relations are based on self-interest: benefits to be gained and losses to be avoided. For the most part, man's politics is determined by his evaluation of material good and evil. Politics results from a conflict of interests, not of consciences. (p. 75)

Echoing this argument, Bell Jr. (1980) asserts that white US political leaders have historically worked to advance racial justice primarily due to self-interest. Arguing that 'The interest of blacks in achieving racial equality will be accommodated only when it converges with the interests of whites' (p. 523), he tracks the development of US civil rights to Cold War soft power campaigns, efforts to secure electoral support and industrialization in the South, and the exigencies created by large wars and the associated necessity for stability and mass mobilization (pp. 524–525).

This analysis correlates with the rhetorical tradition's emphasis on audience-centered tactics. Discussing the world of US campaign politics, Schell (1996) writes, 'the path to power is far smoother if one gives the people what they already believe they want than if one undertakes the arduous business of persuading them to want something else' (p. 72), while Cashin (2005) argues, 'In the ordinary, day-to-day struggle of a political or policy battle, progressives would do better to be realistic about human nature and strategize accordingly' (p. 276). 'Human nature' is here understood as a combination of existing beliefs, and perceived interests. Beliefs can be altered through public advocacy and education, but perceived interests constitute a powerful evaluative factor. In the words of the Reverend Dr. Martin Luther King Jr. (1991), 'freedom is never voluntarily given by the oppressor; it must be demanded by the oppressed' (p. 72). During the 1960's US civil rights movement, Malcolm X (1964) voiced broad scepticism about the political efficacy of appeals to either American morality or the legal system. Asserting 'It is the government itself, the government of America, that is responsible for the oppression and exploitation and degradation of black people in this country', he censured white complacency: 'Don't change the white man's mind – you can't change his mind, and that whole thing about appealing to the moral conscience of America – America's conscience is bankrupt'.

Parallel arguments are justified regarding North American Indigenous struggle. Addressing US dynamics, Tinker (2003) denounces the vested interests at the heart of the political-economic order:

> It should be abundantly clear, to Indian and non-Indian, that Indian people can count on neither the US government, nor the churches of the United States, nor the private-sector institutions of free enterprise to solve any of the problems that these institutions have invested so much time in creating. (p. 4)

I commend work directed towards socio-economic justice on multiple fronts, indigenous and non-Indigenous. There is no magic bullet or simple solution to the problems of cross-generational racism, vested interests, and colonial power. To misquote Mao Zedong, let a thousand flowers bloom. Any contribution is part of a wider landscape. My focus here is specific: communicative strategies for motivating non-Indigenous Canadians to support the expansive project of decolonization/substantive reconciliation. Highly sympathetic to Barker's (2010) assertion that 'confronting oppression requires that some individuals within the hierarchy will have to make significant sacrifices' (p. 322), I worry that such normative claims evade pivotal pragmatic questions. Which individuals will make 'significant sacrifices'? What will these sacrifices entail? And most important, how can such individuals (or corporations, or governments) be motivated to make these sacrifices? Few individual property owners in Canada will voluntarily return title to First Nations communities. Corporations have legal obligations to amass profits for their shareholders. As a relatively minor (although fast-growing) segment of Canada's voting population, Indigenous peoples cannot realign the political/economic system overnight through traditional democratic votes.

So what strategies hold promise? Critical deconstruction of naturalized power configurations (such as the Canadian state) plays a vital role in reconciliation efforts. However, criticism entails also the invention of creative and pragmatic alternatives. In Canada's colonial present, this is a challenging prospect. A number of traditional rhetorical strategies are blunted by asymmetrical power dynamics. Appeals for moderation and allusions to a reasonable middle path have limits when the political landscape is aligned to one's perpetual disadvantage and the dominant party (including federal institutions) has no interest in, or motivation to entertain, serious negotiations. Appeals to inertia (doing nothing is easier than doing something) are counterproductive when the status quo is to one's disadvantage. Accentuating the educational (as opposed to persuasive) dimensions of decolonial pedagogies attains the benefits associated with apolitical truth, but even education has a finite capacity to motivate action (again, education *is* a crucial long-term factor). Finally, reliance on abstraction (for instance, peace, rights, reconciliation) secures the advantages of strategic ambiguity and polyphony. Difficult to attack, such abstractions also attract positive reception from broad and diverse audiences. However, due to their tactical imprecision, such concepts can be easily appropriated by one's opponents. When precisely defined, by contrast, abstractions can lose broader horizons of positive association.

The Canadian state operates from the central premise of federal sovereignty over First Nations. Given this backdrop, motivating substantive political realignments is a vexing challenge. In proposing that communicative solutions derived from a win-win model have the strongest chance of concrete success, I align my project with that of Allen (2004) who argues that 'Distrust can be overcome only when citizens manage to find methods of generating mutual benefit despite differences of position, experience, and perspective' (p. xix). Mutual benefit can take multiple forms, and communicative strategies might profitably target a number of specific frameworks. I below outline a range of potential models. Beginning with more extreme measures rooted in coercion and/or force, I gradually proceed towards an educational model based on a hopeful understanding of Canadian society. These models are not prescriptive; they simply provide an overview of a range of means by which to motivate serious dialogic engagement (including genuine listening and willingness to compromise) in parties not readily prone to such exchange. Crucially, target audiences need only encompass a sufficient number of people (particularly public leaders) to achieve the desired evolution.

Direct action

Direct action constitutes an important means to compel serious dialogic exchange. Such actions can take several forms. For instance, refusal to permit large-scale resource extraction on traditional Indigenous lands puts at risk the very foundation of Canada's economy. Alternatively, global shaming campaigns can spark civic and political discomfort that in turn inspires remedial action. Examples of the latter include the global media attention devoted to the plight of the Attawapiskat First Nation in northern Ontario, and the creation of the Royal Commission Report on Aboriginal Peoples as a result of the 1990 conflict between Mohawk protestors and federal armed forces in Oka, Québec. The tense image of Mohawk warrior (and University of Saskatchewan economics student) Brad Larocque facing off with Private Patrick Cloutier of the Canadian forces destroyed any comfortable national ideas about Indigenous complacency, invisibility, or passive resignation. A significant parallel can be drawn to the 1963 televised coverage from Birmingham, Alabama of white law enforcement officials attacking peaceful young black protestors with fire hoses and police dogs. In both cases, extensively publicized imagery made it impossible for the broader public to ignore ongoing national injustices. The cases of Oka and Birmingham are, of course, distinct. However, a comparative study of socio-political struggles can illuminate transferable insights.

Advocating for a comprehensive approach towards Indigenous resurgence, Kanien'kehaka scholar Alfred (2005) proposes 'non-violent agitation combined with the development of a collective capacity for self-defence, so as to generate within the Settler society a reason and incentive to negotiate constructively in the interest of achieving a respectful coexistence' (p. 27). If one believes that Indigenous nations have no reason to trust the federal government, and can, further, reasonably expect continued discrimination and homeland destruction, there is perhaps justification for this emphasis on self-defence. In the 1892 *Southern horrors: Lynch law in all its phases*, Ida Wells-Barnett (1892) addresses the racially motivated violence and extra-juridical murders common at the time in the US South. Her prescription for African-American survival includes economic development, urbanization (and associated political coordination), and independent media creation. However, she also explicitly advocates that 'a Winchester rifle should have a place of honor in every black home, and it should be used for that protection which the law refuses to give' (p. 20). 70 years later, this sentiment remained central to the civil rights struggle. Speaking in Cleveland, Malcolm X (1964) warned that the junction had arrived whereat the white political establishment had to choose between 'the ballot or the bullet'. I do not advocate for armed rebellion, or indeed any form of violence. Nonetheless, such direct assertions signify the polar opposite of passive submission to an unjust and unchanging status quo. In more moderate terms, ex-member of the Manitoba legislature Harper (Red Sucker Lake First Nation) (1994) once foregrounded the importance of assertive action to compel government cooperation: 'We do not need sympathy, we need action. We need support to force the government to deal with us' (p. 222). The central idea, one with strong warrants, is that disenfranchised groups must apply pressure to compel/motivate dominant institutions to engage in constructive discussions. Problems (including injustices) require concrete articulation before they demand redress.

Common ground

Another way to bring people together is through designation of a shared antagonist. Common ground, in other words, may be constituted by shared resistance to an external force. The key factor in this model is that the enemy cannot be one of the parties. Few individuals or groups are willing to work to their own perceived detriment. However, it is possible to locate a number of agents that might comprise a shared opposition. Highly promising, I believe, is collective Indigenous/non-Indigenous opposition to environmentally damaging governmental and/or corporate practices. A contemporary high-profile example involves widespread Indigenous opposition to the proposed Enbridge Northern Gateway Pipeline. Proposed to run from the tar/oil sands in Northern Alberta across British Columbia (BC) to Kitimat (at the mouth of deep coastal fjords), the project has encountered fierce resistance from First Nations opponents. Following this model, Indigenous knowledge systems might be associated with progressive environmental policy (significant ties might be drawn between traditional worldviews and contemporary environmental science). There is no guarantee that non-Indigenous persons will take the step from respecting Indigenous knowledge to respecting living Indigenous individuals and nations (for instance, many people practice Buddhist teachings without caring deeply about Tibetans' well-being), but this is nonetheless an acutely promising model.

Economic gain

There are also compelling economic reasons for non-Indigenous Canadians to support the aspirations of Indigenous peoples. Grievous

Indigenous rates of school dropout and fetal alcohol syndrome fundamentally harm the whole country. Indigenous youth constitute one of Canada's fastest growing populations. Urban, youthful, and technologically sophisticated, this demographic has the capacity to make significant contributions to Canada's economic and cultural development. First Nations desire a fair share (parallel to that enjoyed by other groups), but also self-governance and the capacity to develop economic self-sufficiency. Moving beyond financial dependence on the state, many Indigenous communities strive to contribute to mutual betterment and multilateral economic development (Kinew, 2012).

Appeals to financial stability and investor confidence have extraordinary potential in an economic environment (such as Canada's) structured around natural resource extraction. One need only look at the severe legal challenges facing the proposed Northern Gateway Pipeline to appreciate the economic leverage of First Nations that refuse to cooperate with federal ambitions regarding unceded territories. Legal settlements (including treaties) can additionally pre-empt future lawsuits. Indeed, it is worth recalling that the federal government's $1.9 billion settlement to IRS survivors (an agreement that included creation of the TRC) was prompted by federal desire to conclude legal liability for the IRS system and its legacy.

Not surprisingly, the BC government has previously employed an interest convergence model that foregrounds economic concerns. In 1990, the province asked PricewaterhouseCoopers to calculate the cost to the province of unsettled treaties. The final report determined that 'uncertainty surrounding unresolved aboriginal rights and title could cost BC $1 billion in lost investment and 1,500 jobs a year in the mining and forestry sectors alone'. The BC Treaty Commission cites a 2009 report by the same organization to claim that 'completing treaties with First Nations will deliver more than $10 billion in benefits to British Columbia's economy over the next 15 years' (BC Treaty Commission, 2009). The federal Minister of Indian Affairs outlined this same argument when he introduced the Nisga'a treaty bill in the House of Commons in 1999:

> By clearly setting out the rights of the Nisga'a people as related to the ownership and use of lands and resources, the treaty provides certainty. This certainty will foster an economic climate conducive to attracting investment and creating jobs while at the same time providing an opportunity for the Nisga'a to protect their culture. I cannot overemphasize the importance of certainty to the future of British Columbia. During the approximately 500 public consultations and information meetings which were held in BC during

the Nisga'a negotiations the business community made one thing perfectly clear: certainty is essential to a strong economic future for the province.

(As cited in Blackburn, 2005, p. 594)

In claiming that Indigenous land claims should be taken seriously for reasons of non-Indigenous material self-interest, the federal government's position aligns with the theory of interest convergence. To be clear, the allusion to Nisga'a efforts to 'protect their culture' reads like an afterthought. Corporate and/or federal interests often don't align with those of First Nations. For instance, one can imagine a mining corporation striving to minimize Indigenous control over traditional territories. My point is not that interest convergence works in all contexts. Indeed, the model may be inappropriate in some settings wherein interests are fundamentally discordant. However, even if not ultimately employed, a communication plan derived from this model will maximize understanding of key actors' motivations, and therefore support an informed strategy.

National mythology

Of course, interests are not solely material, nor economic; there are perhaps more comprehensive models for motivating socio-political realignment. Canada's mythology pivots on ideals of fairness, peace, cultural pluralism, rule of law, egalitarianism, and tolerance. While lived experience often falls short of such ideals, I believe a communicative strategy might productively challenge non-Indigenous citizens to align practice with national mythology.

A compelling tactic involves drawing equivalences between past and present through a demonstrated continuity of habitual values. Knowledge of historical fact is one thing. Appreciation of history's contemporary legacy is another. And despite the powerful appeal of abstractions such as 'progress' and 'forward', prejudicial values may have resilience. A promising educational model might therefore articulate historical injustices' expression into the present. In other words, one might *animate* the past by articulating its contemporary relevance. By acknowledging the story and ethics that informed (justified) historical discrimination, and then linking those values to current practices, an educational campaign might articulate how racism continues to permeate contemporary experience. For instance, one might draw an analogy between the pervasive colonial belief that Canadians of European descent were superior to Indigenous peoples, and present-day instances of governments acting 'on behalf of Indigenous communities' without consultation. By establishing narrative continuity from past to present, one might thereby interrogate the justifications for current socio-political relations, and concretize otherwise transparent ideologies. Here, the distinction between historical injustice and contemporary (often peripheralized) discrimination dissipates. Minow (1999) writes, 'Effective education must connect the histories of mass atrocities with students' own lives and personal experiences' (p. 145). I believe this counsel applies broadly to peacebuilding efforts.

Unconvinced that accenting mythological dissonance is a sufficient motivator, I nonetheless believe promise lies in appeals to *honour*. Honour entails integrity and a commitment to justice and legal standards. I write this with significant scepticism, one day after a Missouri grand jury decided not to indict the white police officer who killed black teenager Michael Brown in Ferguson on 9 August 2014. Due to a long history of unequal treatment, many African-Americans lack faith in the US justice system, and many Indigenous persons in Canada likewise distrust that nation's justice establishment. Serious limitations notwithstanding, and in the spirit of exploring multiple tactics, I believe a promising way forward might take the form of a re-validated centuries-old partnership, one conceptualized in light of the original treaty agreements between First Nations and colonial governments. Struggles for racial and political-economic justice require multiple configurations (extending beyond polite calls for civic discussion). History suggests the limits of disenfranchised communities' reliance upon dominant groups or institutions for major social change. Direct action and appeals to shame or fear have their place, but the restoration of mutual honour might also constitute a reciprocal and positive advance. Above all, a rigorous communication strategy will engage precise contexts with a focused understanding of key audience (and specifically decision makers') commitments.

Closing thoughts

Sinclair (2010) is aware of the challenges facing the TRC. An address to the Canadian Senate in 2010 emphasizes the abstract nature of the Commission's mandate and the ambiguous contours of reconciliation:

> There are no quick fixes. Uncovering the truth will be difficult, but achieving reconciliation will be more-so, because Canadians are not

yet agreed on what reconciliation means or what it will look like. That is a fundamentally important conversation which has yet to happen. ('Presentation' 3)

I whole-heartedly agree with the above. Justice in Canada's colonial present mandates that non-Indigenous citizens seriously listen to alternative (at times uncomfortable) histories. Indeed, political scientist Cairns (2000) argues that because the status quo favours the majority history, non-Indigenous citizens 'have a greater obligation to listen and to practice a self-restraint than do the Aboriginal participants' (p. 40). Although sympathetic to this idea, I believe the task is exceptionally challenging. Listening is never a given. Principles of intercultural respect lie at the heart of democratic community, but ideals can be difficult to actualize. Emerging communication technologies allow political leaders to employ targeted messaging. The same technologies allow individuals to filter information sources. As one's views are confirmed, they may be intensified to the extent that understanding of, and cooperation with, others beyond a self-selected group becomes more difficult. Critical reflection may suffer. Polarization and fragmentation of the populace do not bode well for a democratic system founded upon the ideals that individual participation matters, and that everyone, despite the final result of a given election, has an equal stake in the system and will be protected and respected by fellow citizens (Hollihan, 2009; Howard, 2006).

Temporarily bracketing the challenge of media echo chambers, why should non-Native Canadians seriously listen to Indigenous histories? We live in a world of abundant narratives. And even having listened, what is the likelihood that individuals will be willing to support substantive socio-economic change and a re-envisioning of the political environment? My point is that saying we need to hold a national conversation, and that those in positions of privilege have the obligation to stretch/challenge their worldviews, is quite different from actually motivating individuals to do so. Knowledge of suppressed histories may foster awareness and perhaps challenge stereotypes, yet such knowledge does not automatically equate to a willingness to relinquish material privilege potentially correlated with that history. The trope of conversation is readily employed as a political weapon and/or distraction; calls for dialogue may circumvent demands for concrete action.

The core challenge is to make a dovetailed transition from accurate historical knowledge to a more just societal configuration. Although the Canadian TRC's mandate is to create public forums for Indigenous voices and histories, its work revolves around issues of economic and institutional reform. By exploring one aspect of the TRC's efforts to foster broad support for substantive socio-political evolution, I have taken a moment to reflect on the power of narrative-based education. Knowledge *can* initiate political change, and dialogue *can* foster understanding. However, it may be counterproductive to presuppose these outcomes. Outlining an approach to peacebuilding that is both hopeful *and* pragmatic, the chapter encourages scholars and practitioners of peace education to pause and contemplate the translucent relation between knowledge and socio-political change.

References

T. Alfred (2005) *Wasáse: Indigenous Pathways of Action and Freedom* (Toronto: University of Toronto Press).

D. Allen (2004) *Talking to Strangers: Anxieties of Citizenship since Brown v. Board of Education* (Chicago: University of Chicago Press).

E. Barkan and K. Alexander (eds) (2006) *Taking Wrongs Seriously: Apologies and Reconciliation* (Palo Alto: Stanford University Press).

A. Barker (2010) 'From Adversaries to Allies: Forging Respectful Alliances between Indigenous and Settler Peoples', in L. Davis (ed.) *Alliances: Re/Envisioning Indigenous–non-Indigenous Relationships* (Vancouver: UBC Press) pp. 316–333.

BC Treaty Commission (2009) Financial Issues, http://www.bctreaty.net/files/issues_financial.php, date accessed 27 May 2015.

D. Bell Jr. (1980) 'Brown v. Board of Education and the Interest-Convergence Dilemma', *Harvard Law Review*, 93, 519–533.

C. Blackburn (2005) 'Searching for Guarantees in the Midst of Uncertainty: Negotiating Aboriginal Rights and Title in British Columbia', *American Anthropologist*, 107, 586–596.

C. Blackburn (2007) 'Producing Legitimacy: Reconciliation and the Negotiation of Aboriginal Rights in Canada', *Journal of the Royal Anthropological Institute*, 13, 621–638.

J. Borneman (2002) 'Reconciliation after Ethnic Cleansing: Listening, Retribution, Affiliation', *Public Culture*, 14, 281–304.

A. Cairns (2000) *Citizens Plus: Aboriginal Peoples and the Canadian State* (Vancouver: UBC Press).

G. Campbell (1990) 'The Philosophy of Rhetoric', in J. Golden and E. Corbett (eds) *The rhetoric of Blair, Campbell, and Whately* (Carbondale: Southern Illinois University Press).

S. Carmichael and C. Hamilton (1967) *Black Power: The Politics of Liberation in America* (New York: Vintage Books).

S. Cashin (2005) 'Shall we Overcome? Transcending Race, Class, and Ideology through Interest Convergence', *St. John's Law Review*, 79, 253–291.

K. Coates and G. Poelzer (September 6, 2012) 'We are all Responsible for the Plight of Canada's First Nations', *Globe and Mail*.

T. Farrell and M. McPhail (2005) 'Reparations or Separation?: The Rhetoric of Racism in Black and White', in F. V. Eemeren and P. Houtlosser (eds) *Argumentation in Practice* (Philadelphia: John Benjamins Publishing Company) pp. 231–250.

S. Hall (1982) 'The Rediscovery of "Ideology": Return of the Repressed in Media Studies', in M. Gurevitch, T. Bennett, J. Curran and J. Woollacott (eds) *Culture, Society and the Media* (London: Metheun and Co) pp. 354–364.

B. Hamber and G. Kelly (2004) 'A Working Definition of Reconciliation', *Democratic Dialogue*. Accessed at, http://cain.ulst.ac.uk/dd/papers/dd04recon-def.pdf.

E. Harper (1994) 'Keynote Address', in A. Morrison (ed.) *Justice for Natives: Searching for Common Ground* (Montréal: McGill-Queen's Press) pp. 219–227.

S. Harper (2008) Prime Minister Harper Offers Full Apology on Behalf of Canadians for the Indian Residential Schools System, http://www.pm.gc.ca/eng/news/2008/06/11/prime-minister-harper-offers-full-apology-behalf-canadians-indian-residential, date accessed 27 May 2015.

P. Hayner (2001) *Unspeakable Truths: Facing the Challenge of Truth Commissions* (New York: Routledge).

T. Hollihan (2009). *Uncivil Wars: Political Campaigns in a Media Age* (Boston: Bedrod/St. Martin's).

P. Howard (2006) *New Media Campaigns and the Managed Citizen* (New York: Cambridge University Press).

International Center for Transitional Justice (2014) https://www.ictj.org/our-work/regions-and-countries/canada, date accessed 27 May 2015.

W. Kinew (2012) *8th Fire*, CBC.

King Jr., M. L. (1991) 'Letter from Birmingham City Jail', in H. Bedau (ed.) *Civil Disobedience in Focus* (New York: Routledge).

R. Kipling (1899). The White Man's Burden, http://www.fordham.edu/halsall/mod/Kipling.html., date accessed 27 May 2015.

K. Ladner (2009) 'Reconciling Constitutional Orders', in A. Timpson (ed.) *First Nations, First Thoughts* (Vancouver: UBC Press) pp. 279–300.

J. Lederach (1997) *Building Peace: Sustainable Reconciliation in Divided Societies* (Washington, DC: United States Institute of Peace Press).

J. Leslie (1978) *The Historical Development of the Indian Act*, 2nd edn (Ottawa: Department of Indian Affairs and Northern Development, Treaties and Historical Research Branch).

J. Lutz (2009) *Makúk: A New History of Aboriginal-White Relations* (Vancouver: UBC Press).

X. Malcolm (1964) The ballot or the bullet, http://www.edchange.org/multicultural/speeches/malcolm_x_ballot.html, date accessed 27 May 2015.

J. Miller (1996) *Shingwauk's Vision: A History of Native Residential Schools* (Toronto: University of Toronto Press).

M. Minow (1999) *Between Vengeance and Forgiveness: Facing History after Genocide and Mass Violence* (Boston: Beacon Press).

G. Myrdal (1944) *An American Dilemma: The Negro Problem and Modern Democracy* (New York: Harper and Brothers).

J. Schell (1996) 'The Uncertain Leviathan', *The Atlantic Monthly*, 278, 70–78.

M. Sinclair (2010) For the Child Taken, for the Parent Left Behind: 9th Session of the United Nations Permanent Forum on Indigenous Issues, http://www.trc.ca/websites/trcinstitution/index.php?p=14, date accessed May 27 2015.

M. Sinclair (2010) Presentation to the Senate Committee on Aboriginal Peoples, http://www.trc.ca/websites/trcinstitution/index.php?p=14, date accessed May 27 2015.

G. Tinker (2003) *Spirit and Resistance: Political Theology and American Indian Liberation* (Minneapolis: Augsburg Fortress).

Truth and Reconciliation Commission of Canada (2010) For the Child Taken, for the Parent left Behind, http://www.trc.ca/websites/trcinstitution/File/pdfs/TRC_UN_Speech_CMS_FINAL_April_27_2010.pdf, date accessed 27 May 2015.

I. Wells-Barnett (1892). Southern Horrors: Lynch Law in all its Phases, http://www.gutenberg.org/files/14975/14975-h/14975-h.htm, date accessed 27 May 2015.

K. Wilson (2004) 'Is there Interest in Reconciliation?', *Rhetoric & Public Affairs*, 7, 367–377.

11
Pakistani Cultural Characteristics: Updated VSM Scores and Facework Geared towards Increasing Women's Access to Education

Rebecca Merkin

Social science has many specializations including psychology, sociology, anthropology, and communication studies and while they have all claimed their individual domains, these fields all include the concepts of culture, conflict, and peace education. The interdisciplinary nature of culture, conflict, and peace education is natural because social scientists from all fields have varying perspectives on how to study phenomena. For example, psychological researchers observe cultural differences that result in different value perceptions. A number of psychologists study the relationships among different value types, (such as individualism and collectivism) and the conflicts and compatibilities experienced when pursuing them (Hofstede, 2001, Schwartz, 1994). They create structures that relate systems of value priorities, as an integrated whole, to conflicts and tend to apply peace education based on this perspective. Cultural sociologists focus on societal aspects of conflict and peace education, focusing on human rights violations, social bases of conflict such as race and ethnicity, immigration, gender, identity, development, and culture, and associated remedies for peace. They also study how schools as institutions teach about peace reflecting societal objectives for peace education. Anthropologists observe, study, and describe thick culture based on participant observation in which they become a part of what they are studying. Through subjective cultural analysis their observations allow them to go deeply into the details of the cultures they live in and study. For example, anthropologists may move to a developing country and join a local NGO and report on it. Anthropologists may also employ critical analyses of societal aid programs in a similar way to sociologists, with a more anthropological focus. Finally, intercultural communication researchers analyse how people from different cultures encode and decode messages differently (Hulbert, 1994) and like psychologists, study how varying cultural dimensions influence human behavior (Triandis and Albert, 1987). They also teach cultural values to apply them to peace education.

Besides the different perspectives of different social scientific fields, there are also multiple methods of collecting and analysing data to study culture, conflict, and peace education. There are qualitative and quantitative researchers in psychology, sociology, anthropology, and communication and critical researchers in all disciplines. As a result of the large number of methods possible to examine culture, conflict, and its impact on peace education, one can view peace education from a variety of interdisciplinary perspectives.

Importance of the deconstruction and reconstruction of current ideologies in peace and conflict education

Part of the reason there are conflicts in the world is because people who have differing ideologies on education, for example, become entrenched in their positions. Each party stakes out their territory and the resources they want to keep and will not give in to the other party's needs or demands. However, different perspectives can be attained by opening up the minds of the parties in a conflict through construction and deconstruction of each other's words. This can be accomplished by identifying how their construction of a concept (in this case, the education of women in Pakistan) is perceived. Then deconstructing or portraying how they their rhetoric is implying one thing but is actually saying something else. In addition, deconstruction allows one to highlight the authors' of texts actual perspective further by challenging the denotative meaning of their utterance; or by pointing out particular aspects that are left out of their statement to expose the other person's position in order to argue with it. In this vein, this chapter will give some background on the fight to improve education for women in Pakistan, including the famous case of Malala Yousaphzai, then highlight the Pakistani government's newly enacted constitutional amendment, known as the *Right to Free and Compulsory Education Act*. A deconstruction of this Act will be carried out to explain how this text is not enough to improve education for women in Pakistan. In addition, cultural dimensions will be analysed and explained using data collected using Hofstede's (1994) Value Survey Module (VSM). This quantitative study was carried out to update and explain the present cultural characteristics in Pakistan in comparison to the US. The results of the data calculated will be applied to focus more specifically on the current situation in Pakistan. Finally, given Pakistan's cultural characteristics, this chapter concludes with ideas for possible peacebuilding efforts to improve the education of women in Pakistan.

Deconstruction

Recently, a lot of press has been given to Malala Yousafzai's situation in Pakistan's Swat Valley. When Malala was young, her hometown remained a popular tourist spot that was known for its summer festivals. However, as she was growing up, the area began to change as the Taliban tried to take control. Malala attended a school that her father, Ziauddin Yousafzai, had founded. The Taliban is against girls going to school and getting educated. Consequently, the Taliban staged a campaign to shutter or bomb hundreds of schools in Pakistan's remote Swat Valley. Malala's reaction was to give a speech in Peshawar, Pakistan, in September 2008. Her talk was entitled, *How dare the Taliban take away my basic right to education?* Malala's activist activities continued in early 2009, when she began blogging for the BBC about living under the Taliban's intimidation and threats to deny her an education. In order to hide her identity, Malala used the pseudonym Gul Makai. However, she was revealed to be the BBC blogger in 2009.

Malala continued to find opportunities to speak out about her rights, and the rights of all women, to an education. However, in October, 2012, after Malala boarded her school bus in Swat Valley, Taliban gunmen asked for her by name, then fired three gunshots at the left side of her head. In the days immediately following the attack, she remained in a critical condition, but later her condition improved enough for her to be flown to a hospital in Birmingham, England for intensive rehabilitation. An immense outpouring of international support for Malala occurred after the shooting, which continued during her recovery.

Although a large number of Islamic clerics in Pakistan issued a fatwā against those who tried to kill her, the Taliban reiterated its intent to kill Yousafzai and her father. On her 16th birthday Malala gave a speech at the United Nations on women's rights to education and the negative acts of the Taliban, which further ignited their ire. In response, a top Taliban spokesman said in a telephone interview that the group would continue to look for opportunities to harm the 16-year-old girl, as long as she remained an outspoken critic of efforts to impose strict Islamic law in Pakistan (Craig and Mehsud, 2013).

While the Taliban claims that their concerns and stance against education are based in Islamic law, theorists claim that Pakistani policies and laws on marriage and women's education are actually methods of control to protect power and property (Akhtar and Métraux, 2013). Clear provisions exist in both Islam and the 1973 Pakistani Constitution to provide respect, safety, and equal rights for women; however, Pakistan remains a male-dominated culture where women still struggle to attain their rights (Akhtar and Métraux, 2013). Pakistan is a traditional Muslim country characterized by patriarchy (Awan, 2012) and gender segregation (Yasin et al., 2010). On the one hand, the government has made continuous efforts to provide basic education to its citizens (Latif, 2009). On the other hand, in Pakistan's traditional society, with few links to the outside world, many girls are prohibited from getting an education and most women are kept at home or in low-paying jobs (Nosheen, 2011). However, better Internet access, an increased presence of global corporations, and a proliferation of television and radio stations, has increased Pakistanis' awareness of how other societies treat women.

Nevertheless, in Muslim societies such as Pakistan there is a tendency for people to dichotomize what they do from how they speak about themselves (Mernissi, 1987). The first has to do with the realm of reality while the second has to do with identity (Mernissi, 1987). Given the strong tendency within Muslim cultures to 'save face' (Merkin and Ramadan, 2010), what people say and what people do in Muslim societies tend to differ (Mernissi, 1987). Therefore, opening up Pakistani society to women's education and work may receive lip service but lukewarm efforts. On the other hand, Malala's story has given rise to greater support for women's education in Pakistan through the government enacted additional constitutional amendment (Article 25A) in 2011, known as the *Right to Free and Compulsory Education Act* which makes education a fundamental right for Pakistani citizens. The article states:

The State shall provide free and compulsory education to all children of the age of five to 16 years in such manner as may be determined by law.

This text states that education will be provided to all children. However, what is omitted and not clear is how the provisions of this amendment are actually carried out. The statement in the text 'as may be determined by law' leaves the law's interpretation of how educational practice is determined up in the air. What is meant by law – civil law or strict Islamic law? As long as the notion of women's education is unclear, no one can be held accountable. No one feels exposed and nothing will necessarily be changed. As long as the interpretation of compulsory education is left unclear, no one is required to respond to the law and nothing must be done about it. Another reason no one is required to respond to the compulsory education law is that the wording indicates that the *State* is required to provide education to its citizens. The entity called the *State* implies no personal responsibility, is ambiguous, and is hard to pin down. This lack of clarity and account-ability make it difficult to accomplish what is needed to carry out the *Compulsory Education Act*.

While the existence of this actual law is a step forward for Pakistan, there are cultural mores that explain why the educational system, particularly for girls, is so regressive in Pakistan. In collectivist cultures, individuals base their sense of self on their in group (Hofstede, 2001). Consequently, if the group is the unit of accountability, individuals tend to not feel person-ally responsibility to make a difference and fight towards helping women's education. In fact, collectivist values in Pakistan militate against a civil human rights approach to handling the treatment of women, owing to the focus on what is perceived as community interests as opposed to individual autonomy (Critelli, 2010). What's more, because traditional gender roles predominate in Pakistan, women are more likely to avoid uncertainty and feel discouraged from directly confronting issues publi-cally or at all.

Updated VSM scores

To better understand Pakistani culture, this analysis employed Geert Hofstede's (1980) classic research, which defines the dimensions of culture that shape significant variations in cultural identity. Hofstede's values include individualism-collectivism (values on group member-ship), power distance (values on how to relate to authority), uncertainty avoidance (the need to reduce uncertainty), and masculinity-femininity (values on using competitiveness versus cooperativeness). Cultures fall on points along a continuum of these values. Hofstede's investigation of culture is undoubtedly the most extensive and comprehensive cultural study undertaken to date (Burgmann et al., 2006). Even though there are various criticisms of Hofstede's study (McSweeney, 2002), his rank-ings have heuristic value (Sigal et al., 2005) and have been validated in replication studies (Vishwanath, 2003).

While a number of cross-cultural theorists analyse cultures on the basis of Hofstede's cultural dimensions (Luthar and Luthar, 2007, Merkin and Ramadan, 2010), which are measured by matching coun-tries to Hofstede's (1980) rankings, it is also possible to actually measure cultural attributes using Hofstede's Value Survey Module (VSM 94) to see if his 1980 cultural characterizations of Pakistan still hold. This study, therefore, employed questionnaire data using Hofstede's (1994) VSM 94 instrument which was distributed to an employed mixed-gender middle-class Pakistani convenience sample (n = 146) as well as to a similar population in the US (n = 156). The VSM 94 is essentially a ranking instrument so it must be calculated relative to at least one other culture. Thus, Pakistan's values will be compared to US values as a reference point.

Findings of this investigation (see Table 11.1) showed that Pakistani VSM 94 rankings are quite similar to Hofstede's (1980) original cultural rankings in that Pakistan is a *collectivist* culture that is relatively high in power distance and uncertainty avoidance. Thus, culturally, the collectivist aspect of Pakistani values explains that they are more likely to follow the norms of their in-group. To stick out is an individualistic concept. By contrast, in collectivist cultures there is value in blending into the group and protecting the group's face against outside parties.

Pakistan's strong power distance (Hofstede, 1980) is responsible for the culture's belief that one should respect authority. Challenging authorities on how they manage women's education, therefore, is frowned upon generally and should be carried out in such a way as to not make lawmakers lose face.

The descriptive statistical results calculated in this study with recent VSM 94 data (see Table 11.1) corroborate and explain that *high uncertainty avoidance* values are partly behind the situation in Pakistan. This aspect of Pakistani culture contributes to the fear associated with trying out new educational initiatives and taking chances. However, once educational ideas are carried out and habituated, citizens would be likely to slowly get used to new ways of functioning.

Table 11.1 Hofstede's and VSM rankings

	US		Pakistan	
	VSM 94	**1980 Rank**	**VSM 94**	**1980 Rank**
Individualism	76	91	37	14
Masculinity	39	62	94	50
Power distance	-39	40	-30	55
Uncertainty avoidance	41	46	50	70

Note: VSM = Value Survey Module.

Pakistani governmental authorities are respected or at least given respect because of the *strong power distance* present in Pakistan as evidenced by the VSM 94 data indicated in this study. Residents are willing to overcome their cultural mores to give grander license to authorities by demanding societal change partly because the Talibans' actions are so extreme they are causing life-threatening harm. Other forces, such as poverty and the corresponding need for women to become part of the workforce are also catalysts behind behavioral change despite the strong forces against promoting education.

The Pakistani sample diverged from Hofstede's original ranking by scoring particularly high in *masculinity*. The high Pakistani *masculinity* score indicates that roles differ strongly between what men do and what women do (Hofstede, 1980, 2001). Given that this score is very high, it is likely that these differences have increased. In fact, in a report on gender differences in education in Pakistan showed that there is gender bias against female children found at all levels of education (Qureshi, 2012). This finding is comparable to findings in Pakistan that show differences between the lesser expenditures spent on a girl child's nutrition, health, and education than on her male siblings. Pakistani gender differences also exist from when a girl steps out of the house to work, gets married, and is not given freedom to work or make her own decisions (Hill and King, 1993). Interesting findings show that returns to education are higher for females than males in Pakistan (Aslam, 2007, Aslam et al., 2008). However, the issue of whether girls get educated seems to be dependent on the education level of her mother because women who are better educated tend to give their girls more education (Qureshi, 2012). What is more, because Pakistan is so culturally masculine, corresponding paternalism where social and familial control is exerted over women, keeping them economically dependence on men, and restricting their mobility determines the differential access that males and females experience vis-à-vis education (Roomi and Parrott, 2008).

Education is of particular interest because it is a means of socialization and identity development through which the transmission of knowledge, skills, values, and attitudes are disseminated across generations (Smith, 2011). The Pakistani government statement that 'the State shall provide free and compulsory education to all children of the age of five to 16 years in such a manner as may be determined by law' has not yet been successfully carried out without disruption. In some places, like Swat Valley, for example, schools have been blown up by the Taliban and girls have lower overall rates of school attendance than boys

(Ray, 2002), despite the compulsory clause in the *Right to Free and Compulsory Education Act*.

On the one hand, well-performing communal systems have been shown to combine non-violent conflict, democratic governance, and highly productive and self-sustaining development. Monty Marshall (2011) found consistent correlations between qualities of conflict, governance, and development in societal-systems. Thus, people socialized in developed societies like the US do not want to endanger their organized systems of governance nor risk upheaval to their productivity by engaging in conflicts that could result in armed conflict. This is evidenced most recently by US citizens' public preference for not attacking Syria for its heinous crimes (Karam and Dozier, 2013).

On the other hand, poorly-performing societal systems are characterized by high levels of violent conflict and weak autocratic governance, characterized as being in the center of the democratic continuum, low productivity, and income (Marshall and Cole, 2011). Consequently, countries like Pakistan tend towards violence. An example of this is the recent case of Malala's shooting for encouraging other girls to go to school and the Taliban's overall threats and violence. It is worse in Afghanistan, where the Taliban forbids women from leaving their homes unless accompanied by a close male relative, and forces them to wear to wear burqas (a head to toe covering with a mesh opening to see through). This group is so vehement that they have consistently imposed or attempted to enact vicious restrictions on women in Afghanistan forbidding them from being employed, going to school (which means eliminating existing schools for girls) and for women in cities, going to university. Women who violate Taliban edicts are reportedly beaten.

Another block to education is the Islamic fundamentalist belief that women's education has destroyed the traditional boundaries and definitions of space and gender roles (Mernissi, 1987). However, it is women's education that could improve Pakistan's economy by increasing the presence of more skilled laborers. On the one hand, economic prosperity could reduce conflicts arising from scarce resources or competition for employment. On the other hand, deeply religious male members of Pakistani society may feel threatened by modern cultural values. While their wives go out and work out of economic necessity, they are also harassed in the Pakistani workplace for being outside their homes. Such conflicting forces discourage education and outside employment.

By contrast, US citizens believe in freedom of speech and the freedom to act as we please within the law. We also believe in equal rights for all.

We believe that women deserve an education and that no one has a right to dictate to others how to live their lives. Nevertheless, there are strong forces in other societies who disagree. There are individuals who believe that women have a role in the home exclusively. There are societies that harbor fundamentalists who believe that women do not deserve the same civil rights as men. Salmon Rushdie described the fundamentalists of the ilk of the 9/11 bombers who were from the area of Pakistan:

> Whatever the killers were trying to achieve (those who carried out 9/11), it seems improbable that building a better world was part of it. The fundamentalist seeks to bring down a great deal more than buildings. Such people are against, to offer just a brief list, freedom of speech, a multi-party political system, universal adult suffrage, accountable government, Jews, homosexuals, women's rights, pluralism, secularism, short skirts, dancing, beardlessness, evolution theory, sex.
>
> (Rushdie, 2001, p. A25)

Reconstruction

Citizens of collectivistic societies have identities that are interdependent with their in-groups. Consequently collectivists defer to their group and have a strong need to save face (Merkin et al., 2013). Face needs could explain why in Pakistan, people dichotomize what they do from how they speak about themselves (Mernissi, 1987).

Pakistanis, who are collectivistic, also have a strong power distance and high uncertainty avoidance which are likely to be responsible for feeling threatened by outside agendas, programs, and cultures. The immense contrast in religious and economic values between Pakistani and US cultures are likely to result in conflict and distrust. For example, Rushdie (2001, p. A25) pointed out that: 'fundamentalists believe that we believe in nothing. In his worldview, he has his absolute certainties, while we are sunk in sybaritic indulgences'; Such value differences are hard to bridge.

In order to intercede and move towards peace between ourselves and Pakistani authorities to convince them willingly to adopt Western notions of women's rights, it is imperative that we try to understand each other's perspectives and learn how to communicate in each other's languages. More specifically, because individualists (for example, those from the US) have independent selves, they tend to show most concern for maintaining their own face and reputation as opposed to that of others (Ting-Toomey, 2005). In contrast, collectivist cultural members

(for example, those from Pakistan) view face as prominent during negotiations because of its important social role (Hwang, Francesco, and
Kessler, 2003). Employing tactics to save face during negotiations or
conflict management could help parties to increase understanding of
each other's position more clearly as well as break down barriers erected
by parties afraid of losing face. Clearly, if we speak in a manner that
threatens people's face (by speaking directly), they will quickly tune us
out. Thus, upholding others' face is essential to peacebuilding processes.
This is because once people feel that their face is being threatened, they
are likely to dig in their heels and stubbornly stand their ground while
writing off the others' viewpoints. Conversely, once people come to
know and recognize that other parties will not humiliate them in public
and can be trusted to uphold their face with language that is not explicitly condemning them, they can meet to talk peacefully with trust.

The trouble with this approach is that individualistic cultures also
tend to be low-context cultures (Boyacigiller and Adler, 1991, Hall,
1976) and share the belief that exposure is the way to shame people
into changing. Individualists sharing this perspective need to change
their natural modes of communication and be more subtle. An intervention of training needs to be carried out with individualists who do
not understand that the Pakistanis would not want to explicitly discuss
their biases towards women's education. Though they have threatened
to hurt Malala and her father (Craig and Mehsud, 2013), the Taliban
would not admit, 'Yes we agree, we are violent'. Alternatively, the
heinous actions carried out by some Pakistani groups are hard not to
condemn – particularly by people who are accustomed to be able to
react to injustice with free speech.

Dialogic space for reducing conflict and promoting education, and peacebuilding

An alternative approach might be to try to influence the Pakistani
authorities to agree to use mediators to reflect on the conflict at hand
through a third party. In low-intensity conflicts, for instance, communication strategies may be more effective; but if the conflict becomes
particularly heated, more active, manipulative strategies may be carried
out by a mediator (Bercovitch and Kadayifci, 2002). Bercovitch and
Kadayifci (2002) point out that time pressure, mediator credibility,
and previous relations between parties all may determine the best
strategy. To be effective, mediation strategies and communication need
to correspond with the cultural values of participating parties.

Besides for direct talks or mediation, a more subtle approach might be to help Pakistani women apply for women's educational grants and UN programs established specifically for the cause of women's education. The influx of money might help alleviate the issue of a lack of family funding which has been determined as a deterrent for spending on education of girls (Qureshi, 2012). The tertiary recipients of funding – for example, the actual school – might also motivate others in Pakistani society to advocate for women's education.

Another more indirect approach is advocated by researchers who found that to foster development, multi-agency cooperation is required (as opposed to direct confrontation). The media, educational policy makers, and government agencies could join forces to offer better access to business development services and the enabling of local, regional, and national networks for women entrepreneurs, thereby assisting them to become more integrated into the mainstream economy (Roomi and Parrott, 2008). The idea of employing advocate groups allows individuals to save face because the amorphous entities pronouncing the initiatives are not the same groups whose face is threatened on the ground in Pakistan. The focus away from political groups could help the political groups feel that less is at stake in promoting women's education through neutral aid organizations. Taking strong cultural needs to save face into account may be more successful in moving initiatives for women's education forward in Pakistan.

On the other hand, as Pouligny (2005) points out, any kind of outside interventions must keep in mind that the local people on the ground in Pakistan need to feel empowered by such support. It is important to be aware that both international and local actors interact in post-conflict contexts and be sure to closely analyse larger political ambiguities that emerge. It is crucial to follow up any effort with active communication and mindfulness so that the efforts put into worked-out initiatives don't fail. Once the improved economics of educating women become clear to households in Pakistan, the associations created could garner more support for educating girls.

Education and peacebuilding

Education may be a catalyst of conflict by stimulating grievances, stereotypes, xenophobia, and/or other resentments but can also be a way of moving towards conflict transformation and peacebuilding (Smith, 2011). For example, the struggle for better education of girls has been the cause of armed conflict between the Taliban and Pakistani girls' schools but communications through lobbying and blogs have resulted in the *Right to Free and Compulsory Education Act*. In turn, though the wording of this amendment is vague, this first step may hopefully become the beginning of more fruitful actions supporting the promotion of girls' education.

New legislation to comprehensively address issues of access, quality, and equity of education for all children of Pakistan is still needed in all provinces and federal areas in Pakistan (Shah, 2003). In particular, present legislation needs to be expanded to explicitly define norms for quality education services, roles, responsibilities, and how the implementation process will work; unlike the present *Right to Free and Compulsory Education Act* draft being used today. The legislative process also needs to be transparent and inclusive and involve a nationwide debate and consultation. It may not be possible, however, given the cultural need for indirect communication, to progress along a direct route. On the other hand, attitudes in Pakistan towards education for girls are changing. The laws just need to catch up and nudge the situation on the ground even further.

References

N. Akhtar and D. A. Métraux (2013) 'Pakistan is a Dangerous and Insecure Place for Women', *International Journal on World Peace*, 30, 35–70.

M. Aslam (2007) 'Rates of Return to Education by Gender in Pakistan', *Global Poverty Research Group*, GPRG-WPS-064.

M. Aslam, G. Kingdon, and M. Söderbom (2008) 'Is Female Education a Pathway to Gender Equality in the Labor Market? Some Evidence from Pakistan' in M. Tembon and L. Fort (eds) *Girls' Education in the 21st Century* (Washington D.C.: The World Bank) p. 67–93.

S. Awan (2012) 'Role of Civil Society in Empowering Pakistani Women', *South Asian Studies*, 27, 439–458.

J. Bercovitch and A. Kadayifci (2002) 'Exploring the Relevance and Contribution of Mediation to Peace-building', *Peace and Conflict Studies*, 9, 21–41.

N. Boyacigiller and N. J. Adler (1991) 'The Parochial Dinosaur: Organizational Science in a Global Context', *Academy of Management Review*, 16, 262–290.

I. Burgmann, P. J. Kitchen, and R. Williams (2006) 'Does Culture Matter on the Web? Marketing Intelligence and Planning', *Journal of Marketing Practice: Applied Marketing Science*, 24, 62–76.

T. Craig and S. Mehsud, (2013) Taliban Renews Threat against Pakistani Teen Malala Yousafzai as Nobel Decision Nears, *Washington Post,* http://www.washingtonpost.com/world/asia_pacific/taliban-renews-threat-against-pakistani-teen-malala-yousafzai-as-nobel-decision-nears/2013/10/08/cb8f58d4-3030-11e3-9ddd-bdd3022f66ee_story.html, date accessed 8 October 2013.

F. M. Critelli (2010) 'Women's Rights=Human Rights: Pakistani Women against Gender Violence', *Journal of Sociology and Social Welfare*, 37, 135–160.

E. T. Hall (1976) *Beyond Culture* (New York: Doubleday).

M. A. Hill and E. M. King (1993) 'Women's Education in Developing Countries: An Overview' in E. M. King and M. A. Hill (eds) *Women's Education in Developing Countries: Barriers, Benefits and Policies* (Washington, DC: The World Bank) p. 1–50.

G. Hofstede (1980) *Culture's Consequences: International Differences in Work-related Values* (Beverly Hills, CA: Sage).

G. Hofstede (1994) *Value Survey Module* (Maastricht, Netherlands: Institute for Research on Intercultural Cooperation).

G. Hofstede (2001) *Culture's Consequences: Comparing Values, Behaviors, Institutions, and Organizations across Nations*, 2nd edn (London: Sage).

J. E. Hulbert (1994) 'Overcoming intercultural communication barriers', *Bulletin of the Association for Business Communication*, 57, 41–44.

A. Hwang, A. M. Francesco, and E. Kessler (2003) 'The Relationship Between Individualism-Collectivism, Face, and Feedback and Learning Processes in Hong Kong, Singapore, and the United States', *Journal of Cross-Cultural Psychology*, 34, 72–91.

Z. Karam and K. Dozier (2013) Syria Chemical Attack Evidence Leaves Doubts in Public Opinion, *Huffington Post*, http://www.huffingtonpost.com/2013/09/08/syria-chemical-attack-evidence_n_3890120.html?utm_hp_ref=world, date accessed 27 May 2015.

A. Latif (2009) 'A Critical Analysis of School Enrollment and Literacy Rates of Girls and Women in Pakistan', *Educational Studies*, 45, 424–439.

H. K. Luthar and V. K. Luthar (2007) 'A Theoretical Framework Explaining Cross-Cultural Sexual Harassment: Integrating Hofstede and Schwartz', *Journal of Labor Research*, 28, 169–188.

M. G. Marshall and B. R. Cole (2011) *Global Report: Conflict, Governance, and State Fragility* (Vienna, VA: Center for Systemic Peace Press).

B. McSweeney (2002) 'Hofstede's Model of National Cultural Differences and Their Consequences: A Triumph of Faith – a Failure of Analysis', *Human Relations*, 55, 89–118.

R. Merkin and R. Ramadan (2010) 'Facework in Syria and the United States: A Cross-Cultural Comparison', *International Journal of Intercultural Relations*, 34, 661–669.

R. Merkin, V. Taras, and P. Steel (2013) 'State of the Art Themes in Cross-Cultural Communication Research: A Systematic and Meta-Analytic Review', *International Journal of Intercultural Relations*, 38, 1–23.

F. Mernissi (1987) *Beyond the veil* (Bloomington, IA: Indiana University Press.)

H. Nosheen (2011) 'Violence against Women', *Dialogue*, 6, 290–299.

B. Pouligny (2005) 'Civil Society and Post-Conflict Peacebuilding: Ambiguities of International Programmes Aimed at Building 'New' Societies', *Security Dialogue*, 36, 495–510.

M. G. Qureshi (2012) 'The Gender Differences in School Enrolment and Returns to Education in Pakistan', *Working Papers and Research Reports*, 84, 2012.

R. Ray (2002) 'Simultaneous Analysis of Child Labour and Child Schooling: Comparative Evidence from Nepal and Pakistan', *Economic and Political Weekly*, 5215–5224.

M. A. Roomi and G. Parrott (2008) 'Barriers to Development and Progression of Women Entrepreneurs in Pakistan', *Journal of Entrepreneurship*, 17, 59–72.

S. Rushdie (2001) Fighting the Forces of Invisibility, *The Washington Post,* http://groups.yahoo.com/neo/groups/sept11info/conversations/topics/2514?var=1, date accessed 27 May 2015.

S. H. Schwartz (1994) 'Are There Universal Aspects in the Structure and Contents of Human Values?', *Journal of Social Issues,* 50, 19–45.

D. Shah (2003) 'Country Report on Decentralization in the Education System of Pakistan: Policies and Strategies', *Academy of Educational Planning and Management Ministry of Education.*

J. Sigal, M. S. Gibbs, C. Goodrich, T. Rashid, A. Anjum, D. Hsu, and P. Wei-Kang (2005) 'Cross-Cultural Reactions to Academic Sexual Harassment: Effects of Individualist vs. Collectivist Culture and Gender of Participants', *Sex Roles,* 52, 201–215.

A. Smith (2011) 'The Influence of Education on Conflict and Peace Building', *Education for All Global Monitoring Report.*

Ting-Toomey, S. (2005) 'The Matrix of Face: An Updated Face-Negotiation Theory' in W. B. Gudykunst (ed.) *Theorizing About Intercultural Communication* (Thousand Oaks, CA: Sage) p. 71–92.

H. C. Triandis and R. D. Albert (1987) 'Cross-cultural Perspectives', in F. M. Jablin, L. L. Putnam, K. H. Roberts and L. W. Porter (eds.) *Handbook of Organizational Communication: An Interdisciplinary Perspective* (Newbury Park, CA: Sage) pp. 264–295.

A. Vishwanath (2003) 'Comparing Online Information Effects A Cross-Cultural Comparison of Online Information and Uncertainty Avoidance', *Communication Research,* 30, 579–598.

G. Yasin, I. Chaudhry, and S. Afzal (2010) 'The Determinants of Gender Wage Discrimination in Pakistan: Econometric Evidence from Punjab Province', *Asian Social Science,* 6, 239–255.

12

Constructing Frostburg's 'Cooler' Future: Sustaining Campus and Community through a Dialogue Series in an Appalachian College Town

Elesha L. Ruminski

The City of Frostburg's letterhead reads, 'Maryland's Mountain City, "It's Just Cooler Here!"', and recently, several faculty and administrators of Frostburg State University (FSU) have included 'Frostburg ... It's Just Cooler Here' in their university email signatures. A large banner with the phrase was also hung above the door of City Place, a town community centre in Frostburg, on the annual town clean-up day supported by the City and FSU, 'Beautify the 'Burg', in 2013. The slogan, created by an action group that emerged that year during the Sustaining Campus and Community Dialogue Series held in Frostburg, Maryland, has stuck, and in doing so constructs a dialogic identity of 'coolness' that promotes a non-violent culture of social sustainability, despite interpretive differences. The phrase helps people to frame experience through metaphor, which Lakoff and Johnson (2003) suggest 'structure what we perceive, how we get around in the world, and how we relate to other people' (p. 3). What is meant by 'cooler' in this context, and do all community members agree it is truly 'cooler' in Frostburg? What are the benefits of and the insights gained by constructing a shared sense of a 'cooler' Frostburg together? And, importantly, what will sustain that 'coolness' in the future now that the two and half year dialogue series is over?

This chapter will examine how metaphoric outcomes, in particular a community slogan ('Frostburg . . . It's Just Cooler Here!'), has prompted dialogue and deliberation about a particular college town's identity while supporting a broader initiative sponsored by the Maryland Judiciary's Mediation and Conflict Resolution Office (MACRO, 2012).

The questions the slogan raises about the community inspire a dialogic process that calls for Frostburg community members to continue to ask themselves—and each other—who they are and what is unique and important to them; in this way, the slogan inspires an opportunity to create partnerships dialogically and to consider what it takes to keep those relationships going. As an experiential learning project for students at FSU, this series and reflection on the community slogan provides an opportunity to examine dialogic spaces rhetorically better to understand the outcomes and opportunities for learning linked to dialogic peace education.

Frostburg is located in the Appalachian Highlands in Allegany County, which is the second western most county in the state; it is a two-to-three hour drive from the major cities of Pittsburgh, Washington DC, Baltimore and the state's capital, Annapolis. From its inception in 1812, Frostburg was a prominent stop on the National Road, and in 1852, on the railroad (Bowman, 2011). FSU, the westernmost of the University System of Maryland universities, was originally a State Normal School; now the comprehensive university offers a doctoral degree in Educational Leadership among many other programmes in Education, Liberal Arts and Sciences, and Business ('About FSU', 2014). FSU has been recognized as a university of distinction (2012) known for its civic engagement and service orientation ('Wins First-Ever Higher Education Award', 2000) that offers 'student-centered teaching and learning ... featuring experiential opportunities' (FSU Mission, 2014); this often places students within the surrounding community to serve, so campus-community partnerships are important to local co-existence.

Authentic 'partnership' in a campus community environment is defined by the Curry School of Education at the University of Virginia as two or more individuals working together with clear timelines, benchmarks, and evaluation processes; a plan to show how the partnership will be sustainable; and evidence that 'non-university partners have participated in all stages of planning and implementation' (UCARE, 2012, p. 24). Sustainable partnerships that build on creativity are vital for the future of government and educational institutions, which are in survival mode in this second decade of the twenty-first century. Creativity means being open to approaches and resources that are new and that were perhaps not previously available. It involves collaboration and constructivism to contribute to a safe, cooperative climate and positive community relations. For example, in Frostburg there is an annual partnership between campus and community for Beautify the 'Burg, through which year-round residents and students come together to do some Spring-time sprucing up of the downtown and local neighbor-hoods. Another example was a 'University Neighbors' group composed of neighbours (locals and students) living adjacent to campus that was formed through a Leadership Studies course project to keep long-term and short-term residents near campus interacting through regular channels of communication, typically through monthly meetings.

Despite such partnerships, communicating differences can be chal-lenging within any university town. Set that university town within the Appalachian culture of Western Maryland, in a town of approxi-mately 9,000 residents (County Quick Facts, 2014) with a mid-sized comprehensive state university of approximately 5,426 students (FSU Enrollment, Fall 2010–2014) that draws students from the Baltimore–DC 195 corridor as well as the tri-state region, and conflicts emerge from communicated differences everywhere—on the streets of local neighbourhoods, in the residence halls, on the editorial page of the local newspaper and on Facebook walls. And although many avoid sharing or acknowledging differences to avoid conflict, or avoid engag-ing in conflict as communicated differences emerge, many others are bravely learning how to 'reboot their framework' concerning com-munication about conflict as peace education and alternative dispute resolution resources have become increasingly available in the region in the past decade. A local community mediation centre, university courses and events, community events, and the recent community dialogue series have contributed to constructing Frostburg's '"cooler" future' as 'town and gown' come together through various initia-tives with support from various resources to strengthen campus and community partnerships. However, the Frostburg-FSU partnership can be further strengthened, especially now that the University Neighbors group has dissolved and the MACRO-funded dialogue series has ended.

As a dialogic understanding of campus-community identity emerges, the community will become more and more able to adapt to the increasingly challenging fiscal and social needs of the community. Partnerships can be achieved through stakeholder consensus building, which is possible, as the Public Dialogue Consortium established in the town of Cupertino, California, through 'small group discussions, interviews, forums, training, team-building sessions, and establishment of a community organization dedicated to continuing the dialogue process' (Littlejohn and Domenici, 2007, pp. 200–201). This is what the Sustaining Campus and Community Dialogue Series attempted to do.

Its outcomes are still in progress, with possible ideas suggested including revival of a town and gown council or creation of a community-based group that keeps the conversations going. Collaborative leadership in a town and gown context is possible by doing what Komives (July–August 1996) says, linking 'classroom learning to experiential activities, including service learning, where individuals and groups can test their impact and collaborate in diverse contexts to learn how their leadership makes a difference and facilitates change' (p. 3). The result is that higher education supports student knowledge of and experience with citizen leadership, democratic processes, and peacemaking processes in this way.

This chapter will examine a particular outcome of the Sustaining Campus and Community Dialogue Series project, a community slogan, to better understand how it demonstrates the dialogic process and contributes to the ongoing construction of a community's identity. First, the project's objectives, sponsors, and process will be discussed. Then, an analysis of the Frostburg community slogan as an outcome conceived within one of the dialogue action groups and grappled over by multiple community members will be conducted. Finally, reflections on the considerations and implications for the dialogue process and its outcomes for peacebuilding and peace education that focuses on sustaining campus and community will be offered. This examination will reveal how peacebuilding was conceptually deconstructed and co-constructed through intentional, collaborative, sustained efforts that were at moments interrupted by 'ruptures' or 'hiccups' resulting from participants' aversion as well as their willingness to engage in conflict so they could learn from those conflicts and each other. Themes of recovery, pride, and resilience were revealed through discussions of community history and the metaphoric implications of symbols, slogans, and ideas that arose as constructive outcomes from the dialogue process. What resulted and what will be shared here is how this small community in Western Maryland created, in episodic moments, 'critical dialogic space for construction of a multi-perspectival outlook towards peace education in a global world', as this collection asserts is important.

A purposeful call for dialogue

To have constructive change led by citizen leaders, community members must be willing to take time to communicate differences.

Typically, they must overcome perceptual barriers that block under-standing of differences as part of that process, and it takes time to talk and listen to get past those initial perceptions to the place where deeper conflict emerges. Community members, including long-term local residents and partial-year student residents, have access to the free mediation services of Mountainside Community Mediation Services (MCMC). Most local mediations involve long-term local residents. Courses are also available in the Conflict Communication Studies track of FSU's Communication Studies major, although only a small number of students can take the class, since only one course offering for 20 students is available each academic year due to department size and faculty resources.

To create an additional opportunity to bridge students and towns-people, sessions of the Sustaining Campus and Community Dialogue Series began in Spring 2012. The series, sponsored through 2014 by MACRO, FSU, and MCMC, was initiated to help the Frostburg commu-nity work through concerns after some incidents of violence and trag-edy that, although unusual and seemingly confined to a certain sector of the student population, set off a chain of interactions online and in person that highlighted cultural tensions that had been brewing under the surface of messages, interactions, and behaviours.

On 18 April 2010, an FSU student shot two other FSU students off campus, injuring 21-year-old Ellis Hartridge and taking the life of 20-year-old Brandon Carroll (White, 2010). Then, in the middle of the night on 3 December 2010, a fire broke out in a building on Main Street in Frostburg, killing two FSU students, Alyssa Salazar, and her boy-friend, Evan Kullberg (Kay and Markus, 2010). The following year, on 6 November 2011, 19-year-old FSU student Kortneigh McCoy was stabbed to death by another FSU student (Taylor, 2011). Then, tragi-cally, FSU again lost another student when Lateef Gazal died in a house fire near campus on 14 February 2014; two residents, also FSU students, escaped the fire (Lewis, 2014).

Following the tragic death of McVeigh, a member of the executive leadership of MACRO reached out to the author, who is a faculty mem-ber teaching within the Communication Studies major at FSU and who was then the board president of MCMC, to invite her to do a community dialogue series to address the violence happening in the community. Before this dialogue series, vigils and an initial campus conversation about the violence were coordinated for students by FSU's Student and Educational Services and Residence Life. The campus community responded constructively through a slogan that appeared on campus windows and Facebook walls that autumn: 'I believe in Frostburg'. In the FSU *Profile* alumni magazine, one student, Matt Renwick, expressed the sense of community that the college town offered him: 'I believe in Frostburg. This is my school, and it's also become my home' ('Last Word', 2012).

As part of the preparation for the dialogue project, MACRO supported the training of the project manager through a Public Conversations Project (PCP) workshop. PCP identifies the role of dialogue in public life as 'talking that serves a distinct purpose' that honours listening without interruption (Herzig and Chasin, 2006, p. 1). Herzig and Chasin recognize that dialogue is a form of communication less understood that debate and activism yet that has a vital role 'in a resilient and civil democratic society' (p. 1). Tenets of dialogue they offer were the basis for the dialogue series in Frostburg:

- Careful, collaborative planning that ensures clarity about what the dialogue is and isn't, and also fosters alignment between the goals of the dialogue and the participants' wishes.
- Communication agreements that discourage counterproductive ways of talking about the issues and encourage genuine inquiry.
- Meeting designs that include supportive structures for reflecting, listening, and speaking questions that invite new ways of thinking and talking about issues.
- Facilitation that is informed by careful preparation and responsiveness to the emerging needs and interest of the participants. (Herzig and Chasin, 2006, p. 3)

After a grant from MACRO to support the four dialogues in the Spring of 2012, a two-year memorandum of understanding (MOU) was set forth with the following purpose:

Under this project, Frostburg State University and the Maryland Judiciary's Mediation and Conflict Resolution Office will collaborate on a demonstration project engaging nationally known dispute resolution experts to address and resolve ongoing, seemingly intractable, campus-community conflicts through dialogue, training, and facilitated problem solving sessions. By bringing together campus and community leaders, and by focusing on long-term sustainability, this project will create new opportunities for peace, reducing the likelihood of future violent and deadly conflicts. Just in the past academic year, conflicts in Frostburg led to very high profile, resource intensive cases in the Circuit Court of Allegany County. The results have been long-term incarceration and tragedy due to interpersonal disputes that could have been prevented or resolved earlier. We believe changing this conflict culture will attract national attention and serve as a model for campus-community dialogue and dispute resolution nationwide.

FSU's Department of Communication Studies served as the host of the series along with community partner MCMC. Other FSU partners— the Office of the President, Office of Human Resources, Diversity Center, Residence Life Office, Department of Philosophy, and Student Communication Studies Association—indicated their support. The MOU integrated the intention to offer what the university as a state institution could uniquely do, which was to integrate 'experiential learning' across disciplines and campus divisions when holding the community dialogue series. Faculty and staff representatives from Communication Studies, Mass Communication, Philosophy, and the Office of Student and Community Involvement integrated assignments and extra credit incentives for participating in the dialogues. The initiative was promoted through FSU's Department of Publications through local press releases, posters on campus and in the community, and through invitation letters, which were followed up by personal invitations in person or by phone. Bobcat Connect, an online student organization platform, was used to advertise to student organizations, and faculty were asked to encourage student participate as part of their classes to start integrating conflict management education into the curriculum.

This project supported the mission of FSU, which strives to promote education about diversity and inclusiveness: 'Frostburg State University affirms its commitment to a campus environment which values human diversity and respects individuals who represent that diversity. Fostering diversity and respect for difference is a fundamental goal of higher education, ranking among the highest priorities of this institution' (FSU Mission, 2014). MACRO's ability to support 'innovative dispute resolution programs' fits FSU's need: 'MACRO has a diverse, high-level Advisory Board and works collaboratively with many others across the state to advance effective conflict resolution practices in Maryland's courts, communities, schools, state and local government agencies, criminal and juvenile justice programs, and businesses'. By assisting FSU with its educational efforts, leading to taking action as a community to build and sustain dialogue efforts, MACRO fulfils its mission as well (MACRO Mission, 2012).

The project included strategic planning retreats involving key stakeholders each year; two to four community dialogue sessions per academic semester; and two training sessions early in the series about developing dialogue facilitation skills. Experiences of planning, discussing, and building community through dialogue and related initiatives were documented by a videographer and photographer as well as through online Facebook posts by students and community members involved in the experience. Interviews featuring participants offered perspectives on how the community sustained itself over the two-year period. These interviews, along with links to Facebook, Youtube, and Flickr links, offer a Web 2.0 presence to document the experience and expectations of the project.

Central to the project was the invitation of two scholar-practitioners who offered consultation and guidance through this process. They were recommended by the deputy executive director of MACRO (2012) because they are top in the conflict resolution field:

• Frank Dukes, Director of the Institute for Environmental Negotiation (IEN), 'designs dispute resolution and public participation processes, mediates and facilitates, teaches and trains, and conducts research' (see   http://www.arch.virginia.edu/people/directory/frank-dukes). Dr. Dukes, who teaches at the University of Virginia, focuses on sustainability in his conflict resolution work.
• Marvin Johnson is founder of The Center for Alternative Dispute Resolution, the mission of which is 'to promote and provide education and comprehensive approaches to dispute resolution that constructively serve the needs of our culturally diverse society'. Johnson, an African American entrepreneur, has experience working across many contexts to facilitate transitions in communities using personal reflections and perception checking tied to identity.

The project's goals and anticipated outcomes were agreed upon in the MOU but were negotiable as the process ebbed and flowed; for example, one deliverable shifted from gathering documentary footage for a future documentary production to capturing video of interviews with participants for the website instead. The Project Objectives follow:

• To continue the series of dialogues begun in Spring 2012 to build on relationship and community building efforts to date.

- To provide training on dialogue, conflict management, communication, and civility to Frostburg's short- and long-term community members.
- To introduce Western Maryland, via this MOU and collaboration with MCMC, to MCMC's and MACRO's resources.

The project deliverables included the following:

- Documentary video of our experience building community through dialogue in Frostburg
- Web 2.0 presence (through Facebook, Twitter, etc.)
- Final report on experience and outcome, including survey results

Campus and community members were invited in the hope that those involved would form or strengthen coalitions to support continuous dialogue across campus and community to support future work on conflict management and violence prevention education. The desired support would be broad-based, consisting of administration, faculty, staff, students, community leaders, and community members, with representation from various groups and affiliations. Sessions were held in downtown Frostburg and on campus on a few occasions. The hope was that through these efforts, perceptions that were intensified by recent violent and tragic incidents could be examined, permitting an opportunity for relationships to be forged between students and local community members to focus more on problem-solving than on differences. Desired dialogue outcomes discussed but not yet achieved include tangible, institutionalized changes, for example, the creation of an off-campus housing office, a community relations office or position, or a town and gown council. The main outcome was to set into motion more dialogue on peace education in the community, specifically sustaining a community conversation about promoting a safe, non-violent culture in Frostburg.

Frostburg ... It's Just Cooler Here

The Pride in FSU and Frostburg action group resolved to offer constructive signs that they cared about the relationship between the campus and the town. Right before FSU's May 2013 graduation, a local family joined the mayor of Frostburg to paint large, orange paw prints on a street leading to campus. A large paw print stencil, confirmed by the university's Office of Publications as the proper paw print style of the school's mascot, an FSU Bobcat. Paint was donated by a local business.

The paw print painters were greeted by FSU students who lived off campus. The college students expressed gratitude for the local community members and leadership sharing their Bobcat pride.

These paw prints were a constructive, symbolic outcome of the Pride in FSU and Frostburg action group that had formed during the dialogue sessions. Those who stenciled the paw prints represent both town and gown elements: two are FSU students (the mother and son of the local family), one is a landlord who rents to FSU students (the mayor), and two are involved in local leadership (the mother is involved with MCMC board leadership, and the mayor leads the City Council of Frostburg). This example reveals how community member and leader roles overlap in Frostburg often, an indication that the leadership pool is small.

The creative collaboration was a moment of pride and connection, of giving and sharing, and it linked back to another outcome of the Community Pride dialogue action group, the implantation of a new community slogan, 'Frostburg . . . It's Just Cooler Here!' Frostburg, with a cooler climate than most of the rest of Maryland (with the exception the western most county, Garrett County) is even ten degrees cooler than nearby LaVale and Cumberland to the east, which are just ten to 15 minutes away. Metaphorically, in Spring of 2012, Frostburg community members began steps toward conceiving their community as 'cooler' through this slogan. Lakoff and Johnson (2003) indicate that *the essence of metaphor is understanding and experiencing one kind of thing in terms of another* (p. 5), in this case understanding the community ethos as one related to pride, resilience, and uniqueness. In this case, 'cooler' functions as what Redding calls a *conduit metaphor*, through which speakers put ideas into words that mask aspects of the communicative process (pp. 10–12). Frostburg as 'cooler' is meant to focus on the pride, resilience, and uniqueness of the community, not the weather, in other words.

However, while the dialogue series was underway and this action group was formulating these metaphoric solutions to address community pride, FSU was undergoing a rebranding process. A new university advertising slogan, 'One University: A World of Experiences', was launched, announced at the annual university convocation in 2014 and accompanied by a celebration and a promotional video featuring the university president, students, staff, and faculty. At that moment, one community had two slogans, and initially, there was not clear agreement about which to embrace. Faculty were advised to use the university slogan, yet some had already begun to identify with the community slogan that had formed through campus-community dialogue, creating a conflict about how community members identified themselves—as part of a campus brand, or as members of the broader Frostburg community. Some wondered could they embrace both identities? The tension over which slogan the campus should use also prompted questions about community identity. Additionally, the community seemed to wonder how it identified with the campus. The minutes of a Frostburg Business and Professional Association (2013) meeting in the summer of 2013 asked,

> Are we a college town? Take a drive along Main Street ... there's nothing that indicates that we are! Where is the Bobcat Laundry or the University Deli? We discussed increasing that presence, and improving our image as a college town that would include lamppost banners and nice signage in our windows and stores that welcome FSU students, guests, faculty, and staff to our community.

These questions reveal that metaphors must be associated with the experiences of those using them; Lakoff and Johnson (2003) suggest, *'In actuality we feel that no metaphor can ever be comprehended or even adequately represented independently of its experiential basis'* (p. 19). The experience of the metaphoric concept is also linked to the cultural coherence of the concept. Values are embedded, yet 'because things are usually not equal, ... conflicts among the metaphors associated with them' occur (p. 23). Not all groups or cultures in a community share or rank values the same way, thus shared metaphoric understanding is not always shared.

While some in FSU administration encouraged use of the new FSU slogan—'One university, a world of experiences'—instead of the dialogue series generated community slogan, 'Frostburg ... It's Just Cooler Here' wouldn't go away. In addition to the City administration and some faculty and staff using it, as mentioned at the start of this chapter, the phrasing came up in everyday conversations or was an interesting point of discussion and query for campus guests who encountered the phrase.

Frostburg's sense of self as linked to climate is common and long-standing. FSU's former logo emphasized the word 'Frostburg' and featured a mountain peak, but a new campus branding initiative in the first decade of the twenty-first century changed that to an image replicating part of the Compton Science Center's Foucault's pendulum image, the portion that is pointing to north (N). The university's Marketing Advisory Committee indicated that the new logo would remove the focus on Frostburg's mountainous (remote, distant, snowy?)

location; Including Foucault's pendulum emphasized STEM (Science, Technology, Engineering, Math) initiatives as well as a directional indication of finding one's way. The university advertising slogan at the time asked, 'Where are you going?'

By the time the newer slogan, 'One University: A World of Experiences' was launched, it was evident that that 'cool' Frostburg identity had emerged. In an 2 April 2014, April Fool's issue of the student campus newspaper, *The Bottom Line* (titled *The Bottom Lie*, in this case), a section called 'This Week in the Future' noted weather twice when referring to FSU, and in one case, in relation to the identity of the university. First, it mentioned that on 2 April, 'Frostburg suffers near death experience after vicious snowstorm'; next, for 6 April, the article mentioned FSU was 'renamed University of Maryland, Iceburg State University' (p. 5). Far and wide, local residents and newcomers alike brace themselves for the harsh winter season and its snow and ice. But they also claim the advantages of the mountain's outdoor activities and the beauty and natural resources and energy efficiency of the area, including wind towers.

Nevertheless, despite such recognition of the cold climate and mountainous region in the public dialogue of the campus newspaper and the image of a former marketing logo, their remains an ambivalence by campus members at acknowledging the Frostburg name as meaning something cold. For example, one faculty member who sent an email to the faculty email list in Spring 2014 after an extreme amount of snow day cancellations during that semester to offer regional weather data quoted the slogan, asking, 'Does anyone want to rethink our catchy town motto: "It's just cooler here!"?'

There is something to be said about that question. The conflict that emerged from the slogan, which was the outcome of a collaborative, coalition-building process during the dialogue series, spotlights the complexity of perspectives that must be navigated in the Frostburg community. The slogan simultaneously reveals the community's spirit and what sometimes divides the town and gown as well as the regional constraints and opportunities within which everyone lives.

But the significance of the phrase 'It's just cooler here' is what it reveals about the community's identity rather than the climate. The City, in contrast to the university, proudly embraces its location and this phrase. The work of taking care of the city and its community members amid harsh weather conditions is an important part of the City and community's ethos. 'Cooler' is about pride, a resilient image, about invitation, about how people can be better by being part of this place.

Frostburg as 'cooler' offers an invitation to others to enjoy that 'cool' quality while offering a metaphoric climate reference recognizing the region's climate and the challenges that the mountainous region faces together. Its overt nature recognizes that there is an inside joke, localized knowledge about what makes the place unique, but there is also a curious question about how this place faces challenges (like weather or economic constraints) and comes out surviving, in some cases thriving creatively through seasonal loss and renewal, as the Frostburg Grows, a greenhouse project initiated by FSU that links to and gives back to the community, illustrates. The slogan 'Frostburg ... It's Just Cooler Here!' functions as a *container metaphor* to reveal boundaries of interpretation in our visual field (Lakoff and Johnson, 2003, pp. 29–31), that in 'Frostburg', 'here', it is cooler. The 'one university' of FSU as 'a world of experiences' interestingly also functions as a container metaphor.

The slogan has represented community resilience (this mountainous community combats harsh winter weather annually), pride (this is 'the cooler', hipper sustainable community), uniqueness (it's 'cooler' 'here' rather than there), and connectedness (you want to be part of this 'coolness' here). For some, however, it might represent exclusion of newcomers or discomfort with diversity, exuding a 'coolness' rather than hospitality in the small town. Close bonds in a small town can sometimes exclude outsiders despite any intentions for a metaphoric construction to bridge gaps between locals and newcomers. However, the intention of peacebuilding by building relationships still exists because it was communicated as a goal to those who participated in the Sustaining Campus and Community Dialogue Series. Even if the paw prints faded on salted city streets, the community slogan still remains on the City's memorandum header and now FSU banners are hung on downtown lamp posts, imbuing Frostburg with a college town image.

The conversations and relationships that grew and strengthened out of the dialogue series linked to the creation of these metaphors of community pride inspires a move to a constructivist interpretation of how this community is capable of working together, of how campus and community members will step in a constructive direction at the pace they can and in the ways they can. Stern and Ruminski (2014) suggest that 'when hiking in the mountains, you risk falling off the narrow ridge' to clarify how Buber's dialogic frame of common ground and walking the narrow ridge Helps us consider that taking the middle ground, even if it is composed of a very narrow range of common ground between two opposing interpretations, is an alternative to taking extreme positions. The creation of the slogan as an outcome of campus and community collaboration through the dialogue series points to a communicative and dialogic space that might be narrow, but still exists.

Final Reflection: How dialogue reframes conflict and conflict education

As a dialogic approach for discussing concerns and creating new opportunities for collaborative problem-solving and coalition-building in Frostburg, the Sustaining Campus and Community Dialogue Series convened students, year-round residents, local officials, and university leaders in Frostburg in a variety of creative ways. The tensions that arose from these tragedies were the starting points for conversations focused on strengthening community member relationships and campus and community partnerships. Dialogic topics brought more awareness of local culture from past and present, including recognition of the loss and recovery within Frostburg's neighbourhoods and the pride and determination of a resilient, resource-strapped community that maintains close bonds and traditions. The series produced symbolic outcomes, like the paw prints and the community slogan, simple but meaningful gestures of unity, pride, reliance, and connection. The paw prints and the slogan launched an enthusiasm for a dialogue process that can lead to continuing conversations with those across campus and community, but these efforts just scratched the surface— both in terms of outcomes achieved and achievable, imagined, and as yet unfulfilled.

The series aimed to have community members create tangible solutions for deeper-level, sensitive, and structurally challenging town-and-gown tensions that affect safe, secure living conditions and civil relationships between long-term and short-term residents. It was known that progress would take time. Action groups formed included Pride in FSU and Frostburg; Building Relationships; Managing Conflicts, with a focus on alcohol related issues linked to an already existing, separately grant-funded Community Coalition effort; Off-campus Housing Solutions; and Race Relations. Action groups focused on outcomes by organizing using worksheets that helped them frame their membership, mission, actions, and promotion. Some of these efforts were sustained, while others evolved or faded. Additional topics that emerged included formally organizing (reorganizing, or further organizing, depending on perspectives) the campus and community partnership, inviting FSU students to join and grow the local community, recovering the history of Brownsville, a former African American community in Frostburg where part of FSU now sits, loss of respect (and even life) within neighbour-hoods, and respect in race relations.

Throughout the course of the dialogues and the interactions that went on outside of them, conflict was deconstructed and peace was co-constructed across campus and community in Frostburg. Deconstructed and co-constructed understandings of those at the cen-tre of the programme transformed together in subtle and significant ways as they challenged and strengthened their relationships. When conflict pushed past comfort zones or tested shared understandings' confidentiality, some of the campus and community leadership backed away. Even when distance was put into place, and deeper-level changes couldn't be achieved, there were indications that something was dif-ferent. At a minimum, collaborative bonds focused on commitments linked to supporting Frostburg as a community, like the annual Beautify the 'Burg, remained in place; other aspects of commitment across cam-pus and community will need time to tell where they are and where they go.

While conflict during the dialogue process was sometimes perceived as 'drama', so much that disengagement was chosen rather than facing the discomfort of tensions that allow the story of conflict to play out, other times dramatic moments were passed through to manage contin-ued engagement and save face for all parties involved. Once one person disengaged, in a spiralling affect others began to disengage to avoid con-flict in the future, a conflict-averse response to differences that mounted through time to indicate how far participants were willing to go in their understanding of conflict perspectives. However, the management of differences through patience and renegotiated roles and relationships to the project helped participants determine safe, appropriate boundaries, since many of their own personal roles overlapped.

By expressing hopes about how to 'keep the conversation going', stake-holders used what Constantino and Merchant (1996) call mirroring. Mirroring is 'a figure looking glass into organizational leadership and asking questions' so the organization is 'willing to look at itself and articulate what it sees' (p. 225), with the hope of creating a breakthrough of changed culture that promotes 'choice and acceptance of conflict' (pp. 225–226): 'Only through such self-examination can we recognize that we all contribute to and help sustain present levels of conflict in the world around us and that we can all contribute to changing the way we manage conflict' (p. 226).

The dialogue provided an examination of community culture and conflicts surrounding the understanding of that. The teaching of culture comes through inviting conversations across cultural groups and about cultural histories. Dialogues helped participants situate themselves in time and place by recognizing the Appalachian culture, as evidenced by, for example, having local bluegrass musicians play and pastors of local churches speak at some events, as well as by allowing participants to interact with others of different ages, races, and city context (urban and rural).

Local histories were shared, including the history of Brownsville, an African American community that was relocated when the Maryland General Assembly sought to expand the Normal School (Bowman, 2011); Bowman, a local scholar who serves as a commissioner of the Maryland Commission on African American History and Culture, was invited to present her research about Brownsville at a dialogue, revealing the textured racial past unknown to many, especially current FSU students. Another local scholar discussed the challenges created by 'studentification' of neighbourhoods adjacent to campus, for example, 'poorly managed properties, trash, parties,' and the effects of these issues on 'intergroup relations in the neighborhoods near campus' (Powell, 2013, p. 8). These textured views of history and present prompted some conflict—who is responsible, should the histories be recognized formally to recover dignity for local families and newcomers as well as students of color at FSU, how and by whom should alternative histories be told? While some discussed commemoration to this historic community of Brownsville, others questioned whether any oppression occurred. What was recognized in this as many of the conflicts that emerged during the dialogues was that more dialogic spaces are needed to safely allow diverse perspectives on what the community was, is, and can be. As Born (2014) suggests, a conscious effort must be made to deepen community rather than maintain a shallow community or a fear-based one: 'When we develop deep community we can overcome our loneliness and challenge our fear; we can come together to make sense of the destruction around us; we can reach out together and actually do something about it' (p. 26).

Racial identity also emerged as a topic of discussion when student dialogue participants began discussing natural African and African American hair and the reality that there is nowhere to shop for hair care or products in the Western Maryland region as African Americans, even though there is an increasing African/African American student population and an increasing if minority non-white and biracial population in the region. Set in the context of more understanding of the racial history of the town, with more knowledge of Brownsville, and with an awareness of current racial tensions, as evidenced by the KKK rally held on 14 April 2014, in Cumberland, MD, a nearby town and the county seat ('Ku Klux Klan Plans Rally in Cumberland on Saturday', 2014), honest dialogue recognized that our history is more textured than recognized and that some cultural values still clash. Constructively, what emerged is the idea that entrepreneurial opportunities exist, whether formal, as the City provides economic development incentives (City of Frostburg, 2013), or informal; for example, one facilitator mentioned how he, as an African American, used to cut hair for other African Americans in the dorms as a job on the side, an entrepreneurial solution that was culturally and relationally based. Thus, conflict about a community, in this case, a perceived lack of respect for the resources required by diversity, is reconceived as a constructive opportunity.

Creative collaboration and problem-solving through dialogue offers alternative dispute management strategies within a community context by enabling symbolic interactionism. Reality is socially constructed in communion with others. It is not scripted through a set facilitative process, rather created through meeting the moment with patience, reflective listening, and facilitator assistance when needed, which enabled the focus to be on how to keep the conversation going and realities emerging. Facilitators in training had to take risks to initiate conversations, ask questions, make mistakes, and engage in relational repair in some instances as new boundaries were set for those involved in the project.

The nature of conflict is changing and so are peacebuilding efforts, so deconstructing and reconstructing current ideologies of peace and conflict education must be supported. A greater understanding of what resources are lacking for student conflict reduction was recognizable from this dialogue project, as well as student understanding of what sort of conflicts are perceived by the local community in regard to students. The dialogues acknowledged at times that the resources a campus provides might seem insular unless better advertised or integrated as a resource for the surrounding community. Student and Educational Services provides an array of support services, specifically a Diversity Center that supports various activities, including a diversity retreat, workshops, training, and an Enough is Enough anti-violence campaign week in April. FSU has president's advisory committees for Gender-Based Violence and for Diversity, Equity, and Inclusion, which support a variety of campus-wide efforts. Some academic programmes or coursework that supports the teaching of ethics and civility, specifically the Communication Studies major, which offers a relatively new track in Conflict Communication Studies, and the Philosophy Department, which introduces peace studies perspectives through its faculty's expertise. Yet many community members and even students weren't aware of these opportunities. Because FSU is promoting it is 'One University: A World of Experiences', it makes sense that more cooperative approaches are used to get students experiences hands on in their local community, so these resources could be offered through projects supported by these campus programmes.

More work must be done to engage in communicating differences to shift perceptions of conflict as negative and thus something to avoid to viewing conflict as valuable and worth engaging. While several of the same campus and community members showed up fairly consistently throughout the two-and-a-half year period of the project, some didn't attend at all, some who attended eventually couldn't return, and some only attended one or a few dialogues and thus did not have an opportunity to shift from a monologic to dialogic mindset. There must be a shift away from the idea that a single workshop, course or certification helps us achieve knowledge in conflict management; instead, ongoing education and engagement in lived experiences are necessary to better understand how we can transform conflict, not just resolve or manage it. Conflict transformation focuses on concerns about traumas or injustices and seeks to build relationships, empower participants, and develop creative solutions by using 'democratic communication to address underlying causes of conflict and create satisfactory solutions for all parties' (Schirch, 2004, p. 48). Through this shift, we transform the experience of how we ourselves engage in conflict, not just how we encounter and deal with others about it.

Another lesson learned is how some management of difference can be formal and supported by experts from the outside, and some takes informal support from insiders from within the community. Kolb (1992) addresses the constraints of conflict intervention coming from hired facilitators since they are viewed as outsiders (p. 65); instead, she says 'peacemakers' are 'insiders who generally have a far greater knowledge of their colleagues than an outsider could possibly have. Their expertise comes from their insider status, the fact that they understand the psychology of the situation, and the political realities of the systems within which they work' (p. 65). Informal peacemaking becomes an informal process of everyday experiences rather than a designated, formal discussion (p. 66). While the author received messages that she was an outsider as a relative newcomer to the Western Maryland community (even after living in the region for nearly eight years), her experience matches what Kolb proposes are themes in 'behind the scenes peacemaking': getting involved, being located in 'positions where they can learn about emerging problems and conflicts' (p. 77), and being involved in peacemaking activities to assist 'private conflicts to become public' (p. 80) and to thus be negotiated.

An evolution in dialogic space to negotiate public conflict will only come from moving beyond the framework of 'us vs. them' (as in town vs. gown) to embrace a hybridized understanding of the 'other'. A hybridized, localized 'other' would offer a way to achieve a narrow plot of common ground (Stern and Ruminski, 2014). An example of this standpoint is an FSU graduate who stays in Frostburg or the region to grow and build his or her family and/or livelihood and continues to participate in the Frostburg community, as evident through a Facebook group called the 'Bobcats for Safer Student Living', which organized quickly after the most recent house fire tragedy that involved off-campus student residents in Frostburg, killing on African American student. Started by a few alumni of FSU who graduated recently and who share concern about student safety and their alma mater's reputation, the group rapidly grew in membership to over 700 members over a few days, with the aim of emphasizing off-campus housing safety. Group organizers, all Caucasians, were friends linked through Greek life while at FSU, reached out to current campus resources, including the dialogue series, as they organized their group. The group's purpose revealed a similar identity as the Frostburg community slogan does— values of resilience, pride, and invitation—as they sat on the borders of 'town' and 'gown' to help keep the conversation going through an online forum and participation in the dialogue series. Frostburg's 'cooler future', then, is recognizable as that larger stakeholder group that includes younger alumni who can transcend regional and cultural distance through online connectedness and engaged citizen leadership. FSU alumni realize they still want to be linked to this 'cooler' place, virtually, geographically, and importantly, dialogically, and this kind of co-construction of 'peace' in the community is what sustains campus and community in this Appalachian college town. Thus, the 'world of experiences' offered by FSU has included engagement in the local community of the college town, an experience available beyond graduation. The benefits of the Sustaining Campus and Community Dialogue Series, then, include sustaining the well-being and safety of self and others and achieving increased respect and strengthened social ties with any who become part of the Frostburg community.

References

P. Born (2014) *Deepening Community: Finding Joy Together in Chaotic Times* (San Francisco, CA: Berrett-Koehler Publishers).

L. Bowman (2011) *Being Black in Brownsville: Echoes of a 'Forgotten' Frostburg* 2nd ed. (MD: Frostburg).

The City of Frostburg (26 June 2013) Economic Development Program, Handout.

C. A. Constantino and C. S. Merchant. (1996) *Designing Conflict Management Systems: A Guide to Creating Productive and Healthy Organizations* (San Francisco, CA: Jossey Bass).

Frostburg Business and Professional Association (26 June 2013) Meeting minutes.

Frostburg State University (2014) About FSU: History of the University, http://www.frostburg.edu/about/history/, date accessed 27 May 2015.

Frostburg State University (2014) About FSU: Mission of the University, http://www.frostburg.edu/about/univ/, date accessed 27 May 2015.

Frostburg State University (2012) Frostburg State University Recognized as a University of Distinction, http://www.frostburg.edu/home/news/university-news-portal/frostburg-state-university-recognized-as-a-college-of-distinctionpifsu-admitted-to-group-of-institutions-lauded-for-well-rounded-educational-experienceip/, date accessed 27 May 2015.

Frostburg State University (2014) Frostburg State University Trends in Undergraduate and Graduate Enrollment, Fall 2010–2014, http://www.frostburg.edu/linkservid/5230BFBB-4E9C-4289-85467882D38D1020/showMeta/0/, date accessed 27 May 2015.

Frostburg State University (2000) Wins First-Ever Higher Education Award for Leadership in National Service, http://www.frostburg.edu/home/news/university-news-portal/frostburg-state-university-wins-first-ever-higher-education-award-for-leadership-in-national-service/, date accessed 27 May 2015.

M. Herzig and L. Chasin. (2006) Fostering Dialogue Across Divides: A Nuts and Bolts Guide from the Public Conversations Project, http://www.publicconversations.org/sites/default/files/PCP_Fostering%20Dialogue%20Across%20Divides.pdf, date accessed 27 May 2015.

Ku Klux Klan Plans Rally in Cumberland on Saturday (27 April 2014). *Cumberland Times News*, http://www.times-news.com/news/local_news/ku-klux-klan-plans-rally-in-cumberland-on-saturday/article_fa5a47c4-4e33-504b-878e-42440eb51ccb.html, date accessed 27 May 2015.

L. F. Kay and D. Markus (3 February 2010) Building Fire Kills 2 Frostburg Students, *Baltimore Sun*, http://articles.baltimoresun.com/2010-12-03/news/bs-md-fatal-frostburg-fire-20101203_1_annapolis-woman-frostburg-students-early-morning-apartment-fire, date accessed 27 May 2015.

D. M. Kolb (1992) 'Women's Work: Peacemaking in Organizations', in D. M. Kolb and J. M. Bartunek (eds) *Hidden Conflict in Organizations: Uncovering Behind-the-Scenes Disputes* (Newbury Park, CA: Sage), pp. 63–91.

S. R. Komives (Jul–Aug 1996) 'A Call for Collaborative Leadership', *About Campus*, 2–3.

G. Lakoff and M. Johnson (2003) *Metaphors We Live By* (Chicago: U of Chicago P) The Last Word (Spring 2012) *Profile*, 24 (2), 36–37.

K. Lewis (15 April 2014) Lateef Gazal, Frostburg Student, Dies in House Fire, WJLA, http://www.wjla.com/articles/2014/02/frostburg-state-student-from-bowie-dies-in-house-fire-100260.html, date accessed 27 May 2015.

S. W. Littlejohn and K. Domenici (2007) *Communication, Conflict, and the Management of Difference* (Long Grove, IL: Waveland).

MACRO (2012) Frostburg State University and Maryland Mediation and Conflict Resolution Office, Memorandum of Understanding, MOU number 12-001-FSU-CBP.

Mediation and Conflict Resolution Office (MACRO) (2015) http://www.courts.state.md.us/macro/, date accessed 27 May 2015.

K. H. Powell (2013) *In the Shadow of the Ivory Tower: Neighborhood Relations in a College Town* (Baltimore: Graduate School of the University of Maryland).

L. Schirch (2004) *The Little Book of Strategic Peacebuilding* (Intercourse, PA: Good Books).

D. B. Stern and E. L. Ruminski (2014) Moving Town and Gown from Dissent to Dialogue: Sustaining Campus and Community in Frostburg, Maryland, Paper presented at the Annual Meeting of the Eastern Communication Association, Providence, R.I.

A. Taylor (2011) Frostburg Community Mourns Death of Kortneigh McCoy, *Afro*, 9, http://www.afro.com/frostburg-community-mourns-death-of-kortneigh-mccoy/, date accessed 27 May 2015.

This Week in the Future (2 April 2014) *The Bottom Lie*, 5.

UCARE (University and Community Action for Racial Equality) (2012) Institute for Environmental Negotiation, https://pages.shanti.virginia.edu/ucare/, date accessed 27 May 2015.

State and County Quick Facts (2014) U. S. Department of Commerce, United States Census Bureau, http://quickfacts.census.gov/qfd/index.html, date accessed 27 May 2015.

J. White (19 Feb 2010) Frostburg Student from Waldorf Slain after Off Campus Party, *The Washington Post*, http://www.washingtonpost.com/wp-dyn/content/article/2010/04/18/AR2010041802460.html, date accessed 27 May 2015.

13
Jewish-Muslim Women's Leadership Initiative: A Program for Peaceful Dialogue

Jing Lin, Sachi Edwards, and Sahar Khamis

Introduction

Resolving cultural and political conflicts, building peace around the world, and reorienting our societies towards harmony and justice are goals that scholars and practitioners across many fields seek to attain. When faced with challenges such as these, education serves as a promising tool for helping the next generation of global citizens and leaders to develop skills in peaceful cross-cultural communication. This chapter explores one such education initiative – the Jewish-Muslim Women's Leadership Initiative (WLI) – which brought together graduate and undergraduate women from Jewish and Muslim backgrounds to collaboratively explore the possibility for mutual understanding and inter-cultural cooperation. Set in the context of US higher education, the processes and outcomes of the WLI point to several interesting implications for those engaged in peacebuilding and conflict resolution, both within and beyond the field of education. Using qualitative research methods and analyses, this chapter describes the WLI, discusses the theoretical foundations of this type of pedagogical approach, and explores both difficulties and successes of the program with regard to its goals of fostering intercultural communication and collaborative action.

In light of the historical and ongoing reality of the Israeli-Palestinian conflict, pedagogical approaches to Jewish-Muslim dialogue are particularly important. Moreover, given that women are often underrepresented in peacebuilding processes we see a need for greater empirical and practice-based attention to women's potential as leaders in the worldwide peace movement. In addition, college-aged students – as they expand their horizons through higher education and prepare to take on the reigns as future world leaders – represent an especially valuable group to target in peace education initiatives. Thus, the case study presented here focuses specifically on Jewish and Muslim college women, and considers the ways in which they may be uniquely qualified to contribute to global discussions on peace and conflict resolution.

Theoretical foundations of intercultural pedagogies

This research draws upon literature from the related fields of peace education and conflict resolution. To be sure, there is a plethora of literature and research on educational programs that involve Jewish and Muslim students in an effort to increase peace between these two historically conflicting groups. However, the bulk of this corpus of work is dedicated to analysing initiatives set in contexts of violence and overt conflict – i.e., in Israel/Palestine or other Middle-Eastern regions. While we recognize that this type of research and discourse is important, we seek here to draw attention to peace education programs further removed from these conflict zones, where the aim is to build peace and foster unity, rather than to simply reduce instances of aggressive violence.

The contact hypothesis (Allport, 1954) and intergroup contact theory (Pettigrew, 1998) have been consistently supported in empirical literature as helpful frameworks for understanding the necessary conditions and processes for resolving conflict and reducing intergroup bias in a contact situation (Binder et al., 2009; Pettigrew and Tropp, 2006; Shook and Fazio, 2008). These theories – we speak of them together here because intergroup contact theory grew out of and expanded upon the contact hypothesis – posit that in order for contact between conflicting groups to succeed in decreasing feelings of hatred, fear, or resentment towards each other, there are five essential conditions and four essential processes that must be met:

Five essential conditions
1. All participants must have *equal status* in the contact situation
2. Participants must all have a *common goal*
3. They all must *work cooperatively* to reach that goal
4. There must be *institutional support* enforcing equal status of participants
5. The contact situation must be sustained to ensure *friendship potential*

Four essential processes

1. *Learning about the other* in order to create new foundations of knowledge
2. Developing new group norms which lead to *behavior and attitude change*
3. Incorporating *emotions* to help *generate affective ties*
4. Reassessing perceptions of their own group through *in-group reappraisal*

Accordingly, the design of the WLI program (to be described in the next section) purposefully incorporates the conditions and processes outlined by the contact hypothesis and intergroup contact theory.

As peace education scholars point out, resolving conflicts and reducing bias is not only necessary for overtly violent situations, it is also needed in seemingly 'peaceful' situations where there may be underlying misunderstanding and prejudice (Galtung, 1969, 1990; Harris and Morrison, 2003). Addressing conflict at this stage – the 'cultural' stage, according to Galtung (1969) – ultimately prevents prejudiced attitudes from escalating into more extreme atrocities such as war or genocide. As such, the WLI program engaged college women in the United States (a rhetorically peaceful context) in conversations about the situation in Israel-Palestine in an effort to address the root causes of this conflict.

Research approach

This project is a qualitative, exploratory case study. Our guiding curiosity in this research was to understand what our participants experienced during the WLI, what they felt they gained from their experience, and what processes they felt were most beneficial to their learning. However, we largely employed the 'let's see what happens' approach, modeled after Khuri's (2004) research on Arab-Jewish dialogue.

The WLI was designed and conceived by the three authors of this chapter – who all served as facilitators of the program – in order to incorporate the conditions and processes of positive intergroup contact, as outlined by the theories described above. A total of 14 college-aged women (eight Muslim and six Jewish) enrolled in the program, and received one elective credit for their participation. Throughout the program, participant-observation served as an important method of inquiry. Additionally, we analysed participants' online discussions and written reflections as another data source. Lastly, after the WLI ended, we administered open-ended questionnaires that served as post-program evaluations. These evaluations were then analysed in order to ascertain what impact the program had on the participants' attitude, communication skills, intended action or behavior, or perspectives on women's ability to serve as leaders in the peace movement.

What we present below is both descriptive and analytical. Our intention is to draw a clear picture of the WLI so that other practitioners who are looking to develop programs like this can learn from our experiences, successes, and challenges. We also offer reflections on and theoretical analysis of our program, in an attempt to contribute to the larger discussion about intercultural communication, peace education, and conflict resolution represented in this book.

Program implementation

The WLI was a semester-long program, funded in part by the United States Institute of Peace, which brought together Jewish and Muslim female college students to explore their own potential for contributing to peaceful Jewish-Muslim relations in the midst of the ongoing Israeli-Palestinian conflict. The program took place at a large public institution in a cosmopolitan region of the United States with large numbers of both Jewish and Muslim students. Recruitment for participation in the program was done through campus-based Jewish and Muslim student organizations and through our own professional networks. In the end, 13 undergraduate students and one graduate student enrolled in the program. There were three distinct stages to the program:

Stage one: online engagement

The first stage of the program was facilitated online through the university's online course platform. Program facilitators assigned weekly readings, posted weekly discussion questions, and facilitated online conversations about the various topics covered in the readings. Specifically, students learned about and discussed (a) the multiple perspectives on the history between Israel and Palestine, (b) conflict resolution and peacebuilding techniques commonly used in conflict situations around the world, (c) the impact of social media on the Middle East peace process, and (d) the opportunity for women to take leading roles in peacebuilding efforts. Immediately, starting with the first week's reading and discussion thread, students began expressing strong interest in, and emotional reactions to, the material. As a result, the online discussions were very lively, engaging, and thought provoking.

Stage two: full-day workshop

Towards the middle of the semester, all participating students attended a full-day workshop where they (a) engaged in face-to-face dialogue about the major lessons learned in stage one of the program; (b) listened to presentations by local female activists working on peacebuilding in Israel/Palestine; (c) collaborated with each other to develop ideas for peace building projects in their respective communities and/or campus organizations; and (d) learned about existing opportunities for engagement in Jewish-Muslim peace building both on their campus and in their city. The day started in the morning with breakfast and community building activities, and ended with dinner at the on-campus Jewish student center. One student, a broadcast journalism major and motivational speaker, live-tweeted the entire day on her Twitter page to over 8,000 followers.

Stage three: student project implementation

In the third stage of the program, students began implementing the projects they developed during the full-day workshop. Projects included: (a) a Jewish-Muslim co-ed book club, where participants read books pertinent to either the Israeli-Palestinian conflict, or any other issue related to Jewish-Muslim relations around the world; (b) a membership campaign to attract students to the Jewish-Muslim Alliance, a campus-based student organization; and (c) a YouTube video promoting peace between Jews and Muslims featuring all the members of the WLI group, which to date has received nearly 5,000 views. Beyond these projects, WLI participants stayed engaged through Facebook, Twitter, Instagram and other social media outlets to report on successes and challenges of their various projects. They also remained engaged with us, the program facilitators, so that we could help guide them through the implementation of their projects.

Findings

Learning about multiple perspectives

The very first reading assignment and topic of discussion in the online stage of the program was a piece by Katirai (2001) that outlined the history of the Israeli-Palestinian conflict from 1880–2000. In this article, Israeli and Palestinian perspectives on various political and historical moments are presented side by side. In doing so, the contrast between these divergent perspectives is highlighted – for instance, what Israelis celebrate as the 'War of Independence' in 1948, Palestinians call 'The

Catastrophe' (Katirai, 2001, p. 2). This article, and the subsequent discussion amongst the students, was one of the more eye opening and impactful parts of the program because it forced the students – both Jewish and Muslim – to consider how their own perspectives on the Israeli-Palestinian conflict have been shaped by their upbringing. Conversely, they began to consider how others, who were raised in differing familial/cultural contexts, might see the same historical events in an entirely different light.

Through exchanging ideas and reactions to this article, the students, from the very first week of the program, began to engage in deep and critical dialogue across lines of culture and religion. As an example, the following is a small excerpt from the online exchange between a Jewish and Muslim student related to the Katirai (2001) article:

> *The stark contrast between the names given by either side to the numerous conflicts is intriguing. The name gives way to notions, which effectively express the motivations of the incidents. For example, in 1948, with the creation of the State of Israel, the war that ensued is called 'War of Independence' by Israel and yet Palestinians call it the Catastrophe. Obviously, anti-Israel and perhaps even anti-Semitic sentiments are embedded in this loaded terminology.* (Jewish Student)
>
> *I appreciate your point of view; however, I would like to clarify that the Palestinians don't refer to the war as the Nakba because Israel wasn't destroyed, but because that was when they began asserting their independence on the Palestinian people and taking over the land, and ended up being a catastrophe indeed.* (Muslim Student)

Moreover, because these online discussions were monitored and facilitated by us, the facilitators, we were able to interject with pointed questions and constructive critique when necessary. For instance, when the Jewish student (same student as quoted above) made remarks that the Muslim students could have easily taken offense to, one of us interrupted the discussion thread by asking the student to reconsider how others may interpret her comment.

> *What continues to surprise me is the stubbornness of the Palestinian people ... [they] feel entitled to land they originally refused of their own volition, and continue to hold Israel responsible for that mistake through the expression of anger through violent means. However, I am puzzled by their obstinacy in that they continually express their desire for a state. The Israelis were going to give it to them for the guarantee of peace, something which should ideally already be a given!* (Jewish Student)

I think you raise a good point about how terminology can be so loaded and can elicit emotional responses from people. Emotions often get in the way of productive dialogue, so I'd like to delve deeper into that. Can you talk more about how you reacted, emotionally, to the notion that Palestinians call Israel's 'War of Independence' the 'Catastrophe'? Where do those emotions come from and what life experiences have you had that led you to feel that way? On the flip side, how do you think a Palestinian person would react emotionally to the comment that their people are 'stubborn' and 'obstinate'? Where do you think their emotions would be coming from and what life experiences might they have had that led them to feel that way? (Facilitator)

After we put forth these questions, the Jewish student clarified some of her comments, apologized if anyone had misinterpreted her, and opted for language that described her feelings about the situation in a way that was much less aggressive and more respectful. In fact, she explained how Jewish tradition celebrates stubbornness as a characteristic of successful survival, explaining that she did not mean to offend Palestinians by her statement. As this exchange exemplifies, online communication – without the ability to see body language and facial expressions, or to clarify yourself if you notice others reacting defensively – can often be misinterpreted and can lead to unintended negative feelings between participants in an intercultural dialogue such as this. Thus, it was important that we, the facilitators, were active participants in the online discussion threads in order to prevent any potential negative feelings between participants during this stage of the program.

Overall, most of the students stated that reading and discussing this article was very helpful to broadening their understanding of the Israeli-Palestinian conflict. This represented the most emotional, but also the most beneficial part of the class for many of them.

I really enjoyed seeing the views and reactions to everything that has happened in history, side by side. I think most people are aware that the Israeli and Palestinian perspectives are different but when it is laid out in a way similar to this document, it is clearer and easier to understand or analyse. (Jewish Student)

Seeing Israel's perspective right next to Palestine's perspective made me see why each side feels the way that they do. Each side is telling its own story which affects how the historical event is reflected. (Muslim Student)

This article made it clear how there is not one side to the story and that the same event can be interpreted in different ways by different groups. (Jewish Student)

> *To be honest I have always known that different perspectives exist, but reading this just gave me a stark reminder of how bad it was. I wonder how a resolution could ever be reached if the two sides cannot even agree on what occurred. Growing up I was always taught the Palestinian side of things and I didn't even know that a different perspective existed. Now that I see how differently things are viewed I try and read both and internally try and come to a mid-ground to what may have really happened.* (Muslim Student)

Beginning the WLI in this way set a foundation for the rest of the program. It prepared the students to think about how their peers may have completely different perspectives than they do, and reminded them to consider that in future conversations we have about potentially sensitive issues. Of all the topics covered during stage one of the WLI – past and current conflict resolution methods used in Israel/Palestine and around the world, peace activism through social media, the Arab Spring, women's roles in the peace movement, Israeli checkpoints set up throughout Palestine, and Israel's anti-terrorist task force Shin Bet – this first discussion thread was regarded by the students as the most eye-opening.

Gender and religion as unifying forces

During stage two of the WLI (the full-day workshop) we spent a great deal of time talking about how women have contributed, and can continue to contribute to the peace effort in Israel/Palestine. For a portion of the day, an invited speaker discussed feminist perspectives on peace activism, and the importance of female involvement in a male/masculine-dominated field such as conflict resolution. As a Jewish woman who has spent her career working for various organizations promoting peacebuilding initiatives in Israel/Palestine and in various other conflict zones around the world, the students found her stories and her message inspiring.

> *I really think that [the speaker] was a great choice. She really put the conflict into perspective and her immense experience helped a lot.* (Muslim Student)
>
> *The speaker brought terrific insight and was incredibly inspiring.* (Muslim Student)

Aside from her formal presentation, the speaker participated for the entire workshop (including all meals) as an additional facilitator and dialogue member. The students truly enjoyed her company, and enjoyed meeting a woman who was so active in the peacebuilding process. It gave them a new perspective on their own value, as women, in the ongoing struggle for peace.

> *Women have the potential to change the beliefs of the upcoming generation and instill compassion and empathy in others hearts. We can help people understand perspectives.* (Muslim Student)
> *I learned that we are important and vital actors in peace building initiatives. We are a necessary force and all the things that make us different from men are all the things that make us a great balancing force in the peace building process.* (Muslim Student)
> *Sisterhood is key. Through this unique workshop we showed that women have such similarities across the board that by joining together for those commonalities, the politics and the propaganda simply fall away. Women therefore have a unique motivation for peace because our first job is to be mothers. We must protect our families.* (Jewish Student)

The women in this WLI began to appreciate their connection to each other as fellow women, and celebrated their femininity as a unifying force. However, beyond gender, the participants also turned to religion as an additional unifier between them. During our workshop, we watched the movie *Arranged* (Cicala Flimworks, 2007), which tells the story of a Jewish woman and a Muslim women bonding over their commitment to their respective religions. Then, when we asked the women to reflect on what divides Jews and Muslims and what unites them. They talked a lot about their own struggles, as religious minorities, to be understood in the Christian dominant society, and how they were able to relate to each other on this level. This blossomed into a conversation about how, on the surface, religion seems to be a divisive issue between Jews and Muslims, but that in fact Jews and Muslims have a great deal in common with each other – and that the Middle East peace process should focus on these commonalities.

Student impact

At the end of the WLI, we administered program evaluations where we asked students to write open-ended comments about the way they felt they were impacted by their participation in the WLI. Most of the participants' comments surrounded the effect of the program on their attitudes towards conflict (both the Israeli-Palestinian conflict in particular, and inter-ethnic conflict in general) and their skills in productive cross-group communication. Accordingly, this section summarizes their feedback within those two subcategories.

Attitude changes

For both Jewish and Muslim participants, participation in the WLI led to attitude changes. As Pettigrew (1998) suggested, adopting the norms of a new group – in this case, the group of women that comprised the WLI – often requires a behavioral shift, which ultimately leads to a change in one's attitude. In the WLI, participants commented that by learning to see each other as fellow women, rather than thinking about ethnic or religious categories, they began to develop an entirely different perspective on the situation in Israel/Palestine.

> *I gained a new way of thinking about the conflict through this workshop. Instead of focusing on the two sides, Israeli and Palestinian, a lot of the workshop taught me how to analyse the conflict from a woman's perspective, or even a mother's point of view. I think this was able to unite all of us, because we disregarded faith and opinion of the conflict in the Middle East in favor of a perspective on which we could all agree.* (Jewish Student)
>
> *I realized now more than ever how similar we all are despite religious ideas and values that separate us. The general ideas of humanity are the same. After participating in this program I realize the Israeli-Palestinian issue transcends any differences between the two groups. These are political and strategic forces being enacted and the Israeli and Palestinian people are victims of a bigger initiative that has nothing to do with them.* (Muslim Student)

After stepping back and opening up to a new way of approaching the conflict, the WLI participants were able to engage in what Pettigrew (1998) calls *ingroup reappraisal* – where they begin to critically analyse themselves and the sources of their respective opinions. Many of them recognized that their previous understandings of the Israeli-Palestinian conflict had been shaped by their families and communities, which only provided them with one side of the story. This process was particularly difficult for some of the Jewish students.

> *I grew up in a very Jewish environment which taught me the fundamental values of being Jewish. I also gained a deep love for Israel the Jewish homeland and State. Even at a young age I had knowledge of the conflict, especially the Israeli and Jewish perspectives ... I was taught that most*

criticism of Israel is hyperbole and too much condemning criticism is directed at Israel due to anti-Semitism and anti-Zionism. I find it challenging to confront that aspect of what I was taught. (Jewish Student)

However, the WLI helped them to do this type of critical reflection in an environment that was safe and supportive. Ultimately, some of them were able to recognize the biases they were raised with, and, in turn, became more sensitive to the plight of the Palestinians.

Before participating in this program, I had been told both sides of the Israeli-Palestinian conflict, but only in an all Jewish setting, so obviously, my perspective on the issue was a little biased. I had gotten my information about the Israeli-Palestinian conflict from my family, friends, and the Jewish schools that I have attended. I am definitely more sensitive about the Israeli-Palestinian conflict and other people's opinions on this issue (and others). I am more understanding of the dual nature of the conflict and the fact that there is a reasonable explanation for both sides of a conflict and that much conflict stems from emotions. (Jewish Student)

Other participants did not experience the same level of attitude transformation, but nevertheless, expressed appreciation for the time they spent with the group that enabled them to have positive interactions that they had not previously experienced.

My ideas and beliefs have not changed very much ... but I very much enjoyed spending time with the Muslim students and think my interactions may have become a little bit better (Jewish Student).

Through these positive interactions, both Jewish and Muslim students developed a stronger sense of hope for the potential for peace, and for their own role in bringing about peaceful change.

I have much higher hopes for peace in general – regarding any conflict but in this case specifically the conflict in the Middle East (Muslim Student).
   I feel more that as a united group, we will be able to make a difference and hopefully bring the issue to more people (Jewish Student).

New communications skills

Beyond attitude changes, the participants' described some tangible skills for effective cross-group communication that the WLI helped them learn. With religion and politics – commonly known as the most controversial and taboo topics to raise in public conversations – both heavily intertwined in the Israeli-Palestinian conflict, our participants had very little experience ever speaking about the issue with those outside of their own familial or religious communities. Thus, this program represented, for many of them, the first time they were able to directly address this topic with those who had different perspectives than they did. The result, however, was positive because they discovered that discussing the Israeli-Palestinian conflict could be done in a calm and respectful way.

> *Before the program, I had never had a productive discussion on the Israeli-Palestinian conflict with those who had opposing views on the situation from mine, but I learned how to have a good and useful discussion and progress towards peace. After the workshop, I am definitely more sensitive towards the Palestinian viewpoint than I had previously been* (Jewish Student).

Specifically, they learned communication strategies such as circle sitting, establishing common ground and shared goals, and incorporating human emotions. While something as simple as sitting in a circle may seem trivial, the students learned that creating an environment that is conducive to group cohesion and the development of shared energy (as many spiritual traditions recognize circle sitting has the power to do) is an important foundational element to positive inter- and intra-group dialogue.

> *I have learned about the different feminist approaches in relation to peace activism. It is about power with men not over men in the peace building process. I have learned about the technique of sitting in a circle, which is more conducive to cooperation in peace building negotiations.* (Muslim Student)
>
> *I have learned that to be most effective in exchanging peaceful dialogue one must first establish the similarities and common goals. Then moving on to a heated topic doesn't sound so threatening or intimidating.* (Jewish Student)
>
> *Many, I learned that the first step is communication. And once that begins happening everything else sort of follows. I also learned to not stop being a human. Many people involved have put aside their humanity on a shelf so to speak, and I think this is one of the core problems.* (Muslim Student)

Additionally, the WLI participants learned about harnessing their aptitude for social media as another means of sustaining communication with each other even after the WLI was over. By doing so, not only were they able to maintain the momentum they developed with their peace action projects, they were also able to share their work with people outside the WLI group – in other words, they were able to use new media as a new form of peaceful communication and dialogue. These women were extremely proud of the projects they developed, and were excited to use social media as a tool for communicating their efforts with a wider group of people.

I think that the creation of initiatives was the most effective part of the program. We were able to put our creative energies to work! (Jewish Student).

Summary and conclusions

The results of this exploratory research project indicate several interesting points. First, learning about the multiple perspectives on the Israeli-Palestinian conflict proved to be the most difficult part of the process for the WLI participants, igniting emotional reactions from both Jews and Muslims. In turn, it became the most important part of the program for building bridges of understanding between the two groups, establishing a common sense of desire for mutual peace, and inspiring critical self-reflection among the participants. Ultimately, this process allowed the group to feel more connected, better able to communicate, and more passionate about future peace activism.

Secondly, WLI participants chose to focus both on their shared female identity, and their mutual commitment to their respective religious beliefs as a unifying factor between the two groups. As Pettigrew (1998) explains, focusing on a common group membership over identity differences can help change individuals' attitudes towards 'others' – and we certainly saw that here. Moreover, with several strong female role models who are actively involved in the peace process, the WLI students were able to envision their own potential in the Israeli-Palestinian peace movement that has historically been dominated by male/masculine forces.

Finally, participants reported changes in their attitude toward the Israeli-Palestinian conflict, and the development of new skills in cross-group communication. Galtung (1990) reminds us that changes in attitude (i.e., bias reduction and increased understanding of alternative perspectives) is an integral part of preventing future acts of aggressive violence. Moreover, the ability to calmly and respectfully dialogue about highly sensitive issues will enable these women to spread the message of peace more effectively as they continue their journey in peace activism. Also, the assistance of social and new media will help them disseminate this message on an even wider scale, engaging their peers from all corners of the globe in the next generation of peaceful inter-cultural dialogue.

The peace action projects that these students developed through the WLI are just three examples of the type of initiatives young women can undertake within the larger peacebuilding process. The projects included: (1) a Jewish-Muslim co-ed book club, where participants read books pertinent to either the Israeli-Palestinian conflict, or any other issue related to Jewish-Muslim relations around the world; (2) a membership campaign to attract students to the Jewish-Muslim Alliance, a campus-based student organization; and (3) a YouTube video compiled by one of the participants featuring the WLI group which has received nearly 5,000 views so far. By having the students create these projects as a part of the program, we were able to ensure that the peacebuilding efforts continued even after the WLI had come to an end.

While the research presented here deals specifically with college-aged women and the Israeli-Palestinian conflict, the implications of our study are relevant for a broad range of inter-cultural conflicts, both around the world and right here in the United States. The processes we used to implement the WLI represent a tangible, action-oriented approach to working with college-aged students. We see an increasing importance of youth and women's involvement in peacebuilding efforts, particularly in the realm of enacting political and social change – as we saw in the Arab Spring. It is our hope that through sharing experiences such as this, and collaboratively growing our peacebuilding 'toolbox', that collectively we can reach our common goal of peace.

References

G. W. Allport (1954) *The Nature of Prejudice* (Cambridge, MA: Addison-Wesley Pub. Co).

Arranged, 2007, Motion Picture, Cicala Filmworks, USA.

J. Binder, H. Zagefka, F. Funke, T. Kessler, A. Mummendey, A. Maquil, S. Demoulin and J. P. Leyens (2009) 'Does Contact Reduce Prejudice or Does Prejudice Reduce Contact?: A Longitudinal Test of the Contact Hypothesis among Majority and Minority Groups in Three European Countries', *Journal of Personality and Social Psychology*, 96, 843–856.

J. Galtung (1969) 'Violence, Peace, and Peace Research', *Journal of Peace Research*, 6 (3), 167–191.

J. Galtung (1990) 'Cultural Violence', *Journal of Peace Research*, 27 (3), 291–305.

I. M. Harris and M. L. Morrison (2003) *Peace Education* (Jefferson, NC: McFarland).

N. Katirai (2001) 'History of the Israeli-Palestinian Conflict', *Point of View* (American Documentaries, Inc).

M. L. Khuri (2004) 'Facilitating Arab-Jewish Intergroup Dialogue in the College Setting', *Race, Ethnicity and Education*, 7 (3), 229–250.

T. F. Pettigrew (1998) 'Intergroup Contact Theory', *Annual Review of Psychology*, 49 (1), 65–85.

T. F. Pettigrew and L. R. Tropp (2006) 'A Meta-Analytic Test of Intergroup Contact Theory', *Journal of Personality and Social Psychology*, 90 (5), 751–83.

N. J. Shook and R. H. Fazio (2008) 'Interracial Roommate Relationships: An Experimental Field Test of the Contact Hypothesis', *Psychological Science*, 19 (7), 717–723.

Part IV
From Singular/Static to Multiple/Dynamic: Creative and Alternative Communication Approaches to Conflict Negotiation and Social Change

The final part of the volume posits interesting questions about how to approach peace when the conflicts are so varied. Are education and information alone sufficient to engender peace? Which processes should be applicable to which scenarios? Bailey's Chapter 14 provides a solid foundation in conceptualizing gender conflict from an unusual stance, as well as highlights a theoretical approach to combining justice and care towards gender peaceability. Saito's Chapter 15 is even more provocative as he encourages the readers to think beyond reactionary approaches to conflict. He promotes an approach that nips the bud of conflict even before it blooms by choosing to protect and use resources, especially food, in a conscious and intelligent manner. Noorzai and Hale's Chapter 16 introduces peace activism through creative use of the arts. In fact, their study found that activists, in this case singers and poets, consider their artistic work important for giving voice to ordinary people and supporting peace activism. Finally, Uysal's Chapter 17 paves the way for interfaith dialogue that can contribute to ameliorating conflict and advancing reconciliation even when religion is not the central cause of a conflict. Organizing dialogue across religious boundaries enables people of faith to live out what most faith traditions consider as sacred duty to be peacemakers.

14

Differing and Disparate Arguments about Gender Roles: Creating Peace through Talking about Threats and Relational Dialectics

Garry Bailey

Introduction

Gender and sex violence, discrimination, and stereotyping continue to be issues of major concern around the world. When it comes to gender roles, there are cultures and communities of shared views as well as radically different views and approaches in the world. Interestingly, in most cultures, men and women seem to believe strongly that they have the correct view. The issues are important enough to be of primary concern among the United Nations in WomenWatch (information and resources on gender equality and empowerment of women), the Security Council, the United Nations Rule of Law, and in many other international and national agencies, such as the Peace Corps.

As a result of the differing views about gender roles, there are arguments about equal pay for equal work, maternity and paternity leaves, sexual harassment in the workplace, etc. The different views of gender roles reach to the disparate levels of limiting opportunities in education, government, or workplaces, and in many places to forced covering, or even the extremes of culturally, politically, and legally approved rape or executions (Ahmed, 2011). Some would argue that this is the way the world works, so men and women need to deal with it. Others argue that these conditions are social, cultural, and religious constructs that need to be addressed (Alessio, 2011). This chapter will, thus, focus on the interpersonal gender relationships that define gender roles and what it is to be part of a society based on these gender roles. The chapter will explore ways to sustain peace between members of opposing genders. The relational experiences of gender roles, threats, and dialectics will be broached as a productive approach to addressing the differing and disparaging arguments about gender roles.

The threats that people experience vary from the stereotypical (Steele, 2010) to the very real (Stephan and Stephan, 2000). Steele (2010) describes how females are stereotyped as lacking logic and scientific competence but in research on this stereotype, where research indicates that there is no real gender difference in their ability, females typically performed as well as males on the test. It is no wonder that males grow up having discriminatory attitudes toward females. These psychological stereotypes become real threats against women when they regularly deal with anything from being treated as inferior to sexual assault and other physical harm (Stephan and Stephan, 2000). But for the number of problems described in research, there are as many solutions identified.

Suggestions for establishing gender equality around the world range from ensuring that women have equal access to educational opportunities (Ahmed, 2011), to women becoming active participants in local economies, and ensuring that there are equal numbers of women represented in government positions and political processes (Moghadam, 2008). Gender equality advocates in religious contexts suggest that women with strong religious convictions have a voice in participating in and reforming church, synagogue, or mosque policies (Roded, 2012). Moreover, advocates urge that legislation creates clear consequences for gender violence and discrimination in all contexts (Trofin and Tomescu, 2010). These are good goals that will help women seeking greater participation in societal institutions. True change, however, will come from advocating for gender peacemaking at the relational level.

The arguments for change are challenged by the arguments advocating for the legitimacy of patriarchal social orders (Gallagher and Smith, 1999). Arguments that support the status quo and maintain a male-dominant gender role often have roots in perspectives of political, social, and religious traditions as well as perspectives related to physical and psychological capacity (Erden-Imamoglu, 2013). Some arguments supporting these differing gender roles arise from social orders that merged with political governance processes and religious beliefs. These arguments are also supported by claims that women are weaker than men or that they are too emotional to handle 'male' jobs (Hebson et al., 2007).

Because of these differing and often disparate arguments about gender roles, peace is an elusive construct for men and women. Generally, peace can be described in a number of ways including from a feminist perspective. However, none of the described approaches address the concerns of both a masculine and feminine view within relationships. And it is within relationships that people live out their gender role beliefs. These can be very satisfying or horrifying depending on the views. One way to address this is through an integration of two ethical approaches to relational conflicts, the ethic of justice and the ethic of care. These approaches to ethics actually create an appropriate and balanced construct for gender peacemaking. Carol Gilligan, in her landmark book *In a Different Voice* (1982), articulated a vision for ethics in two distinct gender voices. Debates about these ethical views have continued for years (White, 2009). However, there is recognition that the two views have relevance for ethical decision-making (Botes, 2000, White, 2009).

Bringing together a masculine and feminine ethic as an approach to peace enables gender roles within relationships to establish a sustainable peacemaking pattern. Boulding and Boulding (1990) talked about the importance of understanding conflict and peace from a dialectical approach. According to this rationale, gender peacemaking is a patterned process of gender relations in conflict responding to problems through either or both the ethic of justice or care. The result is both parties seeking a balance of fairness and love for each other by initiating dialectical interactions of justice and care. To reach a status of peace, the interactions must work out the balance of justice and care depending on the needs of the parties. Bringing together these masculine and feminine approaches enables both parties to participate in the process of establishing a satisfactory resolution. It is only when this happens that gender peacemaking is successful.

The wide ranging differences of arguments often made regarding gender roles create a context for efforts to change or to maintain the status quo in long standing cultural, religious, legal, and organizational traditions (Martens et al., 2006). Typical approaches to gender role change often have little effect or do not create peace in the process because gender peacemaking is not enacted at the relational level. Peace oriented gender role change is more likely when the parties can work through the relevant threats and use dialectical gender peacemaking processes to build sustainable solutions. While this chapter lays out a rationale for the productive study of gender role conflicts, more research is needed to address the various intersections of gender roles, threats, and dialectical gender peacemaking solutions.

Theoretical frames

Gender roles

Gender relation systems are sensitive to differing perspectives on roles particularly because of struggles related to the interdependence and valence of these roles (Gabriel and Gardner, 1999). As a formal theory, the Role perspective goes back to the work of George Herbert Mead (Mead, 1934) and many others. Mead was commonly referred to as the father of Role Theory. More recently, Role Theory has been applied in a lot of research in the context of gender (Colander and Warner, 2005, Erden-Imamoglu, 2013, Grasham, 1999). Erden-Imamoglu (2013) tested gender role formation among Turkish women. This study showed how women demonstrate masculine and feminine gender role characteristics.

Another way that gender roles are often perceived is through egalitarian or complementarian perspectives. This issue is significant for women because religious socialization impacts their career aspirations (Colander and Warner, 2005). Colander and Warner also suggest that traditionally socialized women, or women taking complementarian gender roles, do not aspire to high level careers as much as women who have a more egalitarian religious orientation. And this is significant because almost every society has a history of religious socialization to gender roles (Noss and Grangaard, 2011). For example, the role of women in the restoration movement varied greatly over time (Grasham, 1999) and these changes are reflective of significant changes in society. It is common and significant for religious research to report on notions of gender roles within religious contexts as exemplified in Grasham's (1999) report about the role of women in the restoration movement.

Because of the significance of early-life socialization in the formation of gender roles, the most appropriate starting point for articulating a view of gender peacemaking is the role of religious differentiation of roles. Regardless of whether a boy or a girl has direct experience of religious socialization, most societies are built on roles that are heavily influenced by religion (Noss and Grangaard, 2011). Therefore, in moving towards a conversation about the gender peacemaking process, it is important to understand the role of religious socialization in creating the differences between men and women. It is in the differences that people in conflict can observe the role of threat in gender roles and engage in gender dialectics interaction to manage the conflicts.

Gender roles have long been an issue of debate in theological circles regarding the participation of women in public Christian worship and the relationship between men and women in general (Grasham, 1999). These views about gender roles have evolved into a framework of four different categories giving a more complete picture of the way differentiation of roles takes place (Shaw and Bailey, 2010). The roles of patriarchalism, hierarchical complementarianism, egalitarianism, and radical feminism are identified as descriptive of typical gender roles in church contexts (Guin, 2007, Osburn, 2001). These categories will be described here but the framework makes more sense as a continuum where relations may be best observed between the categories.

These terms can also vary in meaning, however the purpose for using them here is to identify the range of views about gender roles. The patriarchal view suggests that the gender relationship is organized in a way such that the male parent, or the leading male, is the one with authority in a family. The children and wife follow in submission. Simply put, the patriarchal view is a relationship where men lead and women follow (Osburn, 2001).

Hierarchical Complementarianism is a view that softens the perspective of a patriarchal view. According to this view, while women are still in a subordinate role to men, it would be inappropriate to consider them inferior to men (Guin, 2007). The view holds to the perspective of male leadership and female submission (Shaw and Bailey, 2010), but does not value men as superior.

The Egalitarian view takes the perspective that there is equality between men and women. Those who hold the egalitarian view consider authoritative religious writings to be directed toward a particular historical, geographical, and cultural context (Guin, 2007). This view resonates with many contemporary societal norms but is also not accepted in many contexts around the world.

Radical feminism is a term used to describe the opposite view of patriarchalism. The approach of the radical feminist view is to argue that women are better leaders and should have authority over men. Some feminine views would argue for change that creates equality but the radical view is one that views male leadership and authority as problematic. This view is ultimately prejudicial against men. Interestingly, Osburn (2001) considers patriarchalism and radical feminism as lacking beneficial qualities because of their extreme views.

The range of views about gender roles is significant because these roles define the potential for conflict experiences between men and women. If men and women accepted their gender roles without question, conflict would not be an issue and gender peacemaking would not be necessary. However, any configuration of gender roles in a relationship can pose a threat to the participants in the relationship. People in relationships who hold differing views about gender roles are likely to find themselves subject to threats. Therefore, to work through arguments about gender roles, there must also be a discussion of threats that gender roles may experience. The next theoretical frame addresses the issue of threat.

Integrated Threat Theory

Integrated Threat Theory (Stephan and Stephan, 2000) includes four types of threat: Realistic Threats, Symbolic Threats, Intergroup Anxiety, and Negative Stereotypes. These threats are forms of prejudice that limit opportunities and in some cases promote violence. To promote peace-oriented, positive dialogues, this research context suggests that typical interactions between men and women about gender roles will represent differing and disparaging arguments. The following are descriptions of the four types of threat in the Integrated Threat Theory.

Realistic threats are the kind of actions that people engage in to potentially harm members of the in-group or marginalize their welfare in substantial ways. A realistic threat is a message or an act that can instill fear or create the perception that violence may occur to compromise the wellbeing of those threatened. A man threatening a woman with violence for not complying with expected behaviours is an example of realistic threat. Less typical but also prevalent is the issue of women threatening men (Kumar, 2012).

Symbolic threats are about the perceptions one has of group differences such as morals and values. This kind of threat affects the worldview of group members. It leads members to think that they are not worth as much as others because society seems to value the others more. When a membership group such as a race or gender holds greater symbolic power over another group, they are affected by symbolic threat. In the context of threats regarding gender relationships, men are generally perceived to be a symbolic threat against women. This is less the case in social networks that are largely egalitarian. Men are clearly a symbolic threat in fundamentalist religious contexts, however, where authoritative religious documents make clear that men have authority power over women.

Intergroup Anxiety is a result of group members sensing the potential for negative outcomes because of membership in the group. If members of a group are embarrassed or ridiculed for attempts to participate in social situations, they develop an anxiety about trying to participate. In fundamentalist religious contexts, women are sometimes forbidden from attending schools. Attempts to attend school may result in ridicule and other threats as well. In more egalitarian contexts, women are ridiculed for wanting to participate in masculine oriented sports like NASCAR. Similarly, men are ridiculed for choosing feminine work like nursing or elementary education.

Negative Stereotypes are the condescending expectations someone will have for a member of a group only because he or she is a member of that group. Stereotypes are negative when they look down on or marginalize the value of a person who is a member of the stereotype group. This stereotyping depends on the perspective of the person doing the stereotyping. Women are stereotypically thought of as not excelling in math. or science as much as men so a male response to a math. or science question may be more respected than a female response. A religious group that allows women to lead publicly may be negatively stereotyped as a poor faith group because women lead.

Threats are signs for relationship partners that gender peace is out of balance. The threats are the subject matter that relational partners use to reveal that the relationship is not at peace. Gender peacemaking is engaged when the relational partners identify the threats and seek to rebalance their concerns for justice and care. Any kind of threat can be identified through talk. When relationship partners talk to each other about what threatens their perception of a balance between their view of relational justice and relational care, they will have a greater understanding of the conflict and be positioned to address the problem. When there is a perception that talk is unnecessary because the rules are clear, threats are more common and care is lacking. Likewise, if the relationship partners express care for each other but do not address the rules that discriminate, peace will continue to be elusive. The way partners address the lack of balance in justice and care also matters. It cannot be a single statement made by one partner. Addressing the lack of gender peace also requires a dialectical process. This process is the subject of the next theoretical frame to be addressed. Relational dialectics are key to the process of resolving gender disagreements.

Dialectical theory

The ancient Greeks used dialectical methods regularly and are thought to have given birth to this philosophical approach (Limnatis, 2010). Early uses of the dialectical method identified the three-part process of thesis, antithesis, and synthesis (Wandschneider, 2010). At the turn of the 19th century, Georg Wilhelm Friedrich Hegel became the key philosopher of dialectical theory, suggesting that logic was a dynamic process of moments, including an abstract or intellectual claim, subjecting it to a negative-rational idea, and then producing a speculative positive-rational idea. The systemic process continues in a helical spiral motion (Nuzzo, 2010). In gender relations, dialectical peacemaking is a matter of identifying threats to the balance of peace in a relationship or what threats prevent peace from being achieved in the relationship. Relational partners work through their threats by the dialectical process of asserting the thesis, or making a statement about the threat. The other partner responds with the antithesis by seeking the justice or care-oriented response. The partners then work together through the details to find a synthesis of justice and care that will provide the balance needed for peace in the relationship.

Relational dialectics

The dialectical approach in practice is about managing the opposing forces that exist within every relationship (Montgomery and Baxter, 1998). As men and women navigate their arguments about gender roles, they will be influenced by the relational dialectics that are typically present in their relationships. A relational dialectic is a tension that exists between people because of human nature's opposing forces. By accounting for these dialectical forces in arguments, the threats can be clarified and responses can be sought. The following are three typical relational dialectics present in male and female relationships (Montgomery and Baxter, 1998).

Connectedness is opposed to separateness. In a relationship we often think that a relationship tends to be close or distant. Relationships actually exist within the dynamic of times preferring greater connectedness and other times when separation is preferred. Men and women can seem to have a positive experience of connectedness at one time but the relationship may be better defined as typically experiencing separateness where the man and woman do not spend much time together. Navigating the peace in a relationship includes asserting the justice and care that can manage the ever-changing dynamic of a relationship.

Certainty is opposed to uncertainty. Relationships are often characterized by their need for predictability, or certainty, or by a more typical experience of uncertainty. Sometimes a male/female relationship is well defined by routine so there is very little uncertainty. Most typically, however, the relationship will experience a degree of certainty but with a high degree of certainty will come a degree of need for what is novel or new. The relationship may have more of one or the other but both are likely present in the relationship, which can cause some anxiety. As the threat of either certainty or uncertainty arises, partners can identify the problem and work through the dialectic to a peace oriented condition.

Openness is opposed to closedness. People in relationships will have times when they prefer a greater degree of transparency or openness in the relationship. With much experience of openness, they will likely gravitate to some need for privacy or closedness. Individuals may have a greater experience of one or the other and the more powerful partner may impose their desires on the other. This can also be a source of anxiety for the relationship. And with greater anxiety comes a greater awareness of the threat that exists to relational peace. Partners will then be motivated to engage the conversation that can balance the justice and care for peace purposes.

Men and women experience the opposing forces and respond in a variety of ways. They may work out the conflicts of difference by engaging the dialectical process of moving from a claim of needing justice or needing care to exchanges that satisfy both parties. They may alternatively attempt to resolve differences by resisting the dialectical resolution process in favour of unproductive conflict methods. If the relational partners engage in the gender peacemaking dialectical process, the moments of negative conflict experience will be replaced by an ongoing peace dynamic.

Peace dialectics

In addition to research on relational dialectics, another stream of thinking about this theory is in the area of peace dialectics emerging largely from the field of International Relations. Boulding and Boulding (1990) demonstrate the dialectical nature of peace research in the area of war deliberations. Understanding the dynamics of peace, according to dialectical theory, means understanding the dynamics of conflict. They express that the key to peace is the management of conflict. They describe the conflict continuum and note how each end of the continuum represents that which destroys the other end (Boulding and Boulding, 1990). As a result, peace as a dialectical process can be thought of thus:

> Peace, then is a highly charged dynamic process involving constant negotiation at every level of human interaction from local to global. Peace is *dialectical* in that each resolution of a conflict, or synthesis, creates the basis for dealing with the next conflict. Applying good conflict resolution skills creates the conditions for increasingly productive conflict outcomes in the future.
>
> (Boulding and Boulding, 1990, p. 1)

Dialectical theory is an appropriate approach to thinking about problematic gender roles. While dialectical thinking does not assume a problematic aspect of relationship, it does provide a focus on opposing forces, which includes locating the problematic threats to peaceful relationships. The important issue for this study is how peace can be created through problematic gender role contexts.

Creating peace in problematic gender role relationships

Most gender conflicts are managed between the parties with no third-party intervention. Many cases of mediation address gender conflicts and many gender conflicts are resolved in the courtroom. Men and women have gender role conflicts regularly as they sort out differences and preferences at home, school, workplace, church, or in any other context where men and women interact. Conflict is a natural human process that is very common between the sexes.

Peace can be created between people in many ways but the goal of this work is to explain the theoretically sound method of creating productive, satisfying, and sustainable peace in gender relationships. The gender role literature suggests that conflicts are less threatening and more peaceable when the relationship is egalitarian or hierarchical complementarian (Guin, 2007). Regardless of the degree of threat, creating peace in the relationship is still necessary because conflict is inevitable. However, the relationship is likely to find that more often than not, the dialectical process of working out the threats to peace is much more successful than other forms of conflict resolution.

Creating peace is a matter of balancing justice and care but that does not mean each side requires equal weight. What satisfies a relationship may be a greater emphasis on justice or a greater emphasis on care. The balance for peace depends on the needs of the partners in relationship. The gender role discussion earlier identified patriarchalism and radical feminism as role relationships with typically more threat and less peaceability. However, in some cultural contexts it may be the case that patriarchalism and/or radical feminism does create the most peaceable, nonthreatening, seemingly sustainable gender relationship. A workable model for creating peace in gender relations should be able to accept that a patriarchal or radical feminist relationship does enjoy a sustainable peace without requiring change.

As noted earlier, it is also true that many people struggle with the patriarchal or radical feminist orientation to gender roles. The struggle coheres around the fact that one party supports the role orientation while the other does not. In this case, to create peace, the party who disagrees with the role definition needs to identify the threat. For the sake of clarity in the communication, the identification helps both parties to understand and work through the threat. The clarity enables the parties to move on to the dialectical process of resolving the conflict.

There are also many conflict contexts that will not enable one party to use this process of conflict resolution successfully to create peace in their relationship. Some conflict contexts are intractable. Many women live in a context that prevents them from engaging the conflict resolution process at all without suffering severe consequences. Where opportunities do arise, however, the identification of the threat and dialectical resolution of the conflict are the necessary elements for creating peace. Some countries have allowed female children to be forced to marry an older male with a strong patriarchal view of gender roles. Women in these situations often do not have the opportunity to engage peacemaking processes. Rescue missions have made efforts to let girls and women know what their rights are and how they can engage peacemaking processes.

In western cultures, it is typical for gender conflict to be very problematic but not in ways where young females are forced to marry older men. The problems are common primarily because of the lack of information and skills for resolving conflicts. With adequate training, conflict resolution strategies can be taught for families, schools, churches, and other social institutions. In a context like family, conflict may not be intractable but family members may lack information about how to resolve conflict or have the ability to engage the abilities they have. Families need the training through parenting classes or in other ways to teach children positive methods for resolving conflict. A key institution interacting with families is schools. This is one institution that should take the lead in advocating for positive gender relational peacemaking.

Education is the key for enabling young people to grow up with skills and knowledge necessary for effectively resolving conflict and schools have the opportunity to perform this task. Schools, however, often tend to be institutional contexts where conflict is not managed well. Good conflict resolution education is available for managing school conflict but teachers and administrators need to know about available resources. School curricula should place a high priority on conflict resolution training, including gender peacemaking training. Schools tend to be the social location for western culture to experience romantic gender relationships so they are a critical institution for teaching the appropriate ways gender peacemaking should be conducted.

Religious and social institutions should also find ways to introduce members to gender peacemaking processes. Teaching young people about gender peacemaking will make a significant and positive difference in the experience those young people have as adults. Positive gender peacemaking could have a significant impact on church relations, educational experiences, family relations, and job performance immediately and long into the future.

A common approach to gender role change around the world is to lobby for government to increase the societal opportunities for women. In this societal level context it is critical to address the structural concerns of the ratio of men to women in business, government and legislative roles, and to ensure that educational policies really do give women an equal chance to pursue formal learning. It is also important to teach people how to address the nature of communication between men and women in the context of arguments about gender roles. Many girls and women experience a communication context at home or school, in religious contexts or at work that does not give them information about their rights or skills to make the desired changes. Peacebuilding efforts need to look into these types of contexts that not only prevent peace in gender relations but also marginalize a woman's opportunity to live violence free. These contexts even limit women's access to the privileges men have for education, employment, and an independent voice in citizenship or social contexts.

The place to begin building peace oriented gender relations is in individual gender relationships. 'Peace is dialectical' (Boulding and Boulding, 1990, p. 1), meaning parties initiate, respond, and find synthesis. It is a process where one party identifies the threat of conflict in the relationship and the other party responds with an orientation to justice and care. Relationships experience peace when the partners seek a synthesis of fairness for the relationship and care for one another. Degrees of fairness and care are typically known by the parties in gender relationships and are also necessary for gender peacemaking. Roles vary from patriarchal and hierarchical complementarian to egalitarian and radical feminism. Some gender relationships experience intractable conflict where peace is not possible with normal peacemaking processes. Relationships that have the opportunity and capacity to learn dynamic processes for resolving gender conflict can experience the value of gender peace.

References

L. Ahmed (2011) *A Quiet Revolution: The Veil's Resurgence from the Middle East to America* (Princeton, NJ: Yale University Press).

J. C. Alessio (2011) *Social Problems and Inequality: Social Responsibility through Progressive Sociology* (Burlington, VT: Ashgate Publishing Company).

A. Botes (2000) 'A Comparison between the Ethics of Justice and the Ethics of Care', *Journal of Advanced Nursing*, 32, 1071–1075.

E. Boulding and K. E. Boulding, (1990) *The Dialectics and Economics of Peace: Occasional Paper No. 3.* Fairfax, VA: Center for Conflict Analysis and Resolution, George Mason University.

C. W. Colander and S. Warner (2005) 'The Effect of Egalitarian and Complementarian Gender Role Attitudes on Career Aspirations in Evangelical Female Undergraduate College Students', *Journal of Psychology and Theology*, 33, 224–229.

S. Erden-Imamoglu (2013) 'Gender Role and Social Identifications: The Two Major Factors to Shape Turkish Women', *Education*, 134, 82–93.

S. Gabriel and W. Gardner, W. (1999) 'Are there "His" and "Hers" Types of Interdependence? The Implications of Gender Differences in Collective Versus Relational Interdependence for Affect, Behavior, and Cognition', *Journal of Personality and Social Psychology*, 77, 642–655.

S. K. Gallagher and C. Smith (1999) 'Symbolic Traditionalism and Pragmatic Egalitarianism: Contemporary Evangelicals, Families, and Gender', *Gender and Society*, 13, 211–233.

C. Gilligan (1982) *In a Different Voice: Psychological Theory and Women's Development* (Cambridge, MA: Harvard University Press).

B. Grasham (1999) 'The Role of Women in the American Restoration Movement', *Restoration Quarterly*, 41, 211–239.

J. Guin (2007) Buried Talents: In Search of a New Consensus, http://jayguin.files.wordpress.com/2007/01/buried-talents-9-1-cor-11.pdf, date accessed 27 May 2015.

G. Hebson, J. Earnshaw and L. Marchington (2007) 'Too Emotional to be Capable? The Changing Nature of Emotion Work in Definitions of "Capable Teaching"' *Journal of Education Policy*, 22, 675–694.

A. Kumar (2012) 'Domestic Violence against Men in India: A Perspective', *Journal of Human Behavior in the Social Environment*, 22, 290–296.

N. Limnatis (2010) 'Introduction', in N. G. Limnatis (ed.) *The Dimensions of Hegel's Dialectic* (New York, NY: Continuum International Publishing Group) pp. 1–11.

A. Martens, M. Johns, J. Greenberg and J. Schimel (2006) 'Combating Stereotype Threat: The Effect of Self-Affirmation on Women's Intellectual Performance', *Journal of Experimental Social Psychology*, 42, 236–243.

G. H. Mead (1934) *Mind, Self, and Society: From the Standpoint of a Social Behaviorist* (edited by C.W. Morris) (Chicago, Ill: University of Chicago Press).

B. M. Montgomery and L. A. Baxter (eds) (1998) *Dialectical Approaches to Studying Interpersonal Relationships* (Mahwah, NJ: Lawrence Erlbaum).

V. M. Moghadam (2008) 'Feminism, Legal Reform and Women's Empowerment in the Middle East and North Africa', *International Social Science Journal*, 59, 9–16.

D. S. Noss and B. Grangaard (2011) *A History of the Worlds Religions* 13th ed. (Boston, MA: Pearson Publishing).

A. Nuzzo (2010) 'Dialectic, Understanding, and Reason: How does Hegel's Logic Begin?', in N. G. Limnatis (ed.) *The Dimensions of Hegel's Dialectic* (New York, NY: Continuum International Publishing Group) pp. 12–30.

C. Osburn (2001). *Women in the Church: Reclaiming the Ideal* (Abilene, TX: ACU Press).

R. Roded (2012). 'Middle Eastern Women in Gendered Space: Religious Legitimacy and Social Reality', *Journal of Women of the Middle East and the Islamic World*, 10, 1–17.

L. A. Shaw and G. Bailey (2010) *Exploring the Relationship among Church of Christ Women's Attitudes towards Women's Roles in Religious Contexts, Age, Self-Esteem, and Attachment to God*. Paper presented at the Christian Scholar's Conference, Nashville, TN.

C. M. Steele (2010) *Whistling Vivaldi and Other Clues to How Stereotypes Affect Us* (New York, NY: W. W. Norton and Company).

W. G. Stephan and C. W. Stephan (2000) 'An Integrated Threat Theory of Prejudice', in S. Oskamp (ed.) *Reducing Prejudice and Discrimination* (Hillsdale, NJ: Erlbaum) p. 23–46.

L. Trofin, and M. Tomescu (2010) 'Women's Rights in the Middle East', *Contemporary Readings in Law and Social Justice*, 2, 152–157.

D. Wandschneider (2010). 'Dialectic as the "Self-Fulfillment" of Logic', in N. G. Limnatis (ed.) *The Dimensions of Hegel's Dialectic* (New York, NY: Continuum International Publishing Group).

R. White (2009). Care and Justice. *Ethical Perspectives*, 16(4), 459–483.

15
Ordinary Grocery Shopping for Promoting Peace and Justice: Global Impacts of Being a Conscientious Shopper

Max Saito

Introduction

It is possible to promote peace and justice through the ordinary practice of shopping for groceries. Grocery shopping choices can also address issues of environmental protection, public health, protection of local farms and food systems, and a healthy economy. One important probe for understanding why conflicts occur and how they can be addressed effectively involves critically self-examining possible ways we unintentionally contribute to initiating and aggravating conflict situations. Food and our food choices are of fundamental importance culturally, economically, and politically. This chapter explores how two personhoods—being smart and being conscientious—as expressed while grocery shopping at food co-ops and conventional supermarkets, can generate varying impacts locally, nationally, and globally. This chapter does not address struggles faced by very low-income consumers living in communities without access to fresh, health foods—an issue increasingly being explored by co-ops and communities nationwide.

Theoretical orientations

Many conflicts and wars have occurred due to struggles for strategic and natural resources (Klare, 2004, Goodman, 2004, Shankleman, 2006, Shuman, 2006, Perkins, 2007). Especially since World War II, large US corporations' needs to protect and advance their enterprises have played major roles in initiating and aggravating many conflicts and social injustice globally. Corporations have influenced the US government and other international institutions' policies and actions both publicly and secretly to their advantage, while the rhetoric of the government resonates with popular values of democracy, freedom, peace, and development (Perkins, 2007).

At the basic level, there are at least three ways to conceptualize how conflicts and wars break out: Realism, Liberalism, and Constructivism. Realism points out that sovereign states are like human beings who are inherently prone to act upon their desire to dominate others, especially when they deem they can get away with it; thus, conflicts are inevitable. Liberalism argues that states are often willing and able to cooperate with others, and that democratic societies are less prone to wage wars against one another. This viewpoint suggests that societal structures and governance such as democracy and socialism are essential for promoting peace. Constructivism addresses dialogic interplays between individuals and their living environments that shape and cultivate guiding principles for living, such as cultural beliefs, values, and normative rules (Jess & Williams, 2011). Understanding these three concepts is productive for further analysing how individuals' lifestyles intersect with peace and conflict. States may wish to dominate each other, while at the same time, they may wish to negotiate and cooperate with each other. A state may function like a human being, but at the same time, a state is made up of people with many diverse opinions.

Whether its structure is democratic or not, a government has to secure stable means for providing its population with food. Food that people grow, purchase, and consume is one of the most significant ways that individuals both directly and indirectly engage themselves with other individuals, with their own state, and with other states. Food consumption dialogically reflects how a society interacts with humans, other living beings, the environment, and other nations culturally, economically, and politically (Singer & Mason, 2006). Most people in the US acquire food by shopping in grocery stores. Ordinary grocery shopping can become an active and conscientious civic action that may substantially contribute to the promotion of peace and justice, although the degree of contribution will vary depending on consumers' choices of which store to shop at, and which items to purchase. It is productive to investigate ways in which ordinary grocery shopping as communicative practice may contribute to the promotion of peace and justice.

One productive communication theory for grounding grocery shopping as a civic engagement activity communicationally is Cultural Discourse Analysis. The theory of Cultural Discourse Analysis (Carbaugh & Cerulli, 2013) is a heuristic framework for delineating and analysing what it means to be a consumer who is actively engaged in both civic and democratic society. In particular, the theory invites the analyst to investigate the process in which communicative practices constitute a particular personhood. The four modes of inquiry useful for analysing personhood are: descriptive, interpretive, comparative, and critical modes. In the descriptive mode, the analyst will describe shopping practices of choosing and purchasing certain items. In the interpretive mode, symbolic meanings associated with the description will be explored. In the comparative mode, two or more personhoods will be compared, making taken-for-granted meanings more identifiable. The critical mode involves at least two ways of evaluating personhood: natural and cultural criticisms. Natural criticism is an evaluation from an insider's viewpoint, while cultural criticism is an evaluation from an outsider's viewpoint.

Each mode consists of five radiants: being, relating, acting, feeling, and dwelling. The radiant of being points to a sense of who one is, while the radiant of relating identifies how one relates to others. The radiant of acting is about what one does when shopping, for instance, while the radiant of feeling points out deeply felt emotions associated with shopping. The radiant of dwelling recognizes how one's communicative practices relate to the environment and one's lifestyle. Personhood as a communicative accomplishment has both direct/intended and indirect/unintended functions, reflecting normative rules and cultural premises that guide communicative practices. The theory of Cultural Discourse Analysis helps identify grocery shopping and food consumption patterns by comparing and contrasting between varying senses of who shoppers and consumers are, their motives, and choices that affect various issues.

Theoretical implications

The theory of Cultural Discourse Analysis posits immediate communicative practices as the focal domain of analysis, as opposed to the analysis of economy, politics, and diplomacy that are discursively distant and intangible to many ordinary people who are not professionally involved in the financial industry, policy advocacy, or peace making and building. Many ordinary people may not be conscious of the unintended consequences of the communicative choices they make with the good intention of maintaining a lifestyle of frugality, buying and consuming the lowest priced items. The theory invites the analyst to explicate and delineate communication practices and their structures and associated particular meanings that are reflexively interconnected with important issues, such as environmental stewardship, public health, peace, and justice.

There are at least four theoretical implications. First, this theoretical approach implicates that ordinary grocery shopping is a central force within the context of a capitalist economy and free market. Second, it implicates the power that ordinary consumers have through their grocery shopping as civic engagement. The consumers' purchasing choices function as economic, political, and democratic power that can significantly influence and shape the society to be more peaceful and just. Third, the theory further implicates that for promoting peace and justice, it is essential to make the indiscernible interconnectedness visible and identifiable between grocery shopping, environmental issues, policies, public health, local and food systems, and peace and justice. Ordinary people, while leading busy lives and making ends meet, can promote peace and justice through one purchase and one meal at a time. Fourth, it is important to cultivate and increase awareness of how ordinary communicative actions and styles intersect with fundamental issues that often create conditions in and through which war and conflict become inevitable. This implication may encourage alternative ways of communicative actions and styles that may foster peace and justice as constructive civic engagements. Certain patterned, regular, and sustained individual communicative practices may function— despite good intentions—as both destructive and constructive actions. One such action, which is closely associated with sense of identity, is purchasing and consuming food.

Two personhoods: being smart vs. being conscientious

Food is an integral part of living, relationships, family, growing up, spirituality, and happiness, to say the least. Food is of universal importance, though cultural variances present different meanings associated with different foods. For many Chinese people, eating dumplings invites good luck during the New Year. Having a cup of coffee might mean sharing a good time with a friend in the US, but sharing a cup of coffee in Turkey may signify 40 years of friendship (Gannon, 2004). As a part of New Year's rituals, Japanese and Chinese people eat long noodles for good luck, symbolizing long life. The most refined and revered rice in Japan can be seen as the worst tasting rice in Sri Lanka. At the same time, the smell of cooking parboiled rice may be appetizing for Sri Lankans, while it might be revolting for people who are not used to it. In some countries with a hot climate, spicy food could serve to stimulate the appetite, while in others it just causes physical discomfort. Ackerman (1990) states, '[t]he Masai enjoy drinking cow's blood ... Americans eat decaying cucumbers (pickles), Italians eat whole deep-fried songbirds ... Upper-class Aztecs ate roasted dog' (p. 132). The smell of cheese being baked in an oven might remind some people of dirty socks, if they are unfamiliar with what they are smelling. *Natto* (fermented soybeans) is a delicious comfort food in Japan; its strong smell and slimy texture due to fermentation may make it seem rotten to those who are not used to it.

Some foods may taste really good and comforting, but may be in fact unhealthy. In the US, many people are aware that consuming fast food and soda frequently can cause heart disease and obesity, but at the same time may cherish the good times they share with family and friends associated with these foods. In any case, people universally need food to survive, regardless of their preferences. One of the most convenient and inexpensive ways of acquiring food is to go to a grocery store. Customers develop shopping habits and routines and often choose stores where they can find the best prices on products they are used to buying and consuming.

There are two potentially conflicting ways of being a customer and shopper at a grocery store: being smart and being conscientious (see Table 15.1 for comparison). Being smart, a consumer may choose a supermarket where the prices are generally lower, a greater variety of foods are available, and the customer can spend less time acquiring all the items wanted for purchase. Customers often try to be frugal, while fulfilling their necessities for acquiring and consuming food for maintaining their busy lifestyles. Many stores acknowledge customers' needs by staying open 24 hours a day, seven days a week, making foods affordable, and making the shopping experience as fun and convenient as possible. Customers and stores have mutual relationships of supply and demand. Customers are free to choose where they wish to shop, and stores do the best they can to attract the customers. When choosing what to purchase, they may consider prices, healthiness, taste, nutrients, preferences of people for whom they cook, particular ingredients, occasions, and so forth. Some customers may wish to grow their own food, but for many it is impractical to raise their own food year round, even if they wish they could, due to weather conditions, lack of arable plots, lack of practical knowledge and experiences, and limited

Table 15.1 Personhoods of being smart vs. being conscientious

Modes / Radiants	Descriptive Mode (Grocery Shopping)	Interpretive Mode (Shopping at Supermarket)	Interpretive Mode (Shopping at Food Co-op)
Being	Shopper Customer Consumer	Being smart Being well informed about prices Being frugal	Being conscientious Being well informed about issues Being patriotic
Acting	Choose grocery stores Buy food Consume food	Utilize supermarket Shop at conventional supermarket Choose best deals and values	Own food co-op collectively as a member Shop at food co-op Cultivate and promote peace, justice, environmental stewardship through shopping, while choosing best deals and values
Relating	Customers vs. Business	Promotion of the best and lowest prices	Promotion of holistic relationships among farmers, suppliers, store employees, communities, customers, and important issues
Feeling	Frugality and necessity Customer satisfaction	Stores serve the customers' needs The cheaper the better	Stores and customers share mutual care and responsibility that are reflected in the right prices and co-op deals
Dwelling	Busy lifestyle Enjoy food	Food is necessary for energy, nutrients, good health, and living	Food choices address interconnectedness among consumption, health, environment, social justice, and peace
Direct Functions	Lead good life style Improve health Value frugality Enjoy food	Purchase the lowest-priced items Resist unhealthy food Improve convenience Conserve time Engage in saving money	Practice civic engagement Engage in environmental stewardship Advocate for sustainable policies Cultivate democracy, justice, and peace Energize fair food and economic systems

time and resources. Stores hire employees and purchase from farmers and producers, stimulating and sustaining the economy. Utilizing grocery stores is an effective way of being a productive member of society, while helping support the business and create jobs.

At a food co-op, smart shoppers can be even smarter by being conscientious and well-informed about issues associated with food, especially how and where it was grown and produced, and where it came from. Shopping at food co-op means being patriotic since food co-ops value volunteerism, democracy, economic development, independence, education, cooperation, and community that are all essential for fostering a strong US economy and civil society. Food co-ops are part of a growing network locally and nationally. According to a report produced by the National Cooperative Grocers Association in 2013, in the US there are at least 128 food co-ops operating 165 stores that are owned by over 1.3 million households who are also frequent co-op shoppers. Together, they generate approximately $1.4 billion annually. Anyone can shop at food co-op, even if they are not co-op members paying annual or lifetime membership fees ranging from approximately $25 to $250, depending on membership policies. Food co-ops are democratically operated by member-owners for providing customers with healthy food, building stronger communities, and promoting environmental sustainability for a better world.

This for-profit business model utilizes the power of capitalism for making grocery shopping a community of communication practice that enhances holistic and mutually beneficial relationships among farmers, suppliers, store employees, and customers. Cooperative businesses in general contribute greatly to foster sustainable economies, reduce inequality, and protect the environment. Cooperatives build an economy that is resilient even in times of recession (Nadeau, 2012). 2012 was the United Nations' International Year of Cooperatives. One of the aims was to raise awareness about cooperatives' efforts to build communities, advance democracy, and promote peace. Cooperatives can contribute to fostering both economic vitality and social responsibility.

Food co-ops are much more efficient than conventional supermarkets in sharing reciprocal care and responsibility for promoting a better world of peace and justice with customers, by addressing important issues such as 1) both local and national economy and the food system, 2) public health and environmental stewardship, 3) reducing fossil fuel consumption.

Economic and food systems

First, the way people participate in the free market at a food co-op contributes to promoting a stronger economy and better job opportunities locally and nationally. This perception is contrary to a popular notion that large corporations are job creators. The popular notion suggests that if corporations are large and competitive globally, they will be able to create more jobs in the US. People need jobs to make ends meet, and the nation will prosper economically and politically in the global market. The US is a superpower nation economically, politically, and culturally. Its success is not accidental, and brilliance of US ingenuity and business practices is responsible for the success, grounded in the principles of free market economy and democracy.

One popular perception of the American Dream suggests that with hard work and good luck, everyone has an opportunity to succeed in the US because of its open economic and social system. A supermarket is an American invention that reflects the American Dream. There is an abundance of foods in the store with countless options and choices at low prices. Anyone can shop there and find something good to eat even if they have limited means. Tax cuts and breaks are necessary for large corporations, so that the profits they generate will trickle down to the general public and will decrease unemployment and help achieve the American Dream.

In reality, consumers themselves too are major job creators in the free market system. It takes both consumers and investors to promote a strong economy, and often it is consumer spending that trickles down to stimulate new business initiatives and investments. Business practices tend to be highly conservative when it comes to investing money. People and consumers are at the top echelon of a democratic society. They are the primary movers in the society that funds, supports, and even changes governance and business practices.

Corporations, through their public relations, advertisements, political campaign donations, and lobbying do their best to influence public perceptions, opinions, and even political outcomes. Their influence is enormous, continuously expanding, and possibly unprecedented historically because of emerging conglomerates. In the end, however, it is people as individuals—not corporations—who vote for the politicians who create laws and policies, and it is people who go out and buy goods and services from corporations.

US household purchases make up approximately 70 percent of our Gross Domestic Product (Chandra, 2012). In 2012, US corporations retained $1.45 trillion in capital earnings without circulating it back to the overall economy. It was a ten percent increase from a retained $1.32 trillion in 2011 when the US economy was still stagnating and the unemployment rate was high. If this capital were to be utilized for job creation, it would generate approximately 19 million jobs and would bring down the unemployment rate to five percent (Pollin et al., 2011). In 1960, the average CEO was paid more than 41 times more than non-management workers; by 2000, it was 691 times more. Between 1920 and 2010, workers' productivity has increased, and US corporations as a whole have increased their profits significantly—especially in the last 30 years, due to new technologies and management innovations. Between 1920 and 1970s, the real wages for working class people in the US increased steadily; however, since the 1980s it has stayed stagnant and has never increased.

Many financial institutions used these massive profits to invest in the housing market, which triggered the financial crisis in 2008 (Wolff, 2009). Supporting large corporations through shopping—unless consumers are well-informed about issues and making conscientious choices—may lead to initiation and aggravation of conflicts abroad, although their influences and forms of involvement might vary (Perkins, 2007). In the US, five large supermarket chains dominate approximately 45 percent of all grocery sales, and their political power is vast. Local and small businesses, however, generate more jobs than large national and multinational corporations, and consumers' conscientious choices make a huge difference in how local economies prosper (Shuman, 2006).

Fostering a prosperous local economy is an important alternative to supporting large conglomerates, whose primary purpose is to maximize profits for the stakeholders and investors, rather than protecting the local economy or paying taxes which the US government needs to provide its citizens with necessary services and protections. According to the National Cooperative Grocers Association's 2012 report, food co-ops' positive local impact is much greater than that of conventional stores.

Here, the term 'local products' refers to products that are purchased within the state or transported less than 100 miles to market. On average, at a US food co-op, 20 percent of total purchases are locally sourced, compared with only six percent at a conventional store; 157 local suppliers are involved as opposed to 65 suppliers at a conventional store. At food co-ops, 11 percent of general merchandise is local, while it is two percent for a conventional store; 15 percent of bulk foods are local, while it is five percent at conventional stores; 31 percent of dairy is local, compared to nine percent; 35 percent of co-op deli sales are local, compared with three percent; and meats are 45 percent local at food co-ops, compared with five percent at conventional stores.

At a food co-op, 13 percent of the income on average is donated to local charities, while it is only four percent at conventional stores. The economic multiplier is 1.6 for food co-ops. This means that for every dollar a customer spends, $1.60 goes back to the local community, while it is 1.3 for a conventional store. The number of staff at an average food co-op is 9.3 per $1 million in sales, earning an average of $14.31 per hour, while it is 5.6 staff earning an average $13.35 per hour at a conventional store. 61 percent of workers are full time at an average food co-op, while it is 43 percent at an average conventional store. 68 percent of workers at a food co-op are eligible for benefits, while it is 56 percent at an average conventional store (National Cooperative Grocers Association, n.d.).

There is a myth that fairly traded items imported from abroad such as bananas, coffee, and chocolate are detrimental to local farmers. They actually do not interfere with local farming practices in the US since these items cannot be grown here effectively. Purchasing conventional bananas, coffee, and/or chocolates supports slave-like working conditions for farmers in export countries. Multinational corporations that are involved in growing and importing them may contribute to aggravation of conflicts and social injustice there (Shuman, 2006). The more money each consumer spends at a food co-op, the more money goes back to the community, the more staff are employed with higher wages, the more local business and employment opportunities are created, and the more donations are given to local community non-profit organizations.

Shopping at a food co-op is one effective way to encourage the local food system to remain diverse and prosperous, by supporting and helping local farmers through purchasing their products and produce. When small farms have steady and profitable access to a marketplace, such as at a food co-op, they are able to compete with large agribusiness farms and stay in business. Protecting local food systems is one important way to prevent potential conflicts that may occur due to scrambles for securing arable land and food supplies globally by large agribusinesses, multinational conglomerates, and other nations (Kugelman & Levenstein, 2013).

Public health and environmental stewardship

Being a conscientious consumer and making careful purchase choices promotes public health and environmental stewardship as well. Human health and environmental health are closely interconnected. Low prices of food items come with high and long-term costs to public health, including our own, as well as contaminating the environment. Large agribusiness farms can bring down the prices of their produce; however, the farming methods they use involve heavy use of synthetic chemical pesticides, herbicides, and fertilizers. For instance, the use of pesticides increased from 100 million pounds to well over one billion pounds a year between 1945 and 2001. Pesticides have become 'active ingredients' in produce (Leon & DeWaal, 2001, p. 5). Strong herbicides are needed for growing genetically engineered organisms (GMOs), such as the herbicide glyphosate. This has become so widely used that during the spring and summer it is detected in the air and rain in the US midwest. GMO food's safety is questioned, and laws in 64 nations including the European Union, Russia, Japan, and China (and not including the US) require labelling of such GMO ingredients (Right to Know, n.d.).

According to the US Geological Survey's research conducted in the 1990s, due to the heavy use of pesticides and herbicides, over 90 percent of water and fresh water fish samples contained pesticides. Almost 50 percent of water samples from agricultural streams contained levels of pesticides that exceeded the Canadian guidelines for safety. Although DDT has not been used since 1960s, almost every fish sample still contained DDT (Singer & Mason, 2006).

After crops are harvested, many food items go through processing which can make the food unhealthy, or unsafe for human consumption. Pollan (2008) points out that cooking is the best way to promote good health since it does not have to contain external and artificial chemicals. Regardless of income, race, gender, ethnicity, and other variables, cooking itself is a significant indicator of good health. Fresh food that promotes health is cost-efficient in terms of health care costs for consumers, but for food companies it is more profitable when food products can stay on the shelf for a long time. The longer food items can stay without going bad, the more potential they have to generate profit.

Homemade cookies taste best when they are freshly baked. Even if good quality ingredients are used, cookies baked without additives don't taste good after a while. For many companies, a cheap way to improve taste when food is not freshly produced is to mix in additives and artificial ingredients that are potentially harmful to human health. Consuming large amounts of food that contain high levels of sugar, unhealthy fats, and salt can make consumers sick (Leon & DeWaal, 2001). In the US in 2011, heart disease, which is highly preventable with well-informed and conscientious consumption, killed 596, 339 people, and caused the cost of health care to soar (Hoyert & Xu, 2012).

Public consciousness of the correlation between health and food consumption is increasing. In 2003, according to a study, only 11 percent of Americans said they consumed organic food on a daily basis, but on a weekly basis, 16 percent consumed organic food as part of their meals. Consumption of organic food has been steadily increasing by approximately ten percent a year (Singer & Mason, 2006). Food co-ops often provide cooking workshops for customers and specialize in making organic and natural foods more widely available at more affordable prices than most conventional stores. Consumer purchases of organic and natural foods can send a powerful signal to large corporations that people desire more healthy food, and that corporations should change their business practices in accordance with the customers' needs and wants, beyond immediate costs. Consuming organic foods contributes to promoting safe food production processes, long-term health, and public health, which in turn support environmental stewardship.

Food co-ops are more efficient than conventional stores when it comes to tackling issues of environmental stewardship. An average food co-op's sales per square foot are $10.37, while it is $8.55 for an average conventional store. The Energy Star rating for food co-ops is 82, while it is 50 for conventional stores. Food co-ops release 51 metric tonnes of CO_2 per $1 million sales, while it is 74 for conventional stores. Food co-ops recycle 81 percent of plastics and 96 percent of cardboard, while it is 29 percent and 91 percent respectively for conventional stores. Food co-ops compost 74 percent of food waste, compared with 36 percent for conventional stores (National Cooperative Grocers Association, n.d.).

Conscientious shoppers who purchase organic foods directly encourage organic food production practices. Methods used to grow organic foods prevent depletion and erosion of rich topsoils that are important for environmentally healthy growth of plants. Organic farming methods contribute to maintaining and even improving the quality of topsoils without using chemical fertilizers that require large amounts of petroleum in the production process. Organic farming can ensure biodiversity, while avoiding the use of dangerous pesticides and herbicides that are harmful to human consumption and can easily contaminate the drinking water supply. Organic farming methods typically use less fossil fuels for growing crops and producing dairies, 35 percent and 74 percent less respectively, than conventional farming practices. Conscientious shoppers do not have to buy organic foods all the time, but each choice to purchase can trickle down to stimulate organic farming and corporate practices. This, in turn, will promote a systematic change for fostering public health, environmental stewardship, and becoming more energy independent of fossil fuels that are one of the major causes of conflict internationally.

Reducing fossil fuel consumption

Shopping at a food co-op can contribute to reducing fossil fuel consumption more than shopping at a conventional store, and can therefore help increase resistance to future breakouts of conflict. First, discussing the oil industry's involvement in initiating and aggravating conflicts is necessary to make the connection between oil, public health, environment, and food. Securing oil has been one of the critical national strategic interests and has triggered many conflicts, such as those in Iran, Nigeria, Iraq, the Middle East, and Afghanistan, to mention just a few. Oil corporations' power and influence are so pervasive and omnipresent that they can set oil prices by controlling the number of gas stations and supply, create a lack of viable alternative fuels, compromise democracy, set the agenda for debate on global warming and environmental issues, and even bring the nation to war over oil. Using a large amount of fossil fuel is necessary to produce food, especially conventional food. Food is made available through the global food superhighway that depends on a cheap and secure supply of fossil fuels (Bowman & Harper, 2011). The use of oil makes it possible to import organic produce from abroad and sell it cheaper than local organic produce. Approximately 71 percent of petroleum is used for US transportation and 23 percent for US industrial sectors (US Energy Information Administration, 2013). Many developing nations suffer from a vicious cycle of poverty that often leads to conflicts, especially when government revenues depend on sales of oil. Although ethnic and religious differences are frequently blamed for world conflicts, these are far less significant than oil-related issues, poverty, and unequal distribution of national resources (Shankleman, 2006).

Not all oil-producing nations suffer from overall poverty—Saudi Arabia and the United Arab Emirates are two good examples. They both are considered to be US allies diplomatically; however, 17 out of the alleged 19 terrorists who attacked US targets in September of 2001 were from Saudi Arabia and UAE (Goodman, 2004, Jhally & Earp, 2004).

There are many conflicts in the Middle East caused by the US need to dominate control of oil. Not every country is directly involved in producing oil—for example, Israel is in conflict with Palestine, many Arab nations, and Iran, because it serves the agenda of the US: domination of oil control in the region (Chomsky, 2011). While it is impossible to completely avoid fossil fuel use in daily living, consumers, who contribute to 70 percent of the GDP in the US, can exercise their powerful influence. Grocery shopping might appear to be insignificant; however, shopping at a food co-op can help reduce oil consumption, thereby promoting peace.

Conclusion

In sum, being a conscientious shopper can outsmart being a smart shopper when grocery shopping. There is an intimate interconnection between grocery shopping, democracy, oil consumption, conflicts, local food systems, local economy, public health, environmental stewardship, and promotion of peace and justice both locally and globally. Promoting a local food system that consumes less fossil fuel supports a local economy that is highly resistant to national recession.

Small farms and local businesses together strengthen communities, and they in turn fortify national prosperity, while cutting back oil consumption. Using less oil as a society will effectively address global warming issues and environmental stewardship. Supporting organic farming can directly address issues associated with pollution and erosion of rich topsoils that are inevitable by-products of the conventional agricultural practices that depend on oil use. Consuming organic foods can promote public health that in turn reduces medical costs for individuals and for society in the long run.

Of course, shopping at a food co-op does not solve all of a society's problems immediately. Although the food co-op movement is growing, some consumers still might have to drive long distances to shop at a food co-op. Consumers on extremely tight budgets might be unable to afford natural and organic foods. Food co-ops are still few in number and may appear to be insignificant compared to the power of large conventional supermarkets. Many food co-ops do carry conventional foods in addition to natural, organic, and locally sourced foods in order to respect customers' choices and maintain convenience. Being a conscientious shopper at a food co-op presents, however, an opportunity for grocery shoppers to contribute in a powerful way. Shopping at a food co-op means active engagement in the capitalistic free market, where consumers can exercise their choices, forcing corporations to pay close attention to how they conduct their business.

This business practice has already happened with cigarette compa-nies. The capitalist economy is a powerful force that can transform society. When consumers become more conscientious about intercon-nectedness, their consumer choices can transform the food, economic, and political systems to be more democratic and just. Cooperatives use such a for-profit business model, and shopping at a food co-op taps into the transformative power of a capitalist economy. The small local action of conscientious grocery shopping enables shoppers to become patriotic global citizens who are both job creators and activists for promotion of local economy, national prosperity, public health, environmental stew-ardship, and peace and justice.

References

D. Ackerman (1990) *A Natural History of the Senses* (New York: Vintage Books, A Division of Random House, Inc.).

S. Bowman and R. Harper, Producers (2011) *Food Superhighway.* [DVD] (New York: Films for Humanities & Sciences).

D. Carbaugh and T. Cerulli (2013) 'Cultural Discourses of Dwelling: Investigating Environmental Communication as a Place-Based Practice', *Environmental Communication: Journal of Nature and Culture* 7, 1–20.

S. Chandra (August 14, 2012) 'Growth in U.S. Slows as Consumers Restrain Spending', *Bloomberg Personal Finance*, http://www.bloomberg.com/news/articles/2012-07-27/economy-in-u-s-grows-at-1-5-rate-as-consumer-spending-cooled, date accessed 27 May 2015.

N. Chomsky (2011) *How the World Works* (Boulder: Soft Skull Press).

M. J. Gannon (2004) *Understanding Global Cultures: Metaphorical Journeys through 28 Nations, Clusters of Nations, and Continents*, 3rd ed. (Thousand Oaks, CA: Sage).

A. Goodman (2004) *The Exception to the Rulers: Exposing Oily Politicians, War Profiteers, and the Media That Love Them* (New York: Hyperion).

D. L. Hoyert and J. Xu (2012) 'Death: Preliminary Data for 2011', *National Vital Statistical Reports, Center for Disease Control and Prevention*, http://www.cdc.gov/nchs/data/nvsr/nvsr61/nvsr61_06.pdf, date accessed 27 May 2015.

B. Hurt, Producer (2012) *Soul Food Junkies: African-American Identity & the Politics of Food* [DVD] (Northampton, MA: Media Education Foundation).

N. Jess and K. Williams (2011) *Ethnic Conflict: A Systematic Approach to Cases of Conflict* (Washington: CQ Press, A Division of SAGE).

S. Jhally and J. Earp (2004) *Hijacking Catastrophe: 9/11, Fear & the Selling of American Empire* (Northampton: MA, Olive Branch Press).

M. Klare (2004) *Blood and Oil* (New York: Holt Paperbacks).

M. Kugelman and S. Levenstein (2012) *The Global Farms Race: Land Grabs, Agricultural Investment, and the Scramble for Food Security* (Washington: Island Press).

W. Leon and C. DeWaal (2002) *Is Our Food Safe?* (New York: Three Rivers Press).

National Cooperative Grocers (2012) Healthy Foods, Healthy Communities: Measuring the Social and Economic Impact of Food Co-ops, http://www.uwcc.wisc.edu/pdf/Healthy_Foods_Healthy_Communities.pdf, date accessed 27 May 2015.

E. Nadeau (2012) *The Cooperative Solution: How the United States Can Tame Recessions, Reduce Inequality, and Protect the Environment* (Madison, WI: Independently Published).

J. Perkins (2007) *The Secret History of the American Empire: Economic Hit Men, Jackals, and the Truth about Global Corruption* (New York: Penguin Group).

M. Pollan (2008) *In Defense of Food: An Eater's Manifesto* (New York, NY: Penguin Group).

R. Pollin, J. Heintz, H. Garrett-Peltier and J. Wicks-Lim (2011) '9 Million Jobs For U.S. Workers: The Impact Of Channeling $1.4 Trillion In Excess Liquid Asset Holdings Into Productive Investments', Political Economy Research Institute, UMass. Amherst, http://www.peri.umass.edu/fileadmin/pdf/published_study/PERI_19Million.pdf, date accessed 27 May 2015.

Right to Know (2013) 'Labeling Around the World', http://www.justlabelit.org/right-to-know-center/labeling-around-the-world/, date accessed 27 May 2015.

River Valley Market (2014) *River Valley Market Annual Report to Member-Owers FY 2014* (Northampton, MA: River Valley Market).

J. Shankleman (2006) *Oil, Profits, and Peace: Does Business Have a Role in Peacemaking?* (Washington: United States Institute of Peace).

M. Shuman (2006) *The Small-Mart Revolution: How Local Businesses Are Beating the Global Competition* (San Francisco: Berrett-Koehler Publishers, Inc.)

P. Singer and J. Mason (2006) *The Way We Eat: Why Our Food Choices Matter* (Emmaus, PA: Rodale Books).

The United Nations (2012) *International Year of Cooperatives 2012*, http://social.un.org, date accessed 27 May 2015.

U.S. Energy Information Administration. (2013) 'What are the Major Sources and users of Energy in the United States?', http://www.eia.gov, date accessed 27 May 2015.

R. Wolff (2009) *Capitalism Hit the Fan: Richard Wolff on the Economic Meltdown* [DVD] (Northampton, MA: Media Education Foundation).

16
Promoting Peace through Songs: Peace Activism during the Afghan Conflict

Roshan Noorzai and Claudia L. Hale

Introduction

On a summer day of 1999, I was traveling in a taxi van from the western province of Nimroz to Kandahar. There were approximately ten passengers in the van. Most of them were from the central province of Ghazni, returning from Iran. An hour after our departure, the driver, a bearded man in his mid-30s, while driving searched under his seat and retrieved a tape cassette. He inserted the cassette in the van's player, and in a few seconds, *Abdullah Moqorai's*[1] voice filled the van. The driver turned his face and gave us a big smile. I think he wanted to see if everyone was fine with listening to the music. As a sign of agreement, there was no utterance from our side.

The journey was very long because of the poor condition of the road, and we listened to at least three cassettes. On the way, we had a number of stops; however, on one of them, the driver replaced the music cassette with a Taliban's *Tarani* cassette. Within ten to 15 minutes of the driver's action, we reached a Taliban check post and the car was stopped. It was a check post to the city of Lashkargah, the capital city of Helmand Province. We were told to get out of the car.

The Taliban did a thorough search of all the passengers and the car. They found nothing, and we were told to re-take our seats. A *Talib* asked the driver if he was playing any cassette other than the Taliban's. The driver quickly said with confidence "no way." He mentioned that he had only Taliban recordings. The Taliban let us go. After a few minutes,

---

[1] A well-known Afghan male singer.

the driver, again with a big smile, retrieved and played a cassette from another singer, *Naghma*.[2]

This used to be common practice during the Taliban regime. People would hide cassettes and CDs and would only listen with caution. This was because the Taliban banned all forms of entertainment media, such as music, movies, and television. The only mass medium allowed under the Taliban regime was radio.

The civil war

The armed conflict in Afghanistan started in 1978, when the pro-Soviet party, the Public Democrat Party of Afghanistan (PDPA), took power. The PDPA's government announced radical reforms in line with their socialist ideology (Edwards, 1986). The regime used force in the implementation of the reforms, and in the process, killed thousands of members of the traditional elite and the religious establishment. Soon, the reforms brought about local resistance and resulted in a conflict (Roberts, 2003).

In 1979, Afghanistan was invaded by the Red Army. With the Soviet invasion, the Western countries were dragged into the Afghan conflict. While the Soviet Union forces were deployed in Afghanistan, the US and its allies started supporting the Mujahideen groups. Regional powers, including Pakistan, Iran, India, Arab states, some Islamist groups, and China became involved in the Afghan conflict (Ahady, 1998, Khan, 2007). The Soviet army left Afghanistan after the Geneva Accord in 1988. However, the conflict did not end; rather, it changed to a devastating civil war.

The Kabul regime stayed in power until 1992, and then the Mujahideen came to power. The Mujahideen forces were composed of some 15 different groups and a number of independent commanders (Rashid, 2001). Almost immediately after taking Kabul, Mujahideen groups started fighting against each other, destroying the capital city. During the civil war, most institutions, including media infrastructures, were damaged, and people had to leave the country.

The Taliban emerged in 1994. They were successful in sweeping out Mujahideen groups and gradually extending their control over most Afghan provinces. The Taliban promised to bring peace and disarm different groups, but also promised to impose *Shari'a* law (Matinuddin, 1999). The Taliban were able to bring relative peace to the areas under

---

[2] A well-known Afghan female singer.

their control. As promised, though, they imposed their strict interpretation of Islam, and the civil war, in some parts of the country, continued.

During the Afghan Civil War (1989–2001), a number of initiatives were undertaken to end the conflict and bring peace to the country. The Kabul regime, under Najibullah, started a reconciliation process in 1986, which continued until the fall of the regime in 1992. In addition, a number of attempts were made by different parties, including the UN, to find a political solution to the conflict. Even so, the conflict in Afghanistan did not end.

Media and conflict in Afghanistan

During the conflict, media were used in Afghanistan as a tool of propaganda. Development and control of media had been a focus of the successive governments (Skuse, 2002). Media, particularly broadcasting media, were controlled by the central government (see Noorzai, 2006). The PDPA government considered using media to educate masses and impart new values and a socialist ideology into the society. The Mujahideen also used media for propaganda purposes during fighting with the Soviet army and the Kabul regime.

The main change in programming and content of the government media after the Kabul regime involved the announcement of a national reconciliation process in 1986. For the first time, the regime discontinued most ideological types of publications and programs (Tanweer, 2001). Instead, media were used to promote a policy of national reconciliation (Skuse, 2002).

After the Mujahideen came to power, the RTA building in Kabul was taken by *Jamiat Islami*, the party dominating the government after the fall of Najibullah. However, control of provincial radio and television stations was assumed by different groups and commanders of the Mujahideen. During the fighting in Kabul, the infrastructure, private businesses and government property were greatly damaged or looted. In this period, most of RTA's professional staff left the country (Yun, 2009).

When the Taliban took control of Kabul, the available infrastructure, particularly state institutions, were already devastated. The Taliban's rule, the imposition of their version of *Shari'a* law, further damaged the media institutions in the country. Except for radio, which was used for propaganda purposes, all other forms of media were banned. The Taliban banned playing or listening to music, taking or keeping pictures—particularly of living beings except for passports, national identity cards, and other documents (Yun, 2009)—and watching television. In addition to the ban on music and television, video cassettes and satellite dishes were banned (Rashid, 2001).

Tape cassettes as an alternative channel

Decades of war brought about the destruction of communication infrastructure. This, together with strict rules governing media, resulted in opposition groups and local population depending on small media produced and brought into the country from outside, mainly from Pakistan (Noorzai, 2006). The conflict, particularly under the Mujahedeen and the Taliban, prompted most of the educated Afghans, including artists, singers, and musicians, to flee Afghanistan and take refuge in either neighboring or western countries. This made the emergence of a transnational Afghan music industry possible.

As in other parts of the region (Sreberny-Mohammadi and Mohammadi, 1994), small media were used in the Afghan conflict (Noorzai, 2006). Throughout the conflict, cassettes were used by different groups involved in the conflict to motivate supporters and gain followers, disseminate ideologies, and communicate to the local population. They were also used for other purposes, such as entertainment and education.

Most of the cassettes were recorded in Pakistan, mainly in the two border cities of Peshawar and Quetta. Since tape players were available in most of the houses, in the absence of other mass media, cassettes became popular for entertainment purposes. During the Taliban era, cassettes having political content and/or music could not be accessed over the counter; however, they were distributed through private channels. Typically, the songs were sung both in the Pashto and Dari languages.

Taking into account the importance and use of cassettes and songs during the conflict, this chapter explores how some of the singers used cassettes to distribute messages of peace during the Afghan Civil War. For this chapter, the period from 1989, after the withdrawal of the Soviet Union, to the fall of the Taliban, in 2001, was selected.

Literature review

Protest songs are a genre of political songs, with a distinction that protest songs have a "clear statement of political message" (Denisoff 1983, p. 25). The main difference between protest songs and other types of political songs—such as propaganda songs, ballads, parodies, social commentaries, and patriotic songs—is that protest songs promote social and political change. In fact, the lyrics of protest songs inform, diagnose, and come with solutions for an issue or a problem (Bloodgood and Deane, 2005).

Protest songs are not only "plain speech," but also music (Bloodgood and Deane, 2005, p, 5). Protest songs should be in line with the social context in which they are produced. The social context gives these songs meaning. Members of a movement and the general public can be the target for the protest songs (Denisoff, 1983). Academic research shows that protests songs have a great impact on attitudes and beliefs (Bloodgood and Deane, 2005). Depending on its context, music can bring feelings of happiness, sadness, anger, enthusiasm, or encouragement (Blommestein and Hope, 2013, p. 60). In fact, as Payerhin (2012) argued, protest songs provide listeners "a sense of agency" (p. 30).

Protest songs can be described as observations of what is happening in society. Through these songs, communities can depict their grievances and call for changes. Communities can express their fears, desires, and issues. Protest songs give a voice to the community, with that voice used to express grievances and offer suggestions for change. In song, a community expresses its hopes and fears, wishes, and problems, thereby presenting the collective interest (Makina, 2009). Protest songs provide community members with an opportunity "to share emotional and mental states" (Cochrane cited in Marsh, 2010, p. 148). The precise foci for the songs change along with changes in society (Makina, 2009).

Protest songs have been a subject of academic research. Scholars have identified a number of purposes for these songs, such as "recruitment, communication, commitment, collective action, mobilization, framing, and problem solving" (Bloodgood and Deane, 2005, p. 6). In general, two main purposes have been identified: (1) unifying and strengthening of a movement and (2) communicating with and educating the general public.

Protest songs, having political messages, have been used in anti-war movements, such as in the United States during the Vietnam War (Auslander, 1981). As Marcus (2006) observed, if conflict means incompatibility in terms of ideas, behaviors, roles, needs, desires, values, and so on, then resolving conflict is somewhat related to changes in attitudes, perceptions, beliefs, norms, behaviors, roles, relationships, and so forth.

Recent scholarship on the subject has argued that the effectiveness of a protest song is assessed on the basis of the song's utility in "unifying and strengthening of a movement and its members' beliefs and commitments to a cause" (Bloodgood and Deane, 2005, pp. 6–7).

The scholars pointed out that the communication and education ability of these songs is actually secondary. However, in this chapter, we argue that, in order to understand the effectiveness of protest songs, it is important to understand the environment in which the songs are produced. As Zangana (2009) pointed out, "oral art" is not static and changes with the socio-political and economic situation.

Although more research has been done on protest songs, scholars still believe that more studies are needed (Bloodgood and Deane, 2005). This study tries to understand peace activism in Afghanistan during the years of conflict. Since, during those years, formal media were controlled by those in power and used exclusively for their purposes, this study tries to understand what creative and alternative communication approaches were used by the peace activists. In particular, how singers used their songs as a medium for peace activism.

Methodology

One of the ways to study resistance is through discourse analysis. Discourses are used as means of resistance to domination (Van Dyke, 2007). In order to understand the daily forms of resistance, knowledge of intentions, ideas, and language is essential. Scott (1990) emphasized that these forms of resistance cannot be studied through positivist or structural approaches. He further pointed out that it is difficult to detect everyday resistance.

Scott (1990) pointed out that the "hidden transcript" can provide a way to examine resistance and power relations from the point of view of the subordinate class. For Scott, hidden transcripts consist of offstage speeches, gestures, and practices that might confirm or contradict what appears in the public transcript.

It is important to understand and contextualize the text. As Jackson (2007) pointed out, discourse analysis aims to understand the relationship between text and larger social processes. The purpose of discourse analysis is to examine texts in their context (Bakhtin cited in Wilson, 2001; Van Dijk, 2007).

Researchers need to find forms of communication that contain alternative discourses. In the case of Afghanistan, in the period selected for this study, official transcripts present the discourses of the parties in the conflict; however, there is little in the official records concerning condemnation of the war and peace activism. Therefore, it is important to analyse unofficial transcripts, such as songs, as they served as a primary medium for entertainment throughout the civil war.

For this chapter, a large number of songs were analysed. The songs analysed in this study were produced during the Afghan civil war—1989 to 2001. We focused on the lyrics of the songs. Among the songs available to us, the ones having a message of conflict and peace were selected. As pointed out in the literature and methodology section, the context in which the songs were produced plays an important role in the interpretation and understanding of these songs. In order to understand better the context, six interviews were conducted. Four artists/singers were interviewed. A journalist working with Radio and Television of Afghanistan for the past four decades and a well-known poet whose poems were the basis of some of the most famous songs were also interviewed. Among the four singers whose work was analysed, two were female and two were male.

Discussion

In 1986, with initiating the national reconciliation process in Afghanistan, the pro-Soviet regime in Kabul allowed broadcasting of non-ideological content and started promoting reconciliation (Skuse, 2002, Tanweer, 2001). During this period, Kabul Radio and Television, to a certain degree, loosened its control over cultural products. Participant #5, an employee of RTA, mentioned that this was a time when strict broadcasting policies were abandoned. He said: "The restrictions were left on news and programming during that period." He further pointed out that it was a time when those who were not affiliated with the PDPA could have their voices heard. Participant #2 noted that, at that time, he was able to produce songs protesting against those in power.

Later, when the regime collapsed and fighting started between different groups of Mujahideen, government officials and the residents of Kabul started fleeing that city and the surrounding area, taking refuge in Pakistan, Iran, and other countries. During the Taliban rule, nearly all singers, journalists, and educated people were displaced. All the participants of this research told us their stories of personal suffering and displacement. At the time of this research, three of the participants were living outside the country although they had periodically returned to Afghanistan. Therefore the experience of the participants of this research had an impact on their work.

As previously explained, tape cassettes, used for distributing songs, were a popular medium. Songs, recorded on tape cassettes, remained the main source of mass entertainment during the rules of the Mujahideen and the Taliban. Under the Mujahideen, television programs were reduced. Later, during the Taliban, television and other pictorial media were banned. The only channels that remained were radio and tape players. Radio was controlled by the fighting factions, and tape cassettes were the only medium that could be used by the parties not involved directly in the conflict.

A number of factors contributed to the popularity of tape cassettes as a medium of entertainment. In the period of this study, most parts of Afghanistan did not have electricity; even residents of Kabul City did not have regular electrical service. Tape players run on batteries, which were available at the market. In addition to being the only medium of entertainment, the availability of batteries made tape players, and their associated cassettes, the most accessible vehicle for entertainment.

Although the Taliban imposed a ban on music, they were not able to ban tape players. First, banning tape players was not possible because most of the players came together with radios sets, which was one of the main channels used by the Taliban for communication. Second, the Taliban themselves used audio cassettes to distribute their messages. Third, tape players were built-in in cars, and banning them was not practical. However, during the Taliban rule, playing music in public was banned, and most people would listen to songs only in private.

In most of the songs made about peace and conflict, peace was considered to be not only the end of fighting but also a process through which every Afghan would be provided a chance to live in a peaceful environment. Peace was considered something that would pave the way for a prosperous Afghanistan that could be a place where all Afghans can live.

One of the major themes in the songs selected for this study was the suffering of ordinary Afghans. The killings and suffering of children, elders, women, and the general population were depicted as a way to question the legitimacy of war in Afghanistan. Songs discussed how the war had influenced living conditions in Afghanistan. Hatred of war and those in war was present in all the songs selected and interviews conducted in this research. In the songs, hatred of war was promoted by mentioning that the war meant destruction of the country and misery brought to ordinary Afghans. A famous song, *Dawood Sarkhush*, lamented:

> *I became homeless, went from one house to another*
> *Without you, I have always been grieving*
> *They looted your treasures for their leisure*
> *They broke your heart, everyone on his turn.*

War was considered to be the main issue faced by Afghanistan; bringing an end to war and fostering peace were considered to be the only way for Afghans to rid themselves of their miseries. Participant #2 pointed out that he made songs that said, to those involved in conflict, "The country is your mother; do not kill each other; if you go to any other country, you will be suffering as refugees" (Personal Communication, 3 October 2013).

Participants in this research pointed out that they sang anti-war songs because people demanded such songs. As participant #2 pointed out, people considered these songs a means through which they could have a voice.

> We were saying what people had in their hearts. We were not afraid and were saying what people were saying or what was in our hearts. [We were talking] about people's sufferings. We were seeing it and talking about it. We had our pen, making poetry and songs.
>
> (Personal Communication, 3 October 2013)

Participant #6, a local poet and singer in Khust province, said that he was singing for the sake of ordinary Afghans and that he would continue singing for/defending them (Personal Communication, 2 October 2013).

In protest songs, foreign countries were blamed for the miseries in Afghanistan. The Afghan war was presented as having been fought for the interests of foreign/neighboring countries. The songs condemned the leaders of the warring parties for being in the service of foreigners. For instance, in a famous song, the leaders of fighting factions were condemned for the continuation of war. The song says: "The enemy of the nation; why [you are] killing Afghans; you deserve hell; you will be thrown to the flames."

Another related theme was a call to soldiers to quit the battlefield. These songs were calling on soldiers not to serve the interests of their leaders and foreign countries and to stop the destruction of their own country. These songs considered soldiers to be suffering, just like other ordinary Afghans. The songs attempted to inform them about the destruction that war brings. Nashnas, a well-known Afghan singer, laments:

> *Young man, who are you, firing bullets?*
> *On your father and grandfather's village*
> *In this graveyard your relatives rest*
> *Some were shot yesterday; some were shot before.*

Participants in this research expressed the belief that their work was important and had a major influence on the ordinary people of Afghanistan. Participants #2, #3, and #4 said that many people had mentioned to them that their songs "made them cry." Participant #4 said that a song should be meaningful; songs should be based on emotions," and that is how people find an attachment to them.

The participants in this research did not agree on the effects of protest songs. Although they agreed that, at the personal level, these songs had an impact, they mentioned that there were a number of other issues that kept the fighting ongoing. Although participant #2 argued that his songs had an impact, he also pointed out that larger issues—such as a war economy that benefits a number of people, and bringing up people in a culture of conflict—contributed to the continuation of the conflict. Participant #3 mentioned that songs by other singers, along with her own songs, made her cry, but they did not have an influence on people involved in the fighting.

The participants in this research agreed that songs were helpful in promoting peace in Afghanistan. All of the participants mentioned that they would continue their work and that it was their job to promote peace. They believed that their work had the power to influence perceptions concerning the conflict. As participant #4 pointed out:

> We look at our society; we know people's pulse. This means we, from both sides of the border [Afghanistan and Pakistan], should make the kind of poetry to end this tragedy. We should make a kind of poetry to promote coexistence, love, and brotherhood and to prevent our youth from frustration.
>
> (Personal Communication, 2 October 2013)

In Afghanistan, poetry has an important political and social role to play. The poet enjoys special status as the spokesman of his neighborhood, community, tribe, or people in general, expressing their hopes, aspirations, and problems. In some cases, the role of poetry is equivalent to that of a journalist or a press officer. In other cases, the poet—whether man or woman—can inspire people to act, to defend their country, or simply to unite and love each other.

Conclusion

This chapter argues that, during the years of conflict, particularly under the Taliban, cassettes and songs were used as one of the main channels for artists seeking to promote peace. As we observed, during the Civil War, tape cassettes remained the main source of entertainment for the population in Afghanistan.

As Lipsitz (2007) pointed out that, when the mainstream media is controlled, people will use alternatives. In Afghanistan, because media outlets were controlled by the central government or warring parties, songs were an important means of communication for civil society, particularly singers and poets. Cassette recordings provided a means for them to communicate their messages to the wider population. In fact, popular music was one of the main channels that people in Afghanistan could employ to "engage in meaningful public dialogue about political issues" (Marsh, 2010, p. 12).

This chapter has argued that, in the absence of mass media, civil society actively promotes peace through whatever means are available, in this case tape cassettes. Although little is known about activism and local peace initiatives during the Afghan Civil War, this study shows that civil society groups, such as singers and poets, were active in promoting peace.

Songs remain one of the most effective cultural means of communication. As Blommestein and Hope (2013) pointed out, social movements use music as an effective cultural tool. In Afghanistan, singers and peace activists use music to promote peace and unity. It is a tool that singers and poets can employ to express themselves and connect with others.

It is also important to mention that the channel of communication used by the singers and poets was accessible to ordinary people in Afghanistan. The availability of tape players served an important role for peace activism during the years of conflict. As discussed, particularly during the rule of the Taliban, it was not possible for the Taliban to ban tape cassettes, even though listening to music was banned.

This research identified a number of themes. These themes included depicting the suffering, hatred of war, foreign interference, condemnation of the protagonists, and calls for foot soldiers to quit fighting. This study also pointed out the importance of taking into account the environment in which the songs were produced and distributed.

During the civil war in Afghanistan, civil society was not active; rather, civil society was oppressed. Members of civil society either left the country or had to work underground. In fact, the ongoing war and fear of reprisals made many activists in Afghanistan limit their activities and/or remain silent. The only civil society groups that could promote peace and oppose war publicly were singers and poets. Tape cassettes served as the media that they could use for their peace activism.

Participants in this study pointed out that they wanted to spread the message of peace to the general public and warring parties.

Unlike previous scholarship on activism of this sort that has concluded that the primary target for songs of peace were members of a particular social movement, participants in this research told us that the aim of their songs was to present grievances, inform and educate masses, and reach out to the warring parties. As protest songs "seek to stir emotional responses to an issue among a relevant identified group" (Bloodgood and Deane, 2005, p. 4), the songs produced and distributed during the years of conflict tried to convince the general public to work for peace and denounce fighting.

This study also found that activists, in this case singers and poets, consider their artistic work important for giving voice to the ordinary people and supporting peace activism. During the years of conflict, music and songs were the media through which that political opposition and resistance to the war were expressed. However, it should also be acknowledged that songs were used by the warring parties to maintain the status quo.

This study argues that local peace activism existed during the years of conflict although the official transcript of that time does not mention such initiatives. In fact, singers and poets had important contributions to peace initiatives during the Civil War. This study also found that post-September 11 peace activism in Afghanistan drew on the rich experience and cultural capital of the years of conflict. In fact, resistance against the war, which was present in the years of conflict and after the fall of the Taliban, became major cultural capital for peace activists and provided a cultural space for peace initiatives in Afghanistan.

Lipsitz (2007) pointed out that "popular music should be read as history and interpreting history through popular music" (p. xvi). It is important to understand that the songs should be interpreted in the context and timing that they were produced. In fact, the songs spoke of the politics and present the history of the period in which they were produced.

This chapter recommends that, in a society where mainstream media is controlled and used by warring parties, it is important to find out what alternative approaches to social change are used by peace activists. In particular, local and indigenous peace initiatives should be considered an important part of the strategy for peaceful resolution of the conflict. We recommend that identifying local initiatives and forming coalitions with local civil society groups should be the cornerstone of any peace strategy. Finally, we recommend that initiatives for peace should pay considerable attention to the experience and cultural capital of the local population.

References

A. Ahady (1998) "Saudi Arabia, Iran and the Conflict in Afghanistan," in W. Maley (ed.) *Fundamentalism Reborn? Afghanistan and the Taliban* (New York: New York University Press), pp. 117–132.

H. Auslander (1981) "If Ya Wanna End War and Stuff, You Gotta Sing Loud—A Survey of Vietnam-Related Protest Music," *The Journal of American Culture*, 4 (2), 108–113.

J. Blommestein and S. Hope (2013) "The Language of Songs: The Utilization of Freedom Songs as a Form of Protest in the South Africa Anti-Apartheid and U.S. Civil Rights Movements," *The International Journal of the Humanities: Annual Review*, 10, 59–68.

E. Bloodgood and S. M. Deane (September, 2005) "Where Have All the Protest Songs Gone? Social Movements' Message and Their Voice in Politics." Paper presented at the annual meeting of the American Political Science Association, Washington, D.C.

R. S. Denisoff (1983) *Sing a Song of Social Significance* (Bowling Green, OH: Bowling Green University Press).

D. B. Edwards (1986) *Pretexts of Rebellion: The Cultural Origins of Pakhtun Resistance to the Afghan State (Islam, Tribal Society, Honor, Afghanistan)* (Vols. 1 and II, Doctoral Dissertation AAT 8612257) (US: University of Michigan).

R. Jackson (2007) "Constructing Enemies: 'Islamic Terrorism' in Political and Academic Discourse," *Government and Opposition*, 42, 394–426.

I. Khan (2007) *Pakistan's Strategic Culture and Foreign Policy Making: A Study of Pakistan's Post 9/11 Afghan Policy Change* (New York: Nova Science Publishers, Inc.).

G. Lipsitz (2007) "The Racialization of Space and the Spatialization of Race," *Landscape Journal*, 26, 10–23.

B. Makina (2009) "Re-Thinking White Narrative: Poplar Songs and Protest Discourse in Post-Colonial Zimbabwe," *Muziki*, 6 (2), 221–231.

E. C. Marcus (2006) "Change and Conflict: Motivation, Resistance, and Commitment" in M. Deutsch, P. T. Coleman, and E. C. Marcus (eds) *The Handbook of Conflict Resolution: Theory and Practice* (US: HB Printing), pp. 436–454.

H. Marsh (2010) "'Writing Our History in Songs': Judith Reyes, Popular Music and the Student Movement of 1968," *Bulletin of Latin American Research*, 29, 144–159.

K. Matinuddin (1999) *The Taliban Phenomenon: Afghanistan 1994–1997* (New York: Oxford University Press).

R. Noorzai (2006) *Communication and Development in Afghanistan: A History of Reforms and Resistance* (Athens, US: Master's Thesis, Ohio University).

M. Payerhin (2012) "Singing Out of Pain: Protest Songs and Social Mobilization," *The Polish Review*, 57 (1), 5–31.

A. Rashid (2001) *Taliban: Militant Islam, Oil, and Fundamentalism in Central Asia* (New Haven: Yale University Press).

J. Roberts (2003) *The Origins of Conflict in Afghanistan* (Westport, Connecticut: Praeger Publishers).

J. Scott (1990) *Domination and the Arts of Resistance: Hidden Transcripts* (New Haven: Yale University Press).

A. Skuse (2002) "Radio, Politics and Trust in Afghanistan: A Social History of Broadcasting," *Gazette: International Journal for Communication Studies*, 64 (3), 267–280.

A. Sreberny-Mohammadi and A. Mohammadi (1994) *Small Media, Big Revolution: Communication, Culture, and the Iranian Revolution* (Minneapolis: University of Minnesota Press).

M. A. Tanweer (2001). *Da Afghanistan Tarekh ao Khparawani* [Afghanistan's history and publications] (Peshawar, Pakistan: Sabor Islamic Publication Center).

T. A. Van Dijk (2007) *Discourse and Power* (New York: Palgrave Macmillan).

J. Wilson (2001) "Political Discourse" in D. Schiffrin, D. Tannen, and H. Hamilton (eds) *The Handbook of Discourse Analysis* (Boston, MA: Blackwell Publishers), pp. 398–415.

M. I. Yun (2009) *Afghani Osanai Rasanai 1387–1380* [Contemporary Afghan Media 2000–2008] (Kabul Afghanistan: Yun Koltori Yun).

H. Zangana (2009) "Iraqi Resistance Has Its Songs," *International Journal of Contemporary Iraqi Studies*, 3, 277–286.

17
Peacebuilding through Interfaith Dialogue: The Role of Faith-based NGOs

Nur Uysal

Introduction

Religion is frequently considered as a factor in international conflicts (Kimball, 2011). Many scholars have argued that most conflicts are driven from frictions of cultural identity, largely based on religion. Indeed, the recent violent attacks (e.g., the *Charlie Hebdo* shooting in January 2015; the Wisconsin Sikh temple shooting in August 2012) seem to support the assumption that religion contributes to violent conflict around the world. However, religion can be an invaluable source in promoting understanding and reconciliation, and it can provide a foundation for peacebuilding efforts (Abu-Nimer, 2001). All of the world's major religions have a significant strain emphasizing peace (Coward & Smith, 2004). Yet, the link between religion and peacemaking is less well documented in the literature. Religious traditions have the resources to help promote peace. Religious leaders and volunteers have proven to be key civil society actors in many efforts to resolve conflicts, serving as intermediaries or helping to facilitate peacebuilding. Coward and Smith (2004) use the term *religious peacebuilding* to describe the range of activities performed by religious actors and institutions for the purpose of resolving and transforming deadly conflict, with the goal of building social relations and political institutions characterized by a mission of tolerance and nonviolence (p. 6). In addition to conflict resolution, religious peacebuilding includes individual and grassroots efforts for promoting human rights and cross-cultural and interfaith dialogue.

Interfaith dialogue can be of great value in promoting peacebuilding and advancing reconciliation even when religion is not the central cause of a conflict. In the field of communication, dialogue is conceptualized as both a kind of conversation and a way of relating (Buber, 1960).

In this context, dialogue can be understood as a small-scale communication process in which participants may say or hear something they never said or heard before, and from which they may emerge irrevocably changed (Cissna and Anderson, 2002). This approach emphasizes listening, learning, and the development of shared understandings. Dialogue can take a range of forms and have a variety of goals in mind. It may involve any level of participants from elites to the grassroots. Through discussion, groups and individuals may come to a better understanding of other faith traditions and of the many points of agreement that likely exist between them. These networks will multiply as people from different faiths have recognized the importance of communication to facilitate interfaith cooperation and to end religion-based violence.

Exploring the role of interfaith dialogue in peacebuilding is a significant step in the study of cultural communication and peacebuilding. Every social unit develops a culture, composed of the collection of rules, rituals, customs, habits, and other characteristics that give an identity to the social unit. Given that culture is the social and cognitive cognition process of individuals, cultural attributes are created, shaped, and transmitted through communication. Religious values and rituals are central aspects of the cultural identity of many groups involved in conflict situations. Cultural identity in turn can have a crucial impact on the course of conflicts. As an integral part of culture, religion thus plays a critical role in peacebuilding through communication practices.

In recent years, there has been a resurgence of interest in how religion can be used in both conflict resolution and the peacebuilding process. Building on Abu-Nimer's (2001, 2002, 2003) work on religion as a source of peace, this chapter explores some of the ways in which faith-based organizations can play a key role in contributing to peacebuilding. By conducting a case study on a faith-based organization inspired by a transnational movement originated in Turkey, this chapter aims to explore the value of interfaith dialogue initiated by faith-based NGOs for peacebuilding work. In the light of the study findings, the chapter proposes several directions to advance the research and practice in the field of peacebuilding through interfaith dialogue. The chapter argues that a cultural communication perspective to interfaith dialogue could further increase the role of faith-based NGOs in the peacebuilding process.

Interfaith dialogue: definition and context

The term *interfaith dialogue* refers to cooperative, constructive, and positive interaction between people of different religious traditions (i.e., 'faiths') and/or spiritual or humanistic beliefs, at both the individual and institutional levels (Abu-Nimer 2002, p. 16). Abu-Nimer (2003) further explained that interfaith dialogue is a set of practices, not limited to elites or to formal means of communication, which aims to foster longer-term relationships based in mutual respect and caring. The premise of interfaith dialogue is that violence and conflicts emerge partly due to ignorance and a lack of constructive interaction with the other. Therefore, understanding the religion of the other is a core strategy for promoting peace and reconciliation. Smock (2002) argued that interfaith dialogue is one of the effective strategies that religious organizations can employ to advance peace.

Symbols and ritual forms such as rules, ceremonial idioms, and repertoires of action can unite and integrate the 'meta-group' formed by religious communities. Abu-Nimer (2002) explained that in interfaith dialogue, religious rituals create a mode of dialogue and thus can be powerful tools in the peacebuilding process. Understanding another religion's rituals opens a window onto the meaning system of the other. Participating in another's ritual allows members of the interfaith dialogue group to temporarily experience the other's worldview. In particular, for the members of Abrahamic traditions, rituals and symbols set a framework for interfaith dialogue. In this context, Smock (2002) argued that the use of rituals and scripture in dialogue settings contributes to reaching a deeper level of authenticity. However, the use of rituals and symbols can also pose a challenge for interfaith dialogue. In particular, the lack of common rituals and symbols can hinder interfaith dialogue efforts among ethically diverse communities.

The role of interfaith dialogue in building peace and resolving conflict could be examined at two levels of analysis: micro and meso. At a micro level, Abu-Nimer (2001) identified three elements that are essential for a successful interfaith dialogue effort: (1) an alternative cognitive process through new information and analysis (change in the head); (2) a positive emotional experience in meeting the other through the construction of a safe and trusting relationship (change in the heart); and (3) working together on a concrete task or action that enforces the positive attitudinal change (change through the head). According to Abu-Nimer (2001), to change the perceptions of a conflict through spiritual framework, participants make a deeper human connection with each other through their spiritual encounter. When this 'deeper spiritual connection' is made in the interfaith dialogue, it becomes the main source for the individual's commitment to peacebuilding efforts.

At a meso-level, interfaith dialogue is facilitated in the form of formal interventions. One of the earliest examples of an institutional interfaith dialogue attempt is the Appeal to Conscience Foundation founded in 1965 by Rabbi Arthur Schneier and a group of high-level clergy representing Catholic, Protest, Orthodox Christian, Jewish, and Muslim faiths (http://www.appealofconscience.org). Garfinkel (2008) explained that formal interventions are those planned and designed as an intervention, in comparison to information and individual level interventions that might occur. For example, the primary approach of the Appeal to Conscience Foundation is to function as a neutral third party to religious groups in areas of conflict and thereby facilitate interfaith communication. Keeping the focus on an institutional level of analysis, the next section provides a brief background on faith-based nongovernmental organizations (NGOs)—the leading force behind many of the successful interfaith dialogue projects in the world.

Faith-based NGOs: building bridges through interfaith dialogue

A faith-based non-profit organization (NGO) is not a legally defined term but it is often used to refer to religious organizations and other charitable organizations affiliated or identified with one or more religious organizations (Clarke, 2006). Faith-based NGOs are often founded by a religious congregation (church, mosque, synagogue, or temple) or religious motivated individuals. The second category is broader as it includes organizations motivated by religiously values but not performing religious services. For example, the Appeal of Conscience Foundation, found by Rabbi Arthur Schneier, is a coalition of business and religious organizations representing various faiths such as Catholic and Muslim. Interfaith dialogue is the overarching theme that brings all these diverse organizations together to promote peace, tolerance, and ethnic conflict resolution.

Faith-based NGOs engage in a range of activities, including promoting interfaith dialogue, providing immediate humanitarian aid, and fostering long-term reconstruction and sustainable development (Clarke, 2006). Coward and Smith (2004) categorize these activities into three groups: conflict management (prevention, enforcement, peace keeping), conflict resolution, and structural reform (institution building, NGO development, civil society leadership). Faith-based organizations perform peacebuilding efforts on the ground as well as work at a distance from actual sites of conflicts. These organizations generally have international and local staff or volunteers, and serve anyone in need, doing both tasks without regard to religious affiliation (Pipes & Ebaugh, 2002). For example, the Inter-Religious Council is consisted of members from the four major religious communities in the Balkans, including the Croatian Catholics, the Bosnian Muslims, and the Jews. The organization promotes a peaceful, multiethnic society in Bosnia through interfaith workshops and interethnic communication. Faith-based NGOs thereby aim to enact principles of nondiscrimination and tolerance of difference in their own operations.

A faith-based NGO brings its own resources and perspectives to the conflict situations. The concept thus enables us to incorporate a rich array of spiritualities into groups of different religious traditions. Building upon Cowan and Smith's (2004) concept of religious, peace-building, in this chapter *faith-based peacebuilding* refers to a range of activities performed by actors inspired by faith; and institutions established by these actors with the goal of ending conflicts and promoting nonviolence in both social relations and political institutions.

Several terms appear in the interfaith dialogue literature regarding peacebuilding. Some Western Christian faith-based NGOs overtly adopt the terminology of 'interfaith reconciliation', while Islamic, Orthodox, and secular groups engaged in the same type of work will describe themselves as oriented toward relief and development. For example, CARE International emphasizes this idea in its mission statement:

> Our vision is to seek a world of hope, tolerance and social justice, where poverty has been overcome and people live in dignity and security. CARE will be a global force and partner of choice within a worldwide movement dedicated to ending poverty. We will be known everywhere for our unshakeable commitment to the dignity of people. We strive to serve individuals and families in the poorest communities in the world.

On the other hand, some organizations' mission statements do articulate explicitly religious values. For example, Catholic Relief Services (2014) highlights the role of religion in its mission statement as the following:

> Catholic Relief Services carries out the commitment of the Bishops of the United States to assist the poor and vulnerable overseas. We

are motivated by the Gospel of Jesus Christ to cherish, preserve and uphold the sacredness and dignity of all human life, foster charity and justice, and embody Catholic social and moral teaching.

International Muslim communities have also long traditions of social assistance. Although they may have less experience operating through formally constituted NGOs than their Western Christian counterparts, they have other assets those counterparts lack. The greatest of these is their presence and immense credibility in communities of their own faith, as well as strong negotiating positions with the local authorities of their own faith. For example, Islamic Relief (IR) (2014) is an independent Non-Governmental Organization (NGO) founded in the UK in 1984 engaged in international relief and development charity efforts. 'Envisaging a caring world where people unite to respond to the suffering of others, empowering them to fulfill their potential', Islamic Relief aims to 'exemplify Islamic values through mobilizing resources, building partnerships, and developing local capacity' (Islamic Relief, 2014).

Faith-based NGOs, both local and international, play very important roles as contributors to peace and development in many areas of conflict. Furthermore, these organizations can foster post-conflict reconciliation, bridging ethnic and religious divisions (e.g., in Bosnia and Herzegovina) (The US Institute of Peace, Special Report, 2003). Regardless of its explicit motivations, many international faith-based NGOs are involved in overcoming the inherent barriers and conflicts around the world. In this chapter, I argue that faith-based NGOs could provide the opportunity to build peace and end conflicts. However, the literature in the field (e.g., Abu-Nimer, 2003, Cowan & Smith, 2004) suggests that social actors working for peace should fulfill certain conditions in order to be considered in the category of faith-based peacebuilding organizations. Building upon this literature, I argue that there are at least three conditions to assess the value of faith-based organizations for peacebuilding. The first condition is that these organizations should involve in one of peacebuilding activities including prevention, advocacy, education, and interfaith dialogue. The second condition is that faith-based organizations should perform their peacebuilding activities in both religious and non-religious conflicts, and thereby reaching out not only beneficiary that share their own religious beliefs, but also other parties from different religious communities. The third condition is that members and leaders of these organizations act upon their own religious convictions and values to promote peace and protect human rights. In the light of these conditions, I examine a multinational faith-based organization involved in peacebuilding efforts.

Methodology

In this project, a qualitative case study approach was adopted, as it was deemed the most suitable methodology for illuminating the process of peacebuilding through interfaith dialogue facilitated by faith-based NGOs. Case study is an essential form of social science research that provides an intensive and systematic analysis of an individual unit, such as a person, an event, or an organization (Wimmer & Dominick, 2006). This approach may involve several data sources, such as documents, archival records, and artifacts, depending on the subject of the case study. Often, in studies of this type, focus is on a key case that can shed light on the research phenomena at hand (Yin, 2011). This case study is guided by the explanation building approach that consists of the construction of a description and illustration of the phenomenon under investigation—including causes, processes, and outcomes—based on the theoretical framework chosen to inform the phenomenon (Yin, 2011).

To address the broader question of whether faith-based NGOs are viable opportunities for peacebuilding and conflict resolution, I analyse an international faith-based NGO called Rumi Forum. The research questions that guided the case study include the following: What is the mission of the organization? What are the characteristics of the organization? How does the organization identify itself? How does it describe interfaith dialogue? What strategies and techniques does the organization use to facilitate interfaith dialogue? The data is collected through several qualitative research methods. The author conducted a textual analysis of internal and external organizational communication materials, including website, mission statement, flyers, and written correspondence as well as video recordings of the events. In addition, the author collected data from interviews with Rumi Forum members through non-directive-non-structured method (Abu-Nimer, 2002). Participatory observation method was used during the events at Rumi Forum between August and September 2013. Collectively, the qualitative case study approach allowed the author to gain multiple insights the viability of interfaith dialogue for peacebuilding as it is practiced by faith-based organizations.

The case: Rumi Forum

In this part, I focus on Rumi Forum—a faith-based organization that provides venues for peaceful building and conflict resolution efforts. Founded in 1999, Rumi Forum's mission is 'to foster intercultural dialogue, stimulate thinking and exchange of opinions on supporting and fostering democracy and peace and to provide a common platform for education and information exchange' (Rumi Forum 2014). Rumi Forum describes interfaith dialogue as promoting love and understanding and initiating efforts to find more common grounds among peoples of diverse faiths. One of the goals of Rumi Forum is to support activities pertaining to the better service to humanity such as promoting conflict resolution and peacebuilding. To achieve this goal, the Forum organizes conferences, panel discussions, community engagement, luncheons, publications, and other activities. In particular, the Forum has an interest in issues regarding pluralism, peacebuilding and conflict resolution, intercultural and interfaith dialogue, social harmony and justice, civil rights, and community cohesion. Indeed, the name of the organization was strategically chosen to commensurate with its mission. The Forum takes its name from the 13th Century Sufi philosopher-poet Mawlana Jalaladdin Rumi, whose reach embraced all humanity as personified by his message, 'Come, whoever you are, come ...' Rumi thus represents a symbolic meaning that emphasizes peaceful coexistence. In congruence with this theme, the organization describes its main goals as the following:

> The principal goal of the Rumi Forum is to promote peace in the world and contribute to a peaceful coexistence of the adherents of different faiths, cultures, ethnicities and races. For that to be achieved, we believe that everyone must be respectful to the environment and to all creatures' right to exist, believe in the sanctity of human rights and democracy and use all means at hand to make this coexistence possible. To this end, we promote education, exchange of information, opinions and expertise, with a special focus on including as diverse a range of viewpoints as possible in our activities.

Rumi Forum defines peacebuilding as 'activities like education, interfaith and intrafaith dialogue, advocacy, conflict resolution, and peace education which can create trust and cooperation over ethnic, religious and other divisions' (Peacebuilding Conference, 2013). In this framework, the organization offers a multidimensional vision of peace and social justice that begins with individual virtue and extends throughout the whole world.

Rumi Forum is one of the initiatives of the Gulen Movement, which was established in Turkey in the late 1970s by a Turkish religious leader as a local project based on dialogue and peaceful coexistence and has expanded on a global scale. The Gulen Movement or *Hizmet (Service) Movement*, as it is generally known in the West, is a loose network of civic and humanitarian projects that include schools, hospitals, aid and relief organizations, interfaith and intercultural dialogue organizations, publishing houses, and media outlets (Cetin, 2010; Park, 2008). These initiatives today operate in about 160 countries, serving societies of different religious and cultural backgrounds (Ebaugh, 2010). Some of these countries include the ones, which suffer from internal conflicts and communal divisions, such as Sudan, the Philippines, Kosovo, Northern Iraq, Afghanistan, Cambodia, Tajikistan, South Africa, and Nigeria (Keles, 2007). The Movement organizations and institutions in these countries engage in various peacebuilding initiatives that foster inclusiveness, build capacity, and create shared spaces.

Saritoprak (2009), one of the founders of Rumi Forum, has reflected on the global levels of dialogue and solidarity created by the Gulen Movement in his paper, *Fethullah Gülen and His Global Contribution to Peace Building*. In 1999, Saritoprak helped found the 'Rumi Forum for Interfaith Dialogue' in Washington, D.C. He noted that members of the Turkish-American community spent their own money and voluntarily painted walls and floors for reasons that did not benefit themselves personally. Saritoprak looked at it as communal solidarity referencing a computer engineer who said he volunteered because he sought 'solidarity with other people to build peace'. Within a few years the center was one of the best of its kind in the US (Saritoprak, 2009). Today the Rumi Forum (rumiforum.org) works with six major projects designed to help people to come to know one another and thereby build peace (Gage, 2013). The Rumi Forum establishes relationships with churches and synagogues, sponsors intercultural trips, organizes conferences, shares cultural activities, hosts Ramadan programs for political leaders in Washington DC and works with community leaders in peacebuilding especially within the Islamic context. Interfaith dialogue is at the core of Rumi Forum's peacebuilding work. The Forum approaches interfaith dialogue as a means to create friendships and relationships that then can promote a culture of peace and mutual understanding.

Rumi Forum has effectively utilized joint events to facilitate inter-faith dialogue. Several interfaith interactions are regularly organized to enhance mutual understanding and identify shared values. For example, the Forum annually holds the Rumi Peace and Dialogue Awards in collaboration with other peace and dialogue centers. More recently, in October 2013, Rumi Forum held an international symposium on conflict management and peacebuilding in collaboration with the Peacebuilding and Development Center at the American University and the Woodstock Theological Center at Georgetown University (for details, see http://www.peacebuilding2013.org). More than 200 participants from 20 countries attended the conference, which focused on the societal impact of these peacebuilding initiatives. Particularly, the events at Rumi Forum emphasize the shared values and traditions that are common to the three Abrahamic faiths. For example, in February 2014, the organization held a panel entitled, 'Social Justice in Theology and Practice—the Abrahamic Traditions'. The panel consisted of Rabbi Batya Steinlauf, the Rev. Dr. Carol Flett, and Aisha Rahman, representatives from Jewish, Christian, and Muslim traditions.

Rumi Forum directs its interfaith dialogue efforts at several levels through top-down and bottom-up approaches. At the leadership level, the organization works with the top representatives of religious hierarchies. The organization also works with high-level representatives from the faith communities and middle-ranges of religious leaders. The engagement with these participants in turn influences others. In addition to engagement with religious elites, the Rumi Forum works at the community level. The organization seeks to facilitate dialogue among persons of different faiths at the grassroots. At the individual level, the organization first initiates interfaith dialogue through building personal connections. Members and volunteers often invite their neighbors and colleagues to their houses for informal gatherings. These personal connections are then carried to an organizational level involving faith organizations of the others in the interfaith dialogue. Rituals and symbols are created, such as annual friendship dinners and peace awards, to endorse interfaith dialogue. At the organizational level, these endeavors are aimed at leading positive changes in other faith-based organizations. At a societal level, Rumi Forum creates a platform for understanding the other and respecting religious freedoms. Each of these approaches at multilevel complements the others and addresses an important part of the overall mission of the organization.

The literature on interfaith dialogue suggests that one of the features that distinguishes interfaith dialogue from secular or interethnic dialogue is the use of rituals and religious symbols (Abu-Nimer, 2001). For example, Smock (2002) argued that the use of rituals and scripture in dialogue settings contributes to reaching a deeper level of authenticity. However, the case analysis showed that Rumi Forum deliberately avoids using rituals and religious symbols. Furthermore, a discourse analysis of the organizational communication materials showed no indication of the use of religious scripture and sacred texts, even though the organization is inspired by Islamic thoughts. It could be explained by the organization's emphasis on finding the common grounds rather than the differences, allowing the interfaith dialogue efforts to reach to a wider audience.

The analysis of Rumi Forum revealed that interfaith dialogue plays a multifaceted role in the peacebuilding process. The organization can be categorized as a faith-based peacebuilding NGOs as it fits within the framework described in the literature (Abu-Nimer, 2003, Cowan & Smith, 2004). First, Rumi Forum involves in peacebuilding activities including advocacy, education, intercultural and interfaith dialogue. The case study suggests that the Forum practices interfaith dialogue as both a means and an end in itself. Among other peacebuilding activities of the organization, interfaith dialogue programs have commanded the most attention and resources. Second, Rumi Forum performs peacebuilding activities in religious and nonreligious conflict. As such, moving beyond the Muslim community, the organization reaches out to different religious communities. However, Rumi Forum does not perform activities in the conflict sites (e.g., Syria, Palestine). Rather, the organization sends out global messages of peaceful coexistence of different faiths, cultures, ethnicities and races. Third, the Forum is led by a team of Muslim members and volunteers who are inspired by their own religious convictions to serve humanity. These people are part of a larger religious community who support the cause of peaceful coexistence and respect for human rights. Given the resources and social capital of these organizations, the study suggests that faith-based NGOs could be a viable opportunity for the peacebuilding process.

Conclusion

This chapter explores the role of faith-based NGOs in the peacebuilding process and examines the value of interfaith dialogue in this context. Interfaith dialogue can contribute to ameliorating conflict and advancing reconciliation even when religion is not the central cause of a conflict. Organizing dialogue across religious boundaries enables people of faith to live out what most faith traditions consider as scared duty to be peacemakers. Interfaith dialogue is thus an area that commands more scholarly attention as a tool for building bridges between people of different religious traditions.

Interfaith dialogue as a part of peacebuilding and social change efforts can take different forms and seek different outcomes, identifying peace-building resources within participants' faith traditions. The following principles may contribute to the value of interfaith dialogue for building peace. The dialogue needs to have a clear purpose based on peace and social change; and the participating organizations need to have a clear vision and mission for their dialogue efforts. The dialogue needs to explore both the similarities among the participant faiths as well as the core differences that divide them. Interfaith interactions should go beyond talk to entail joint activities. The use of language in the dialogue communication is crucial. Power dynamics and sensitiveness should be given companionate attention. Dialogue communication should be supplemented by deeds and symbols aimed at transforming relationships.

Faith-based NGO activities that may enhance peacebuilding clearly cover a wide array of organizations and practices. The case analysed here illustrates some of the varied approaches, changing practices, and fluid relationships of faith-based NGOs as they pursue their various goals. Rumi Forum aims directly at interfaith dialogue, working with religious institutions and representatives. Through various efforts, the organization aims to get citizens of different religious and ethnic backgrounds to cooperate in civic engagement. Furthermore, it focuses on interaction and reconciliation at a personal level by encouraging members of different faiths to share their cultural heritage. Moving beyond the benefits of secular dialogue, the organization offers the potential for deeper and more meaningful engagement because of the possibility for spiritual encounter. This in turn may enhance the participants' commitment to peacebuilding.

Grounded in an emic approach, this chapter has argued that motivated by religious goals of seeking peace, religious leaders and faith-based NGOs can play prominent roles as mediators in mitigating conflicts and building peace around the world. Faith-based organization such as Rumi Forum have the potential to exemplify how interfaith dialogue efforts can contribute to building peace by staying above state politics and avoiding mundane power struggles.

Nevertheless, there has been very little scholarly research into strategies and techniques of interfaith dialogue currently practiced by faith-based NGOs. Given the range of approaches and techniques and the wide variety of geographic, political, and social contexts in which interfaith dialogue takes place, it is imperative that there should be more scholarly activity on the effectiveness of these programs.

References

M. Abu-Nimer (2001) 'Conflict Resolution, Culture, and Religion: Toward a Training Model of Interreligious Peacebuilding', *Journal of Peace Research*, 38, 685–704.

M. Abu-Nimer (2002) 'The Miracles of Transformation through Interfaith Dialogue: Are You a Believer?', in D. R. Smock (ed.). *Interfaith Dialogue and Peacebuilding*. (Washington DC: United States Institute of Peace), p. 15–33.

M. Abu-Nimer (2003) *Nonviolence and Peace Building in Islam: Theory and Practice* (Gainesville: University Press of Florida).

M. Buber (1960) *The Origin and Meaning of Hasidism* (New York: Horizon Press).

CARE (2013) Care International Core Values, http://www.care-international.org/about-us/core-values.aspx, date accessed 12 January 2014.

Catholic Relief Services (2014) Mission Statement, http://crs.org/about/mission-statement/, date accessed 12 January 2014.

M. Cetin (2010) *The Gulen Movement: Civic Service without Borders* (New York: Blue Dome Press).

K. N. Cissna and R. Anderson (2002) *Moments of Meeting: Buber, Rogers, and the Potential for Public Dialogue* (New York: SUNY Press).

G. Clarke (2006) 'Faith Matters: Faith-based Organizations, Civil Society and International Development', *Journal of International Development*, 18, 835–848.

H. Coward and G. Smith (2004) *Religion and Peacebuilding*. (New York: SUNY Press).

H. R. Ebaugh (2010) *The Gulen Movement: A Sociological Analysis of a Civic Movement Rooted in Moderate Islam*. (New York: Springer).

T. Gage (2013) The Hizmet Movement's Approach to Peacebuilding in Comparison to Other Initiatives around the World, http://www.rumiforum.org/conference-seminars/call-for-paper-international-symposium-on-peace-building-and-hizmetgulen-movement.html, date accessed 25 November 2013.

R. Garfinkel (2008) *What Works? Evaluating Interfaith Dialogue Programs* (DIANE Publishing).

Islamic Relief (2014) Islamic Relief Mission Statement, http://www.islamic-relief.com/Whoweare/Default.aspx?depID=2, date accessed (12 January 2014).

O. Keles (2007) 'Promoting Human Rights Values in the Muslim World: the Case of the Gülen Movement,' Gulen Conference, House of Lords, SOAS, LSE, retrieved from http://gulenmovement.info/userfiles/file/Proceedings/Prcd%20-%20Keles,%20O.pdf.

C. Kimball (2011) *When Religion Becomes Lethal: The Explosive Mix of Politics and Religion in Judaism, Christianity, and Islam* (California: Jossey-Bass).

B. Park (2008) 'The Fethullah Gulen Movement', *The Middle East Review of International Affairs*, 12, 2–36.

P. F. Pipes and H. R. Ebaugh (2002) 'Faith-based Coalitions, Social Services, and Government Funding', *Sociology of Religion*, 63, 49–68.

Rumi Forum (2014) About Rumi Forum. rumiforum.org, date accessed (24 February 2014).

Z. Saritoprak (2009) *Fethullah Gülen and His Global Contribution to Peace Building*, http://www.fethullahgulen.org/press-room/columns/2433-gulen-and-his-global-contribution-to-peace-building.html, date accessed 18 December 2013.

D. R. Smock (ed.) (2002) *Interfaith Dialogue and Peacebuilding* (Washington DC: United States Institute of Peace Press).

The Gulen Movement (2014) *Gulen's Views*, http://www.gulenmovement.com, date accessed 10 January 2014.

The United States Institute of Peace, Special Report 2003, *Can Faith-based NGOs Advance Interfaith Reconciliation? The Case of Bosnia and Herzegovina.* http://www.usip.org/sites/default/files/sr103.pdf, date accessed 14 February 2014.

R. D. Wimmer and J. R. Dominick (2006) *Mass Media Research: An Introduction*, 8th edn. (Boston: Wadsworth).

R. K. Yin (2011) *Applications of Case Study Research.* (Thousand Oaks: Sage).

Index

Printed and bound by CPI Group (UK) Ltd, Croydon, CR0 4YY